# Inferior Office?

# Inferior Office?

*A History of Deacons*
*in the Church of England*

Francis Young

*For Frances,*

*I hope you enjoy the book,*

*Francis Young*

© 

James Clarke & Co

*For my parents,*
*Alan and Doreen Young*

**James Clarke & Co**
P.O. Box 60
Cambridge
CB1 2NT
United Kingdom

www.jamesclarke.co
publishing@jamesclarke.co

ISBN: 978 0 227 17488 3

*British Library Cataloguing in Publication Data*
A record is available from the British Library

# Contents

# *Preface*

This book is about a group within the clergy of the Church of England that is at once very common and very rare. All clergy spend at least a year in deacon's orders, and indeed continue in deacon's orders for the remainder of their lives. Yet the number of clergy in the Church of England who have chosen to remain as deacons only ('distinctive deacons') is at present very small (fewer than one hundred). The fact that all clergy must pass through a 'diaconal' period in their lives would be enough on its own to justify a study of what being a deacon in the Church of England has meant over the centuries, but there is of course more to the diaconate in Anglicanism than the so-called 'transitional diaconate'. Beginning in the mid-sixteenth century, there existed a persistent minority of clerks in holy orders who remained deacons, and deacons only, for a lengthy period of time – sometimes even for their entire lives. This book shows that such individuals cannot simply be dismissed as freakish exceptions. The existence of lifelong deacons may be a backwater of controversy in the contemporary church, but there was a time in the nineteenth century when the issue repeatedly took centre stage at the Convocations of Canterbury and York, and even provoked a bill in the House of Commons. *Inferior Office?* tells, for the first time, the history of this largely forgotten segment of the clergy, as well as the controversy that has often accompanied it.

This book originally grew out of an interest in marginalised elements of the early modern clergy, an interest that in turn developed from my previous work on early modern popular religion. More often than not, the clergy who got themselves into trouble with the law for engaging in unauthorised practices were not the career priests who held incumbencies, but more shadowy figures of lower status: chaplains, perpetual curates and schoolmasters in holy orders. The clearest way in which a member of the clergy could be marginalised was by being excluded from priest's orders. A study of deacons, therefore, has much to reveal about the little studied social composition of the clergy in the early modern period and thereafter. Rather than a monolithic elite composed of graduates of Oxford and Cambridge, the clergy were a diverse group, and the early modern and eighteenth-century church was constantly suffering from a crisis of manpower. The half-educated individuals who were drafted in to solve this crisis were often those who remained in deacon's orders. In some parts of England, especially the Province of York, ill-educated clergy predominated until the mid-eighteenth century.

Once we acknowledge the presence of a local body of clergy within rural communities, who sometimes maintained a trade alongside their ministry, we are forced to question historical perceptions of the role of the church in early modern society. The parson was often perceived by the local community as a figure of authority, and sometimes as an alien intruder differentiated from the local community by class and origin, but it seems less likely that this was true of the marginalised local clergy who remained as lifelong deacons. The present volume is certainly not a comprehensive social history of the marginalised 'lower orders' of the clergy, but I hope it may provide the stimulus for more research into the diverse educational backgrounds and social roles of clergy between 1550 and 1800.

In addition to my interest in marginalised clergy, curiosity about the almost total absence of deacons in the Church of England stimulated me to write this book. Permanent deacons have been part of everyday life in the Roman Catholic Church in England and Wales since the 1970s, and the idea of permanent deacons assisting the parish priest seems natural to many Catholics. In the Church of England, by contrast, Readers regularly assume many of the same roles performed by deacons in the Roman Catholic liturgy, in spite of the fact that deacons exist in both churches. This seemed to me a curious anomaly in the Church of England requiring a historical explanation, and subsequent conversations with Anglican distinctive deacons convinced me that the history and position of deacons within the church was worth studying. This book is a work of history in which I make historical judgements (rather than theological ones), and it is not my intention to put forward one particular view of the way in which the diaconate should develop in the Church of England. However, this book is intended as a contribution to the ongoing debate about the role of non-priestly ministry within the established church. The year 2014 marked 175 years since Thomas Arnold first proposed a permanent 'order of deacons' in a sermon in Rugby's parish church in 1839, and 2015 marks 30 years since General Synod voted to ordain women as permanent deacons, but there has been little discussion of the diaconate in print since the publication of *The Mission and Ministry of the Whole Church* in 2007. The question of why Arnold's vision has yet to be realised in England in any significant sense, in spite of so much effort by so many, needs to be asked for the twenty-first century.

I have cause to thank many people for the assistance they have given me during the writing of this book. I am grateful to Revd Teresa White and Su Shaw for pointing me in the direction of valuable sources on the contemporary diaconate, and to Revd Pat Wright for her comments on a draft of this book, as well as Revd Jill Mabire for her insights on the diaconate. I am indebted to Richard Noble, the initiator of the process that resulted in the report *For Such a Time as This* (2001), for being willing to be interviewed, for supplying me with a copy of Bishop Stephen Sykes's speech in General Synod and for his comments on the text. I also thank Bridget Nichols for her comments on the text, as well as Revd Jonathan Clark, who supplied me with copies of the Chichester Report and R.P. Clement's dissertation on the diaconate. Dr David Nicholas kindly pointed me in the direction of his superb research on deacon-schoolmasters in the nineteenth century. I thank Max Openshaw for providing the cover photograph. I am grateful to the ever helpful staff of the British Library and Cambridge University Library for their assistance. I also thank those who helped this book to make it into print, especially Evangeline Deavall and Philip Law, as well as Adrian Brink, Lisa Sinclair and all of the staff at James Clarke and Co for their advice and assistance. I am grateful to Dr Liesbeth Corens, Prof. Felicity Heal and the organisers of the 2014 Reformation Studies Colloquium at Murray Edwards College, Cambridge, where I delivered a paper entitled 'The "Lower Orders" of the Clergy in the English Reformation' (largely based on Chapter 1 of this book). My wife Rachel Hilditch, as always, enabled this book to come to fruition through her unfailing support and her patience with my research work.

In order to avoid confusion in the text, I use the term 'Readers' (with an upper case 'R') to refer to lay individuals formally appointed Readers after 1866 (now officially known as Licensed Lay Ministers). Non-ordained individuals who acted as scripture readers before 1866 are referred to with a lower case 'r', since the formal title 'Reader' was sometimes given to ordained ministers before the nineteenth century. All dates given in the text are Old

Style (Julian Calendar) before 14 September 1752 and New Style (Gregorian Calendar) thereafter, with the year taken to begin on 1 January throughout, rather than 25 March. All translations from Latin are my own, unless otherwise stated. I take full responsibility for any errors or omissions in the text.

*Francis Young*
Ely, Cambridgeshire
February 2015

# Deacons in the Church of England
## A Timeline of Events

1549  The Strasbourg Reformer Martin Bucer seeks refuge in England, possibly composing *De Ordinatione Legitima* while a guest of Archbishop Thomas Cranmer

1550  The first English ordination service for deacons, 'The Form and Manner of Making of Deacons', requires all clergy to remain in deacon's orders for one year. John Bradford ordained deacon by Bishop Nicholas Ridley

1552  First revision of the Ordinal

1553  Accession of Queen Mary; the English Prayer Book and Ordinal are made illegal

1555  John Bradford executed by burning

1557  Cuthbert Symson, deacon of a London congregation using the English Prayer Book, is arrested and tortured

1558  Cuthbert Symson executed by burning

1559  The Elizabethan Settlement restores the 1552 Prayer Book and Ordinal

1566  A 'gospeller' (deacon) and 'epistler' (subdeacon) are required to assist at celebrations of Holy Communion in larger churches

1594  Richard Hooker defends the diaconate in his *Laws of Ecclesiastical Polity*

1604  The Canons of the Church of England specify that no one may be ordained deacon and priest on the same day

1626  Nicholas Ferrar ordained deacon by William Laud

1637  Death of Nicholas Ferrar

1642  Outbreak of the English Civil War

1646   Parliament abolishes bishops and the threefold order of ministry; dissolution of Nicholas Ferrar's community at Little Gidding

1662   The Act of Uniformity restores the threefold order of ministry but prohibits deacons from holding benefices

1701   Foundation of the Society for the Propagation of the Gospel

1784   John Wesley ordains his own deacons using an adapted form of the Ordinal

1785   Thomas Clarkson ordained deacon

1838   Pluralities Act makes it illegal for a clergyman to be in secular employment

1839   Thomas Arnold proposes the revival of the diaconate as a solution to the shortage of clergy in the Church of England

1841   St Mark's College, Chelsea, begins training deacon-schoolmasters

1844   A 'Lay Address' to the Archbishop of Canterbury calls for a renewal of the diaconate

1847   Education Act withdraws funding from schools run by a clergyman

1861   Revival of deacons proposed at the Convocation of Canterbury by Francis Massingberd

1862   Elizabeth Ferard licensed as the first deaconess in the Church of England

1866   Creation of the modern office of Reader

1869   Fanny Eagles ordained deaconess by Bishop Harold Browne of Ely

1878   Extension of the diaconate discussed at the second Lambeth Conference

1884   The Convocation of Canterbury approves the ordination of professionals and men of private means as deacons

1886   George Harwood ordained deacon

1887   Sydney Gedge MP unsuccessfully introduces the Deacons (Church of England) Bill in Parliament in an effort to repeal the Pluralities Act 1838

1888    Efforts to revive the diaconate are abandoned when the Convocation of Canterbury ends in deadlock on the issue

1920    The Lambeth Conference affirms that deaconesses are ordained ministers

1929    The Upper House of Convocation calls for the renewal of the diaconate

1955    Michael Jackson ordained as an experimental 'worker deacon' in Sheffield

1968    The Welsby Report recommends ordination of non-stipendiary clergy

1972    Deaconesses permitted to serve as deacons during public worship

1974    ACCM's report *Deacons and the Church* recommends the abolition of the diaconate

1981    The Portsmouth Report recommends the ordination of women as deacons

1985    General Synod votes in favour of the ordination of women as permanent deacons

1987    Women admitted to deacon's orders

1988    Publication of *Deacons in the Ministry of the Church* by Mary Tanner and Stephen Platten

1989    Foundation of the Diaconal Association of the Church of England (DACE)

1994    Women admitted to priest's orders. Most women deacons eventually choose to become priests

2001    *For Such a Time as This* calls for greater efforts towards the establishment of a distinctive diaconate in the Church of England. General Synod sends back the report for further work

2007    *The Mission and Ministry of the Whole Church*, a report of the Faith and Order Advisory Group, recommends the encouragement of vocations to the distinctive diaconate as one part of the church's overall approach to ministry

# *Abbreviations*

ASB      *The Alternative Service Book 1980* (Cambridge University Press: Cambridge, 1980)

Canons 1604      *The English Church Canons of 1604*, ed. C.H. Davis (H. Sweet: London, 1869)

Canons      *The Canons of the Church of England*, 6th edn (Church House Publishing: London, 2008)

DMC      [Tanner, M. and Platten, S.], *Deacons in the Ministry of the Church: A Report to the House of Bishops of the General Synod of the Church of England*, GS 802 (Church House Publishing: London, 1988)

FSTT      *For Such a Time as This: A Renewed Diaconate in the Church of England*, GS 1407 (Church House Publishing: London, 2001)

MMWC      *The Mission and Ministry of the Whole Church: Biblical, theological and contemporary perspectives*, GS MISC 854 (Church House Publishing: London, 2007)

ODNB      *The Oxford Dictionary of National Biography* (Oxford University Press, 2004), 60 vols

# Introduction

Anglican Christianity is distinctive among most other Reformation churches in retaining the threefold order of ministry: deacons, priests and bishops. Most historical accounts of the Church of England, perhaps understandably, pay attention to only two orders of ministry: bishops and priests. The Church of England inherited the diaconate from pre-Reformation Catholicism; historians have led us to believe that it also inherited the late mediaeval church's attitude to the diaconate as a mere formality on the way to priesthood. The Ordinal of 1550 refers to the diaconate as 'thys inferior offyce',[1] reinforcing the idea that all deacons were destined to be priests. A newly ordained member of the clergy might expect to spend little more than a few days as a deacon before admission to the priesthood, and before the late twentieth century, the Church of England was supposedly without a theology of the diaconate or an appreciation of the distinctiveness of diaconal ministry. In an official church report of 1988 that came to be extremely influential, Mary Tanner concluded that for most of Anglican history, 'It was usual practice for the two orders of deacon and priest to be conferred at the same time or within a few days of each other. Only those who were under age for the priesthood or who were felt to need the stimulus of a further examination were required to serve the full year'.[2] As a recent report on the diaconate put it, 'After the Reformation the tradition of having long-term or permanent deacons virtually died out'.[3]

This book questions received assumptions about deacons in the history of the Church of England, presenting evidence that 'lifelong', 'distinctive', 'permanent' and 'long-term' deacons have existed

---

1. 'The forme and maner of makyng and consecratyng of Archebishoppes Bishoppes, Priestes and Deacons' in *The First Prayer-Book of King Edward VI 1549* (London: Griffith Farran Browne, 1891), p. 281.
2. [Tanner, M. and Platten, S.], *Deacons in the Ministry of the Church: A Report to the House of Bishops of the General Synod of the Church of England* (Church House Publishing: London, 1988), p. 16.
3. *MMWC*, p. 59.

throughout the church's history. The 'third order' of ministry was hidden rather than invisible, and evidence of deacons has been overlooked on account of inherited preconceptions about Anglican history. It is certainly true that lifelong or distinctive deacons were non-existent in the Church of England for the first six decades of the twentieth century, but this era was atypical of the period since 1550. When the revival of the diaconate began in the 1960s, most were unable or unwilling to look back beyond living memory to the Victorian church's bold experiments in diaconal ministry, or the older tradition of ministers in deacon's orders who flourished in the sixteenth, seventeenth and eighteenth centuries. The restoration of the diaconate in the Church of England has been portrayed as a borrowing from the Roman Catholic Church, a borrowing from German Evangelical Lutheranism[1] or simply a direct return to the early church.

Missing hitherto from studies of the diaconate in Anglicanism has been any proper investigation or acknowledgement of the significance of deacons in Anglican history. It is the argument of this book that deacons, and thought on deacons, have always existed within the Anglican tradition. However, the meaning and significance of deacons has undergone transformation many times over the course of nearly 500 years, making it well-nigh impossible to give a simple definition of what an Anglican deacon is. The same could be said of the definitions of priest and bishop in the Anglican tradition, but the roles taken by deacons have proved particularly fluid. This difficulty of definition raises important questions about contemporary attempts to revive the diaconate as a permanent order of ministry, which will be addressed in the final part of this book.

## Deacons

The origin of deacons as an order of ministry is a controversial issue, but there can be no doubt that deacons and the diaconate are one of the Christian church's oldest institutions. The Greek word *diakonia*

1. Bruce Lescher, in his article on the spirituality of the diaconate, saw nineteenth-century Anglican interest in the diaconate as a direct consequence of the Lutheran experiments of Johannes Wichern and Theodore Fliedner in the 1830s (Lescher, B., '*Diakonia* and Diaconate' in Sheldrake, P. (ed.), *The New SCM Dictionary of Christian Spirituality* (SCM Press: London, 2005), p. 242). Whilst it is true that the deaconess movement had Lutheran origins, I have found no evidence of a Lutheran inspiration in any nineteenth-century Anglican publication on the revival of a lifelong diaconate for men.

can be translated simply as 'ministry', making it doubtful whether all of the individuals called 'deacons' in the New Testament can be considered members of a specific 'order' of ministry. Traditionally, deacons were traced back to Acts 6, when the Apostles chose seven men to help them in serving the poor and waiting at tables. Stephen, the first martyr, has always been traditionally depicted in the West vested as a deacon. In the East, the Council of Trullo in 692 asserted that there was no identity between the men chosen in Acts 6 and the deacons of the church, who were seen primarily as liturgical ministers. In Rome, the deacons acquired enormous influence as the bishop's 'eyes and ears' and took charge of seven administrative divisions within the city. Indeed, deacons started to acquire or pretend to a status above presbyters, and Jerome protested against this. In 314, the Council of Arles forbade deacons from making the offering (the eucharist), suggesting that the roles of presbyter and deacon were not always differentiated in relation to eucharistic presidency before that date.[1]

In a book that has become immensely influential in theological discussions of the diaconate since its publication in 1990, *Diakonia: Reinterpreting the Ancient Sources*, the Australian theologian John N. Collins questioned the assumption that the early church saw *diakonia* in terms of humble service, and argued that the primary meaning of *diakonia* referred to a 'go-between' or agent of one in authority, ready to perform a duty on behalf of someone in authority or act as an administrator. This interpretation is supported by the prominent role played by deacons in the early church as the influential assistants of bishops. For Collins, the association of the deacon with a ministry of love and humble service was introduced by German Evangelical theologians in the early nineteenth century,[2] while the Second Vatican Council's revival of permanent deacons in the Roman Catholic Church from the 1960s onwards was based on similar faulty assumptions.[3]

According to Collins's interpretation, deacons were the bishop's assistants and administrators, his 'staff', as opposed to the presbyters, who represented the bishop in individual churches in his diocese with delegated authority. Deacons worked for the bishop, whereas presbyters represented him. In the first three

1. Lescher (2005), pp. 241-3.
2. Collins, J.N., *Diakonia: Reinterpreting the Ancient Sources* (Oxford University Press: Oxford, 1990), pp. 8-11. The ordination of a deacon as a bishop was later known as ordination *per saltem*, 'by a leap'.
3. Ibid. pp. 14-20.

centuries of the church, deacons often rose to become bishops themselves (without being ordained as presbyters along the way).[1] Two relics of this era have survived in the western church: the practice whereby the bishop alone lays hands on a deacon in the ordination service, and the title of 'archdeacon' bestowed on the bishop's principal clerical administrators within the diocese (albeit present-day archdeacons in the Church of England can only be priests).[2] The practice of ordaining both men and women as deacons was authorised by the Council of Chalcedon (451) and until the twelfth century, male and female deacons were ordained in the Byzantine church with virtually identical ceremonies.[3] Women deacons seem to have fallen into disuse at this time because their ministry was limited to the baptism of adult female catechumens, which was thought unseemly for male clergy because catechumens were baptised naked. As adult baptism declined in the West, so the ordination of women to the diaconate died out. However, parts of the western church seem to have opposed the ordination of women deacons from early on, and the Synod of Nimes banned the practice in 394.

Whatever the original meaning of the word 'deacon', by the fifth century (at least) the diaconate had been transformed into 'the first step in a successful clerical career through the order of presbyters, up to the rank of bishop, just like the various career grades in the Roman civil service'.[4] In fact, deacon was not the lowest grade of orders, since from late antiquity until the Reformation there were five 'minor orders' below it. In the Roman Catholic Church, seminarians continued to be admitted to the orders of doorkeeper, reader, exorcist, acolyte and subdeacon until 1972. These 'minor clergy' were not ordained; rather, a man was tonsured by the bishop, thereby making him a cleric, and appointed to the minor orders by receiving an object pertaining to each office. Deacons, who were ordained, were considered to be in the lowest of the 'major orders'. All of these orders, major and minor, are mentioned in a mid-third-

1. MacCulloch, D., *A History of Christianity*, 2nd edn (Penguin: London, 2010), p. 134.
2. The situation is different in the Episcopal Church in the United States, where deacons can be appointed as archdeacons in some dioceses (Plater, O., *Many Servants: An Introduction to Deacons* (Cowley Publications: Boston, MA, 1991), p. 142).
3. Pinnock, J., 'The History of the Diaconate' in Hall, C. (ed.), *The Deacon's Ministry* (Gracewing: Leominster, 1991), pp. 9-24, at p. 20.
4. MacCulloch (2010), p. 134.

century letter of Pope Cornelius, quoted by Eusebius in his *Church History* (324). Cornelius reported that the Roman church contained fifty-two exorcists, readers and doorkeepers in addition to its priests, deacons, subdeacons and acolytes.[1]

However, the idea that these orders corresponded to 'ranks' of the clergy, and that ordination into them was sequential, was a later interpretation. Other sources, such as the third- or fourth-century *Traditio Apostolica* (once attributed to Hippolytus of Rome), suggest that while some ministries in the Roman church were conferred by the laying on of hands, others were 'charismatic', taken on by those who believed they had been given a special gift for them. The transformation of the orders of the clergy into a series of ranks was symptomatic of an increasing preoccupation with hierarchy in the late Roman church, which was to continue unabated in the Middle Ages. By the early Middle Ages, deacons tended to be defined by what they were not (priests), rather than by what they were.

From a liturgical point of view, early deacons were ministers of the sacrament of baptism and assisted the bishop or presbyters at the eucharist. Deacons were ministers of the church in the full sense, and the only functions they could not do were those specifically delegated by the bishop to the presbyters, such as presiding over the eucharist. However, deacons were 'concelebrants' of the eucharist in an important sense, their liturgical role being the critical one of mediating between bishop/presbyter and people. The presence of deacons at the celebration of the eucharist was originally a required element of the rite,[2] and a relic of this survives in the requirement for a deacon and subdeacon at high mass in the Tridentine rite used in the Roman Catholic Church before 1965.

Whilst the meaning of the diaconate was inevitably diluted by its transformation into a 'rank' in the church, there were individuals in the centuries that followed who consciously chose to remain in deacon's orders without proceeding to the priesthood. Famous examples include Alcuin, the ninth-century Northumbrian monk who became the architect of the Carolingian Renaissance; Francis of Assisi, the founder of the Franciscan Order; and Gerard Groote, the Dutch mystic and founder of the Béguinage movement. Three popes (Gregory the Great, Leo the Great and Hildebrand) were all elected whilst in deacon's orders. William Wareham, later Archbishop of Canterbury, was a deacon when he was appointed Bishop of London in 1502, and Reginald Pole was a deacon when he

---

1. Eusebius, *Historia Ecclesiastica* 6.43 (*Patrologia Graeca*, vol. 20, 244).
2. Dix, G., *The Shape of the Liturgy* (Dacre: London, 1945), p. 152.

was appointed Archbishop of Canterbury in 1556. The diaconate as ministry survived as an undercurrent within Christian history, and the sixteenth-century reformers took the opportunity to resurrect it. This phenomenon will be examined in Chapter 1 below. Because the minor orders were abolished in England at the Reformation, the diaconate became the most junior rank of the clergy.

On 29 September 1562, the Twenty-Third Session of the Council of Trent discussed the issue of a revived diaconate and decreed 'that the functions of holy orders from the deacon to the porter, which have been laudably received in the Church from the times of the Apostles . . . may again be restored to use in accordance with the canons'.[1] Thomas Goldwell of St Asaph was the only bishop from the Provinces of Canterbury and York in attendance, although his participation was academic, given that Elizabeth I had determined to break with the Roman church. In the end, because no instructions were ever issued on how a revival was to be practically accomplished, a renewal of the diaconate did not take place in the Roman Catholic Church until the 1960s. However, the fact that the Fathers of the Council of Trent, as well as the Protestant reformers, were discussing the diaconate was a mark of a renewed attention to the New Testament, in which deacons are very prominent.

In spite of the fact that it embraced the Reformation, the Church of England did little to revive the diaconate. The service for the making of deacons in the Ordinal of 1550 described the office of a deacon as an assistant to the priest, with a particular concern for the poor and weak:

> It perteyneth to the office of a Deacon to assiste the Prieste in devine service, and speciallye when he ministreth the holye Communion, and helpe him in distribucion thereof, and to reade holye scriptures and Homelies in the congregacion, and instructe the youth in the Cathechisme, to Baptise and preache yf he be commaunded by the Bisshop. And further more, it is his office to searche for the sicke, poore, and impotente people of the parishe, and to intimate theyr estates, names, and places where thei dwel to the Curate, that by his exhortacion they maye bee relieved by the parishe or other convenient almose.[2]

However, the Ordinal also made clear that the diaconate was a temporary ministry for clergy who expected to be ordained priest, since at a deacon's ordination the bishop prayed that deacons 'may

---

1. *Decrees of the Ecumenical Councils*, ed. N.P. Tanner (Sheed and Ward: London, 1990), vol. 2, p. 742.
2. 'The forme and maner of makyng . . . Deacons' (1891), p. 280.

so wel use themselves in thys inferior offyce, that they may be found worthi to be called unto the higher ministeries in thy Church'. Nevertheless, the Ordinal deviated from mediaeval practice by insisting that a man had to remain a deacon for at least a year before his ordination to the priesthood, 'excepte for reasonable causes, it bee otherwyse seen to his ordenarie'. This left a considerable degree of latitude to diocesan bishops.

The Ordinal remained in use for less than three years before the repeal of the Edwardian and Henrician ecclesiastical legislation by Queen Mary's (reigned 1553-1558) Parliament, and when the English liturgy returned under Elizabeth I in 1559, ordination practice differed little from the pre-Reformation era. Although the bishops made attempts to improve standards in the reign of James I, it was not until Laudian efforts to reform the church in the 1620s and '30s that the year-long diaconate was widely (but by no means universally) enforced. However, a minority of clergy remained in deacon's orders for their entire careers. After the Interregnum (1649-60), when episcopacy and the threefold order of ministry were suppressed altogether, diaconal ordinations resumed. The prescriptions of the Ordinal regarding the interval between ordination to deacon's and priest's orders were still widely flouted, largely because the 1662 Act of Uniformity made it impossible, for the first time, for deacons to hold benefices. This made it imperative for men who wanted to advance their clerical careers to be in priest's orders. However, standards of conformity to the canons progressively improved until, by the early eighteenth century, the average interval between diaconal and priestly ordination was well over a year.

The eighteenth century was the era of the long-term deacon, when many men spent three years or more in deacon's orders as they waited for the patronage and preferment that would allow them to obtain a 'title' to priest's orders. Again, a minority remained in deacon's orders for their entire lives, pursuing ministries as diverse as teaching in schools and colleges, preaching, caring for chapels and undertaking foreign missionary work. Ironically, the Anglican clergyman who arguably made a greater positive impact on the world than any other in the eighteenth century, the anti-slavery campaigner Thomas Clarkson (1760-1846), felt that he had to abandon his calling in the church in order to pursue the abolitionist campaign. Ordained deacon in 1785, Clarkson underwent a conversion to abolitionism whilst a deacon that meant that he did not proceed to priest's orders, campaigning instead on behalf of William Wilberforce. However, Clarkson did not renounce his deacon's orders until ten years later, in 1795, when he was attracted to Quakerism.[1] If deacons should be prophetic witnesses to social justice, as a recent church report on deacons has suggested,[2] no better example could be imagined than Thomas Clarkson.

By the beginning of the nineteenth century, changes in the church meant that long-term and lifelong deacons were increasingly uncommon, and the 1838 Pluralities Act forbade the clergy from pursuing secular professions. Since some eighteenth-century deacons had been less educated men who were already in employment, the law now made it difficult for deacons to exist in the traditional form. It was at this moment, however, that Thomas Arnold and many others began to call for a restoration of the diaconate to relieve the workload of the professional clergy. Advocates of the diaconate wanted to see a band of lower-middle-class men added to the clergy, to preach and assist in the running of parishes in the rapidly expanding cities, and to train as schoolmasters. A few experiments were tried in individual dioceses, and a college was set up that eventually trained over one hundred schoolmasters who were ordained deacon. However, apart from this success in education, by the end of the nineteenth century, the many proposals put forward for deacons in other ministries had come to nothing, and the number of lifelong deacons remained very small. Discussions continued into the twentieth century, but by this time the terms of the argument had changed. Talk of non-professional clergy was now focussed on expanding the priesthood, while talk of deacons moved to the question of whether women could or should be ordained to the diaconate. There was also much debate on whether deaconesses, who had existed in the Church of England since 1861, were deacons in the true, sacramental sense.

The issue was finally resolved in 1985 when General Synod voted to admit women to the diaconate, although the first women deacons were not ordained until 1987. A sudden flurry of documents and teaching on the diaconate followed, but the discussion soon turned to ordaining women to the priesthood. This occurred in 1994, leaving behind a small 'rump' of male and female deacons. General Synod took note of a report that called for the development of more 'distinctive deacons', *For Such a Time as This*, in 2001, but no positive decision was made to adopt the report's recommendations and encourage a larger body of deacons in the church. A subsequent report, *The Mission and the Ministry of the Whole Church* (2007) acknowledged that the church should encourage vocations to the

1. Brogan, H., 'Clarkson, Thomas' in *ODNB*, vol. 11, pp. 937-41.
2. *FSTT*, p. 54.

distinctive diaconate but presented this as just a small part of the Church of England's strategy for ministry. At the time of writing, the number of distinctive deacons within the Church of England remains tiny (around one hundred), with deacons mostly confined to the dioceses of Chichester, Portsmouth and London. However, all ordained ministers in the Church of England are ordained to the diaconate before they are admitted to the priesthood.

The Church of England is in communion with a number of similar churches where the diaconate has developed quite differently. In the Episcopal Church in the USA (ECUSA) and the Church of Sweden, both of which maintain the threefold order of ministry and ordain both men and women to the priesthood, the number of lifelong deacons runs into thousands. One purpose of this book is to shed light on why a distinctive diaconate has failed to prosper in the Church of England as it has in other parts of the Anglican Communion. However, it would be pre-judging the issue to assume that the diaconate is undervalued in the Church of England just because there are very few distinctive deacons. There is no *prima facie* reason why the traditional 'transitional' diaconate of one year may not be a valuable ministry in its own right. In reality, however, the vast majority of transitional deacons still serve as curates, essentially acting as priests who are unable to preside at Holy Communion.

## Speaking of deacons

The use of terms such as 'distinctive deacon' and 'transitional deacon' is just one example of the linguistic difficulties into which any historical study of deacons is bound to run. These are terms of very recent coinage, while the diaconate itself is very ancient indeed. It is an irony that those who make the loudest claims in favour of the restoration of an ancient order sometimes make the heaviest use of newly coined language to refer to deacons. In the Roman Catholic Church, which revived the ministry of lifelong deacons in 1967, such deacons are referred to as 'permanent deacons'. The vast majority of permanent deacons are married men, so the permanence of their diaconal orders is necessitated by Roman Catholic Canon Law, which does not permit married men to be ordained to the priesthood in the Latin rite. The Church of England has rejected the use of the term 'permanent deacon', since there is no canonical or theological reason why an individual ordained to the diaconate could not choose, at some later time, to be ordained priest. Furthermore, every ordained minister in the Church of England is a 'permanent deacon', since deacon's orders are permanent. In order to avoid confusion, I use the term 'lifelong deacon' in this book to refer to individuals who remained in deacon's orders, without receiving priest's orders, for the rest of their lives. The term 'distinctive deacon', currently favoured in the Church of England, seems anachronistic when applied to deacons before the twentieth century.

The term 'distinctive deacon', generally preferred to 'vocational deacon' or Karl Rahner's 'absolute deacon', emerged from the Portsmouth Report of 1981, which recommended the ordination of women to the diaconate, and it has been used ever since in the Church of England as the preferred means of distinguishing those who will remain deacons only from those who are transitional deacons. The difficulty created by the use of these terms is that they give the impression of two distinct orders of ministry, when in fact deacons are a single order. 'Transitional' could imply that men and women who are ordained deacons cease to be deacons when they are subsequently ordained priest, but the Church of England's doctrine of sequential and cumulative ordination would indicate otherwise. In this book I have spoken of individuals choosing 'to remain in deacon's orders' rather than choosing 'to remain deacons', since this would imply that priests and bishops are not deacons. Likewise, I write of the 'interval' between diaconal and priestly ordination rather than 'the duration of the diaconate', since the latter implies that a minister's diaconate comes to an end when he or she is ordained priest.

The prevalent assumption that transitional deacons are mere priests-on-probation, whose diaconal ministry is more symbolic than real, is a recent one. In telling the story of the diaconate in the Church of England, it is important to avoid the glib assumption that the transitional diaconate was 'merely' a probationary period for priests, thereby denigrating it. Just as it would be wrong to assume that pregnancy is an insignificant event in a woman's life because it is temporary, so it is wrong to disparage the experience of so-called 'transitional deacons' just because their time in deacon's orders ends in priestly ordination and the apparent sublimation of diaconal into priestly ministry. A historical approach that concentrates solely on the distinctive diaconate is in danger of underestimating the impact on priests of their diaconal ordination. Advocates of a distinctive diaconate must not be tempted to create the impression that transitional deacons and priests are not 'real' deacons, since this attitude subverts the threefold order of ministry itself.

## Histories of the diaconate

The most influential account of deacons in the early church remains the Australian theologian John N. Collins's *Diakonia* (1990), which has informed almost all subsequent scholarship in the area as well as the thinking of several churches regarding a revived diaconate. Collins's work was preceded by the less academically rigorous but still influential *The Diaconate: A Full and Equal Order* by J.M. Barnett (1979), which has had a strong impact in the United States. Indeed, the extensive development of the diaconate in both the Roman Catholic Church and the Episcopal Church in the USA means that there is more English-language literature published on the diaconate in America than anywhere else. Ormonde Plater's *Many Servants: An Introduction to Deacons* (1991) includes a historical study of deacons in the ECUSA, and in the second edition (2004); Plater also provides a good overview of the recent history of the diaconate in the Anglican Communion as a whole, although his primary focus remains America.[1]

The history of deacons in the Church of England has been very little studied, and knowledge of the subject is very poor. One recent Anglican author declared that 'There is no need to say much about deacons after the fourth century', and used the wording of the ordination service for deacons in the 1662 *Book of Common Prayer* as evidence that deacons were never anything more than 'apprentice priests'.[2] Brief accounts of the history of the diaconate appeared in Mary Tanner's contribution to the report *Deacons in the Ministry of the Church* (1988), presented to General Synod,[3] as well as in the collection of essays edited by Christine Hall, *The Deacon's Ministry* (1991), in the form of an article by Jill Pinnock.[4] Subsequent official and semi-official documents, such as *For Such a Time as This* (2001) and the Diocese of Salisbury's *Distinctive Deacons* (2003), have been derivative of Mary Tanner's work and contain no new research.[5] Rosalind Brown's *Being a Deacon Today* (2004) is the only book currently in

1. Plater, O., *Many Servants: An Introduction to Deacons*, 2nd edn (Cowley Publications: Plymouth, 2004).
2. Turner, H.J.M., *Holy Orders and Completeness of the Church* (Melrose Books: Ely, 2005), p. 77.
3. *DMC*, pp. 14-18; *FSTT*, pp. 4-9.
4. Pinnock (1991), pp. 9-24.
5. *FSTT*, pp. 4-9; [Brown, R.], *The Distinctive Diaconate: A Report to the Board of Ministry, the Diocese of Salisbury* (Sarum College Press: Salisbury, 2003), pp. 43-5.

print dedicated to the diaconate in the Church of England that is not an official report, but its focus is pastoral and theological rather than historical.[1] A notable example of fine scholarship on deacons in the Church of England is David Nicholas's ground-breaking work on the training of nineteenth-century deacon-schoolmasters.[2]

Reliance on the work of Tanner and Pinnock by other authors has meant that historical knowledge of the diaconate in the Church of England has not advanced since the early 1990s. Tanner made a number of observations that are challenged in this book, since they are not supported by the evidence I have encountered. Tanner is hardly to be blamed for this, since *Deacons in the Ministry of the Church* was not intended primarily as a work of historical scholarship. However, it is regrettable that it has subsequently been treated as such, without any further effort at investigation. Tanner argued that it was the norm for deacons to be ordained priest after a few days or weeks in the seventeenth, eighteenth and nineteenth centuries, which is not supported by the evidence. However, she conceded that a 'greatly attenuated version of a permanent diaconate existed in the Church of England, in the ancient English universities whose fellows had by statute to be in holy orders, which in many cases meant the diaconate'.[3] She offered the example of Charles Dodgson (who wrote under the name Lewis Carroll), the author of *Alice in Wonderland* (1865), as someone who remained in deacon's orders. Whilst it is true that deacons existed in the universities, this was by no means the only ministry in which deacons were engaged in the eighteenth and nineteenth centuries.

Tanner recognised that there were some categories of clergy in the Church of England in the seventeenth and eighteenth centuries, such as academics and government servants, who either remained in deacon's orders for a significant period of time or never proceeded to the priesthood. However, the authors of *Deacons in the Ministry of the Church* seem to have been unaware of the extensive Anglican theological literature on the diaconate produced in the nineteenth century, apart from Barry Rogerson's solitary reference to the 1878

1. Brown, R., *Being a Deacon Today: exploring a distinctive ministry in the Church and in the world* (Canterbury Press: Norwich, 2004).
2. Nicholas, D., '112 years of professional disability: an under-examined aspect of the 1846 Education Minutes', *History of Education* 39 (2010), pp. 319-41. This article was based on Nicholas's PhD Thesis, 'Derwent Coleridge (1800-83 and the Deacon Schoolmaster', Institute of Education, University of London, 2007.
3. *DMC*, p. 16.

Lambeth Conference in the Preface to the report.[1] In fact, research into the nineteenth-century call for a revival of deacons did exist at the time, in the form of Patrick H. Vaughan's unpublished 1987 doctoral thesis on the origins of non-stipendiary ministry.[2] Although Vaughan's focus was not specifically on deacons, but rather on the wider question of how the church came to authorise non-professional clergy, his and Nicholas's research was until now the only serious research into the Victorian movement for lifelong deacons.

Although no published studies of nineteenth-century deacons exist, research has been conducted into the Victorian deaconess movement, most recently by Henrietta Blackmore.[3] Research into deaconesses was stimulated by the growing recognition of the value of women's ministry in the late twentieth century, and scholars such as Blackmore have seen a process of evolution at work within the church, arguing that the deaconess movement foreshadowed the ordination of women to the priesthood in the 1990s. However, women's path to ordination was less than direct, and the status of deaconesses remained ambiguous right up to the ordination of women deacons in 1987, an act that was in itself a clear statement that deaconesses were *not* deacons. A narrow focus on the development of deacons as a byway of the study of women's ministry has the danger of obscuring the fact that two separate historical streams converged in the admission of women to the diaconate: the growth of women's ministry and the ongoing call for deacons, both men and women, in the Church of England. The former is now well understood, but the latter much less so.

The most complete account of the diaconate in the Church of England published to date has been the collection of essays *The Deacon's Ministry* (1991), edited by Christine Hall. Although these essays were inevitably coloured by the fact that making sense of the role of women deacons was a priority at the time, they are undoubtedly of lasting value. They include discussions of the theology of the diaconate from an Anglican perspective by Robert Hannaford and

1. Ibid. p. 2.
2. Vaughan, P.H., 'Non-stipendiary Ministry in the Church of England: A History of the Development of an Idea', PhD Thesis, University of Nottingham, 1987.
3. Blackmore, H., 'Autonomous Ministry and Ecclesiastical Authority: The Revival of the Female Diaconate in the Church of England, 1850-1900', DPhil Thesis, University of Oxford, 2004; Blackmore, H., *The Beginning of Women's Ministry: The Revival of the Deaconess in the 19th-century Church of England*, Church of England Record Society 14 (Church of England Record Society: London, 2007).

Antonia Lynn,[1] as well as discussions of the diaconate from the points of view of pastoral care, liturgy, education and Canon Law.[2] The volume also contained contributions from Orthodox and Roman Catholic authors. Jill Pinnock's article on the history of the diaconate offered an excellent account of the diaconate in the early church and touched upon the revival of the diaconate since the 1960s, but she spent little more than a paragraph on deacons between the end of the Middle Ages and the late twentieth century.

If the history of deacons in the Church of England between 1550 and 1987 has been woefully neglected, that is not because there are no available sources for such a history. The most useful secondary sources for a history of the diaconate are studies of ordination practices, such as Kenneth Fincham's study of the Jacobean bishops and William Marshall's study of the dioceses of Hereford and Oxford between 1660 and 1760.[3] These regional studies draw on diocesan ordination registers, but registers are of limited usefulness for discerning patterns of ordination on a national scale. Ordinations of deacons and priests were recorded separately, and since lifelong deacons were not distinguished from those who expected to go on to the priesthood, calculating the number of lifelong deacons from ordination registers would require an extremely time-consuming cross-referencing process. Even then, a priest might not be ordained in the same diocese in which he received deacon's orders.

Fortunately, the contemporary historian can draw upon the diligent work of an earlier scholar. John Venn (1834-1923) was the Master of Gonville and Caius College, Cambridge and is now most famous as the inventor of the Venn diagram. In his lifetime, however, Venn was a notable historian, editing the definitive list of alumni of Cambridge University between the foundation of the university and 1900, *Alumni Cantabrigienses* (1922-54). Although Venn began this

---

1. Hannaford, R., 'Towards a Theology of the Diaconate' in Hall (1991), pp. 25-44; Antonia Lynn, 'Finding Images' in Hall (1991), pp. 103-22.
2. Bardwell, E., 'The Pastoral Role of the Deacon' in Hall (1991), pp. 45-66; Burnham, A., 'The Liturgical Ministry of a Deacon' in Hall (1991), pp. 67-87; Cullen, J., 'The Educational Ministry of Deacons' in Hall (1991), pp. 89-101; Leeder, L., 'The Diaconate in the Church of England: A Legal Perspective' in Hall (1991), pp. 123-45.
3. Fincham, K., *Prelate as Pastor: The Episcopate of James I* (Oxford University Press: Oxford, 1990); Marshall, W., *Church Life in Hereford and Oxford, 1660-1760: A Study of Two Sees* (Carnegie: Lancaster, 2009), esp. pp. 158-87. See also Hayes, G.M., 'Ordination Ritual and Practice in the Welsh-English Frontier, circa 1540-1640', *Journal of British Studies* 44 (2005), pp. 713-27.

work just a year before his death, it was completed by his son, John Archibald Venn, who included as much information about alumni as possible and scoured ordination registers for the dates of their diaconal and priestly ordinations. Venn and his son thus gathered into a single place a vast amount of data on ordinations that would otherwise have been scattered in individual registers. An online version of Venn's *Alumni* now exists, the ACAD database, to which still more data has been added by contemporary editors.[1]

The ACAD database and Venn's original volumes are by no means a perfect resource, but since the vast majority of clergy between 1550 and 1900 matriculated at or graduated from Oxford and Cambridge, a significant proportion of all clergy ordained in England and Wales during this period appear in Venn's pages. Venn may have relied on imperfect records, and it must be borne in mind that Cambridge graduates were not necessarily representative of the clergy as a whole, but Venn's *Alumni* remains one of the best general sources for ordination statistics available. During the course of this book, I have endeavoured to balance my reliance on Venn with the surviving evidence for less educated clergy, who were more likely to remain in deacon's orders than the university graduates who made up the bulk of professional ministers.

In addition to the data on ordinations provided by Venn, I have drawn upon controversial literature and accounts of individual deacons, such as Cuthbert Symson and Nicholas Ferrar. However, material on deacons is meagre until the nineteenth century, when there was an explosion of literature on the subject. I have identified no less than twenty books and pamphlets published on the subject of a revived diaconate between 1841 and 1919, and this excludes the far more numerous articles in magazines and newspapers. For the purposes of this study, I have relied on *The Times* for a record of nineteenth-century convocations and public reaction to them, as well as the extensive pamphlet collections of the British Library and Cambridge University Library.

As this history approaches the present, I have relied upon official reports, online sources and, in the case of Richard Noble, the originator of the report *For Such a Time as This*, a personal interview. There is a small but important secondary literature on deacons in the period 1987-94, when the distinctive diaconate in the Church of England was almost entirely confined to women, some written

---

1. 'A Cambridge Alumni Database' (ACAD), *Cambridge University Library*, accessed on 27 September 2013: http://venn.lib.cam.ac.uk/Documents/acad/intro.html.

at the time and some afterwards.[1] This literature consists primarily of studies based on surveys of women deacons conducted by sociologists of religion intrigued by the unusual position of women clergy in the church, although not all of these scholars understood or appreciated the history of the diaconate. Indeed, the impression that emerges from this literature is that many of the women ordained to the diaconate during this period had little or no understanding of the theology and significance of the diaconate, since their primary calling was to the priesthood. This is hardly surprising, given that the elephant in the room in official documents such as *Deacons in the Ministry of the Church* (1988) was the unresolved question of whether women should be ordained to the priesthood.

There are a number of pitfalls for the church historian which I have endeavoured to avoid in this study. This book is neither a confessional history nor a manifesto for deacons in the Church of England; much less is it a report, official or unofficial, into the state of the diaconate in the contemporary church, because I have not undertaken any quantitative research of my own into contemporary deacons. Instead, *Inferior Office?* is an attempt to tell, objectively, the history of a marginalised institution, and a marginalised group of clergy, within the Church of England. Nevertheless, since some readers (lay and clerical) will have more than a merely academic interest in the future of the church's ministry, in the book's Conclusion I have offered two arguments based on the evidence presented in this book: the first against the idea of reviving a distinctive diaconate in the Church of England, and the second for it. This balanced approach seems preferable to transforming a historical investigation into a work of theology by advocating a single personal view. At the same time, it would be dishonest to pretend that the practice of church history does not have theological consequences, even if church historians are not theologians.

Professor Eamon Duffy, who has revolutionised the historical study of Roman Catholicism in England, has argued convincingly that a better understanding of history is good for the church: 'The

---

1. Aldridge, A., 'In the Absence of the Minister: Structures of Subordination in the Role of Deaconess in the Church of England', *Sociology* 21 (1987), pp. 377-92; Aldridge, A., 'Discourse on Women in the Clerical Profession: The Diaconate and Language-Games in the Church of England', *Sociology* 26 (1992), pp. 45-57; Francis, L.J. and Robbins, M., *The Long Diaconate 1987-1994: Women Deacons and the delayed Journey to Priesthood* (Gracewing: Leominster, 1999); Treasure, C., *Walking on Glass: Women Deacons Speak Out* (SPCK: London, 1991).

richness of the Church's past is a liberation, not a straitjacket'.[1] In other words, contemporary Christians should neither fear nor be constrained by history. Since the 1960s, some church leaders, both Roman Catholic and Anglican, have felt that delving into history is an irrelevance to a church that must look forward. In Duffy's view, however, an honest appraisal of the church's history will reveal multiple strands of opinion, often at odds with one another. Whilst some of these have rightly been consigned to obscurity in the contemporary church, others may have a great deal to teach the church in the present. We cannot naïvely assume that recent ideas are new, for they may have been suggested many times before; nor should we assume that novel solutions are better than those that were proposed in the past.

At the same time, there is sometimes a tendency in the Church of England for theological writers to depend almost entirely on the last report prepared by the House of Bishops of General Synod, instead of delving into the deeper historical and theological background to an idea. The parallel tendency in the Roman Catholic Church, which Duffy criticises, is the belief that the statements of the current pope should be relied upon to the exclusion of the magisterium as a whole.[2] The great treasure that the Church of England (and the Anglican Communion generally) shares with the Roman Catholic Church is a centuries-old tradition that can be drawn upon as an almost inexhaustible source for challenging current practice and assumptions inherited from the recent past. The past can often provide the most powerful witness to challenge the wrongheaded assumptions of the present. One example is the mediaeval practice of using church naves for secular purposes, an historical argument now used in many dioceses to challenge the Victorian view that the entirety of a church is, and must always be treated as, sacred space.

The significance of history to the present is an issue particularly acute in relation to the revival of the diaconate. If Anglicans assume that the diaconate should be revived at all, should that revival be an attempt to reinstate the diaconate as it existed, say, in the early church of the fourth century? An antiquarian revival of something so ancient may not be possible in contemporary society, or even desirable. Or should the Church of England simply establish a diaconate that fulfils the vision set out in the Ordinal of 1550 as a lifelong ministry? Or should it revive the diaconate in the form that it existed in the eighteenth century as an option for a minority of

---

1. Duffy, E., *Faith of Our Fathers* (Continuum: London, 2004), p. x.
2. Ibid. pp. 78-87.

clergy doing something other than parish ministry? The resuscitation of the diaconate has been a work in progress for so long (it began in 1839) that theological ideas have changed dramatically during the course of the process – yet what earlier advocates of revival said and believed must be taken seriously by contemporary exponents of the same idea.

Recently, Martyn Percy has rightly criticised accounts of the development of ministry in the church that try to establish 'one single meta-narrative of how orders came to be' by eliminating competing interpretations. Thus J.M. Barnett's assurance in *The Diaconate: A Full and Equal Order* (1995) that 'The charisma of the Holy Spirit was fully at work in the Church, guiding its development' would suggest that 'all "histories" of the diaconate can only be read theologically'.[1] A church historian who asserts that the development of the church is guided by the Holy Spirit not only cuts off church history from mainstream historical scholarship but also forestalls critical analysis: that which was guided by the Holy Spirit is presumably not open to criticism. Percy observes that Barnett's 'providentialist' reading of church history is used to support the restoration of the diaconate in the contemporary church, as if the re-emergence of any aspect of the early church in the present is automatically validated by the assumption that the Holy Spirit is working to perfect the church.

In reality, Percy argues, the re-emergence of the diaconate 'may also be part of a complex and problematic ecclesial economy'.[2] Clearly, he has in mind here the Church of England's revival of the diaconate in the 1980s, which had as much (or more) to do with accommodating the aspirations of women who felt a call to the priesthood as it did with valuing the diaconate for its own sake. Likewise, the existence of lifelong deacons in the sixteenth, seventeenth and eighteenth centuries was a consequence of bishops' concerns about the inadequate education of certain ordinands, or their need to legitimise the ministry of lay readers in remote parishes, and did not reflect a coherent theology of the diaconate. Yet the use of the diaconate as a tool to enable new and creative models of ministry in the church is itself a part of its history, and the fact that the purpose of the diaconate was rarely articulated in this period does not mean that it was not serving a purpose. The fact that

---

1. Barnett, J.M., *The Diaconate: A Full and Equal Order*, 3rd edn (Trinity Press: Harrisburg, PA, 1995), p. 44.
2. Percy, M., *Clergy: The Origin of Species* (Continuum: London, 2006), pp. 19-20.

many men chose to remain deacons for a period of several years, and even permanently, demonstrates that the diaconate was thought of as a fruitful identity enabling a number of possible ministries. Deacons existed, and therefore the actions of deacons constituted their ministry.

Such an approach is open to the accusation that the historian is reifying a diaconate that did not exist in anything like the same sense in which the diaconate exists in the Church of England today. However, it is in the nature of church history (and indeed religious history in general) that ideas and practices pass in and out of active life, their continuity enabled by the process we call 'tradition', which allows ideas and practices to be passed on even when a particular era or generation has lost touch with their original meaning. So, for instance, the parish communion that takes place in most Anglican churches on a Sunday in the twenty-first century did not exist in the eighteenth century in a form that most contemporary worshippers would recognise. But its elements, and the more ancient traditions upon which it draws, have existed in every age since the Apostles. The contemporary theology of the diaconate is a revival – but any revival must have genuine historical sources.

The assumption that no 'real' diaconate existed in the Church of England before the late twentieth century may be one reason why nothing more than a superficial attempt has been made to tell the story of deacons in England and Wales. Another reason may be the intense focus on the ministry of bishops that has been part of recent debates about the consecration of women to the episcopate. Whatever the cause, it is my hope that this book will mark the beginning of more serious investigation into the history of the diaconate, and indeed into a related field: the marginalised clergy. Clergy have traditionally been seen as a privileged group in history, but as the example of under-educated deacons demonstrates, there were marginalised individuals among the clergy as well, undertaking less remunerative ministries or unable to attain preferment. It is a contention of this book that this portion of the clergy is under-studied and worthy of further investigation.

The most recent fashion amongst writers on the diaconate in the Church of England has been to eschew historical analysis in favour of a return to the New Testament sources. I shall outline current theological developments in detail in Chapter 5 below. This change of emphasis from the 1980s is perhaps understandable, given the absence of any good quality historical research on the diaconate in the established church. However, it is questionable whether such an approach is truly Anglican, given the Anglican emphasis on the importance of tradition. If the diaconate in the Church of England has a history of its own – and this book makes that argument – then it is incumbent on Anglican theologians to take that history and spirituality into account when considering the future direction of the diaconate. If the diaconate is to be reinvented for the twenty-first century, then previous incarnations of the diaconate cannot simply be dismissed without argument.

## Structure and scope of the book

The book's approach is chronological, beginning in 1550 and dividing the history of the diaconate into five eras: the Reformation period, from the Edwardian reform beginning in 1549 to the outbreak of the English Civil War in 1642; the 'long eighteenth century', from the Restoration of the Monarchy in 1660 to the Great Reform Act of 1832; the Victorian era (1837-1901); the twentieth century to 1994; and finally, the era of the contemporary distinctive diaconate from 1994 to the present day. The book's primary focus is the Church of England (including Wales before 1920), and it is not my intention to provide a history of deacons in the Anglican Communion as a whole. However, I refer from time to time to the impact of changes in other churches on the Church of England, especially in relation to the Lambeth Conferences of the nineteenth century. Furthermore, it is helpful at times to compare developments in the Church of England with those in its geographically proximate sister churches, the Church in Wales and the Scottish Episcopal Church.

Chapter 1 examines the theological sources for the 'Making of Deacons' in the Ordinal of 1550 and presents an analysis of ordination practice in the late sixteenth and early seventeenth centuries, based on the Venn data and other sources. The chapter considers the significance of deacons to Gospeller congregations in the reign of Queen Mary, drawing on the evidence in John Foxe's *Actes and Monuments* (1583). It presents evidence that the new theology embodied by the Ordinal did create genuine vocational deacons, even if the words of the Ordinal implied that the diaconate was only a temporary ministry. However, although Elizabethan apologists for conformity such as Richard Hooker upheld the need for diaconal orders as a key part of their defence of the threefold order of ministry, the Elizabethan and Jacobean church generally treated the diaconate no more seriously than the mediaeval church had done. The liturgical theology of Lancelot Andrewes and George

Herbert, combined with the Laudian bishops' reform of ordination practices, made space for a better appreciation of the diaconate in the 1620s and '30s, a process that culminated in the ordination of Nicholas Ferrar (perhaps the Church of England's most famous lifelong deacon), but was cut short by the English Civil War.

Chapter 2 presents evidence that lifelong deacons formed a sizeable minority of clergy (around 10 per cent) between the 1662 Act of Uniformity and the middle of the eighteenth century. The most common form of ministry in which these deacons were engaged was teaching in schools and universities. Furthermore, long-term deacons who waited three years or more before being ordained priest were common in this period. The chapter examines the ministries in which these lifelong and long-term deacons were engaged, and argues that the diaconate was a means for eighteenth-century bishops to deploy less educated men in parish ministry, even if no coherent theology of the diaconate can be said to have existed during this period. Ordination to the diaconate 'made honest men' of lay readers whose ministry was only partially authorised by canon. The eighteenth century was also a time when intriguing experiments with diaconal theology and ministry were attempted at the fringes of the Anglican tradition by the Non-Jurors and Methodists.

Chapter 3 examines the repeated calls for a revival of the order of deacons that began with Thomas Arnold in 1839 and continued throughout the nineteenth century. Victorian legislation made it harder for a diaconate of the kind that existed in the eighteenth century to survive, but a movement for a renewed diaconate commanded widespread support from both clergy and laity. A college for the training of deacon-schoolmasters, St Mark's, Chelsea, was established in 1841. The issue of deacons was raised at the Convocation of Canterbury in 1861 and a resolution was achieved in 1884. By 1888, however, divisions on the issue meant that discussions ended in stalemate, and the matter was shelved until the early twentieth century. The chapter examines the various arguments on both sides and tries to explain how, with so much support behind it from both clergy and laity of all shades of churchmanship, the Victorian campaign came to nothing and is now virtually forgotten.

Chapter 4 examines the call for the renewal of the diaconate at the Lambeth Conferences in the twentieth century and the reasons why that renewal was less successful in the Church of England than in other provinces of the Anglican Communion, in spite of a handful of bold experiments. It will trace the process by which General Synod approved the admission of women to deacon's orders in 1987, and the subsequent attempts to recover a coherent theology of the diaconate to enable the ministry of women to be as wide as possible in the church. The chapter will examine the key documents involved in this process and assess the extent to which late-twentieth-century Anglican thinking on the diaconate valued the diaconate for its own sake, or made use of it as a vehicle to deliver the aspirations of women seeking ordination.

Chapter 5 deals with the development of Anglican thinking on the diaconate since the admission of women to priest's orders in 1994, concentrating on the report presented to General Synod in 2001, *For Such a Time as This*, and the subsequent report, *The Mission and Ministry of the Whole Church* (2007). The chapter will examine the reasons behind General Synod's reluctance to endorse *For Such a Time as This* and the debate that was ignited by both reports. Finally, the Conclusion draws upon the evidence of history to present the twin cases for and against an active revival of the distinctive diaconate in the Church of England.

# 1

# *Deacons and the English Reformation, 1550-1642*

The history of deacons in the Church of England begins with the publication of the first English Ordinal in 1550. Prior to that date, the Roman Pontifical remained in use for ordinations in Henry VIII's Church of England. For the first time, the English Ordinal articulated the reformed English church's official understanding of the orders of ministry, including the diaconate. 'The Form and Manner of Making of Deacons' remained in the 1662 *Book of Common Prayer*, virtually unaltered from its original form, and thus it still stands as an official embodiment of the Church of England's doctrine of orders, even if it has been superseded in practice, in almost every case, by the ordination service of *Common Worship*, a version slightly altered from the *Alternative Service Book* of 1980.

The two earliest lifelong deacons in the Church of England, the martyrs John Bradford and Cuthbert Symson, dedicated themselves to pastoral care of the poor and a prophetic witness on their behalf, but experiments in diaconal ministry launched in England by Martin Bucer in the early 1550s were cut short by Mary I's I's reversal of the recent ecclesiastical changes. When the English Prayer Book and Ordinal returned with the Elizabethan Settlement in 1559, Protestant deacons came back too, but Puritans who were dissatisfied with the 'purity' of the English Reformation called into question the threefold doctrine of orders and the validity of episcopally ordained deacons. Richard Hooker responded by defending the diaconate against its detractors, providing the Church of England with a theology of the diaconate that focussed on a teaching ministry rather than a ministry to the poor. The 1580s and '90s marked the nadir of the transitional diaconate, and it was a time when many – perhaps most – clergy were ordained priest within a day of receiving deacon's orders, and frequently on the same day.

During the reign of James I, the prescriptions of the Ordinal regarding the interval between diaconal and priestly ordinations began to be more strictly enforced, although it was not until the late 1620s that a year in deacon's orders became normative for most clergy. This may have been as much to do with the increased difficulty of obtaining benefices as it was to do with a conscious effort on the part of the bishops to honour the year-long diaconate. However, William Laud and some other bishops began to demand higher standards from candidates for ordination, and Laud himself was supportive of the idea of ordaining men to a lifelong diaconate. In 1626, as Bishop of St Davids, Laud ordained Nicholas Ferrar, the founder of the Little Gidding community and the best known of all Anglican deacons. However, both Laud's reform of the Church of England and Ferrar's experiment in religious life were cut short by the English Civil War in 1642 and the abolition of episcopal government of the church in 1646.

## Deacons in the Ordinal

The Canon Law of the mediaeval English church did not require men to be ordained priest before they were appointed to a benefice, and it was commonplace for individuals to be admitted to the order of acolyte or subdeacon at a young age in order to secure preferment before they proceeded to the major orders of deacon and priest. However, the centrality of the mass to late mediaeval spirituality meant that most incumbents went on to be ordained priest at some point, and were often ordained deacon and priest on the same day. For poorer clergy, who were without benefices, it was critical to be in priest's orders, since among the few sources of income were becoming a curate (saying mass for an absentee incumbent), a chaplain to a religious house or hospital, or a chantry priest, paid to say private masses for the souls of a donor or donors. The significance of diaconal ordination in the late Middle Ages was that it marked admission to major orders, and therefore a commitment to lifelong celibacy. It was the 'point of no return' that indicated that a man was definitively choosing a career in the church. A man could be in minor orders, as an acolyte or subdeacon, and still marry and pursue a secular profession.[1]

---

1. The Act of Parliament authorising the Ordinal of 1550 made provision for the creation of minor orders, 'other ministers of the Church' below deacons,

It was an abiding theme of the European Reformation that the mediaeval church had allowed once significant institutions to become stagnant and corrupt. Bishops and priests, once true pastors, had become parasites who lived off the incomes of their dioceses and benefices without pastoral concern for the people. Although the reformers differed on the question of when the church had become corrupted, and when the popes had become Antichrist, they were at one in their view that the Reformation was not about innovation but about the revival of the purity of the primitive church. In this respect, the Reformation went hand in hand with the revival of learning and critical scholarship that went under the name of Renaissance Humanism. Whilst scholarship of the Bible always came first, the reformers were also diligent students of the Church Fathers. After all, Luther's doctrine of salvation by faith alone, the keystone of the Reformation, was underpinned by his reading of St Augustine.

It was quite natural, therefore, that from their reading of the New Testament and the Church Fathers, the reformers drew a model of the diaconate rather different from a peremptory rite of passage for would-be priests. The first hint that the Church of England would adopt an attitude to deacons different from that of the mediaeval church emerged as early as 1543, when an official publication of Henry VIII's church, entitled *A Necessary Doctrine and Erudition for any Christian Man* (commonly known as *The King's Book*), said of deacons: 'Their office in the primitive church was partly in ministering meat and drink and other necessities to poor people found of the church, partly also in ministering to the bishops and priests, and in doing their duty to the church'.[1] The idea that deacons should be involved in the service of the poor had by this time entirely disappeared from the instructions of the Roman Pontifical, so this insight derived from the reformers' renewed emphasis on the belief and practice of the early church,[2] even though Henry VIII's Church of England remained a profoundly conservative institution.

The most influential reformers, as far as the Church of England's doctrine of orders was concerned, were Martin Bucer and John Calvin. The ex-Dominican friar Martin Bucer (1491-1551), who began his reforming career in Strasbourg and remained associated

but this never happened (Smyth, C.H., *Cranmer and the Reformation under Edward VI* (Cambridge University Press: Cambridge, 1926), p. 231).

1. Bradshaw, P.F., *The Anglican Ordinal: Its History and Development from the Reformation to the Present Day*, Alcuin Club Collections 53 (SPCK: London, 1971), pp. 10-11.
2. Ibid. pp. 35-6.

with that city all his life, played an especially intimate role in the composition of the Ordinal of 1550. In April 1549, Bucer fled Strasbourg, which had been conquered by the army of the Emperor Charles V, and sought refuge in England as a guest of the Archbishop of Canterbury, Thomas Cranmer. Bucer took up the position of Regius Professor of Divinity at Cambridge University, and produced two important works during his time in England. *De Ordinatione Legitima* ('On Lawful Ordering'), a treatise on the ordering of overseers, presbyters and deacons, may have been written just before Bucer came over to England or just after, when he was staying in Cranmer's house. David Wright noted in 1993 that the question of where the treatise was written remains unresolved, although Bucer's use of the term 'our church' (*ecclesia nostra*) to describe Strasbourg might suggest that he was writing for an English context.[1] Bucer favoured the retention of the titles 'bishop', 'presbyter' and 'deacon', in spite of the fact that he regarded them all as presbyters.

Although he believed that there were three orders of presbyters in the church, Bucer insisted that there were just two ministries: 'The one includes the administration of the Word, the sacraments, and the discipline of Christ, which really belongs to the overseers or elders. The other consists in the care of the poor (*curatio egentium*) which is entrusted to those who are called deacons'.[2] Bucer's deacons are, therefore, a specific type of presbyter to whom the care of the poor is especially delegated. Bucer's bishops or overseers were the first among equals, but Bucer did not regard the work of deacons as in any way inferior to that of the presbyters, who had responsibility for preaching and dispensing the sacraments. Indeed, care for the poor occupied a prominent position in Bucer's theology. Deacons were assistants to the presbyters, but only because the presbyters did not have the time to be burdened with the care of the poor.[3]

Bucer's treatise *De Regno Christi* ('On the Reign of Christ'), which he completed in October 1550 as a Christmas gift for Edward VI, set out his ideas on the diaconate in more detail. Bucer emphasised deacons' role in relieving the poor, and set out an apostolic ideal according to which all Christians would contribute alms to a common

---

1. Wright, D.F., 'Martin Bucer in England – and Scotland' in Krieger, C. and Lienhard, M. (eds), *Martin Bucer and Sixteenth Century Europe* (Brill: Leiden, 1993), vol. 2, pp. 523-32, at p. 527.
2. Quoted in Bradshaw (1971), p. 36.
3. Van't Spijker, W. (trans. Vriend, J. and Bierma, L.D.), *The Ecclesiastical Offices in the Thought of Martin Bucer* (Brill: Leiden, 1996), p. 389.

fund, to be distributed by the deacons. However, deacons also had a disciplinary and admonitory role: they were to maintain a list of the poor and examine the lives of those on the list, removing them if they were lazy or indigent. Contrary to what was then current practice in England, Bucer argued that deacons should be chosen by the congregation for their exemplary piety, rather than selected by the bishop.[1]

Bucer regarded the ordination of overseers/bishops, presbyters and deacons as essentially the same ceremony: it should take place by the laying on of hands, although deacons should be ordained with less solemnity than presbyters or bishops, since more authority was committed to these latter ministers.[2] Willem Van't Spijker has argued that Bucer's deacons took a pivotal role in the eucharist by presenting the offertory, thus bringing care for the poor into the heart of the church's worship: 'the diaconate transfigures everything', because the human suffering of the poor is united with the suffering of Christ. Furthermore, the care of the poor was made an integral part of the church's work, which happened 'by divine right' rather than as an activity additional to the sacraments.[3]

The English text of 'The Form and Manner of Making of Deacons' in the Ordinal of 1550 bears a strong resemblance to the Latin text of *De Ordinatione Legitima*, to the extent that Cranmer seems to have borrowed extensively from Bucer's writings.[4] Paul Bradshaw has noted that, in spite of language in the Ordinal that clearly indicates that deacons are expected to continue to the priesthood, its compilers nevertheless envisaged the diaconate as 'something rather different from the mere stepping-stone to the priesthood which it had become in the course of the Middle Ages'.[5] The diaconate is differentiated from the priesthood by the language used: deacons are 'made', while priests are 'ordered' and bishops are 'consecrated', reflecting Bucer's belief that while each ordination was essentially the same ceremony, the language and gestures used should convey greater solemnity if the authority being imparted was greater. The ordination service

1. Ibid. p. 434.
2. Ibid. p. 414.
3. Ibid. p. 439.
4. Ibid. p. 347. For the text of the original service in the Ordinal see *The First and Second Prayer Books of Edward VI* (J.M. Dent and Sons: London, 1910), pp. 293-302.
5. Bradshaw, P.F., 'Ordinals', in Sykes, S., Booty, J. and Knight, J. (eds), *The Study of Anglicanism*, 2nd edn (SPCK: London, 1998), pp. 155-65, at pp. 161-2.

for deacons does not contain the overt references to the bestowal of the Holy Spirit found in the services for priests and deacons. As Paul Avis has noted, the 'imperative formula . . . which suggested a particular moment of ordination' is different for deacons: 'Take thou authority' for deacons, rather than 'Receive the Holy Ghost' for priests.[1] Furthermore, the establishment of deacons in the church is attributed to divine providence rather than the Holy Spirit:

> The diaconate was here viewed [in the Ordinal] as a creation of divine providence working through the Apostles, in which the authority of the Church to minister was given to men who had already received the Holy Spirit, in contrast to the priesthood in which the Holy Spirit was given to the candidates just as it had been bestowed upon the Apostles by Christ.[2]

Bradshaw has argued that Cranmer viewed the diaconate and the priesthood not as two consecutive orders, 'but as two completely separate orders of ministry'. Whereas in the ordination of priests, the laying on of hands was intended to confer the Holy Spirit on the candidates, in the ordination of deacons, 'candidates are expected to have received the Holy Spirit before hands are laid on them'. Cranmer thus distinguished between two different sources of power in ordination: 'The power or authority given to deacons at the imposition of hands was the permission of the Church to exercise certain functions for which they were fitted. This power originated in the Church, which by divine providence working through the Apostles had created the office of deacons'.[3] The implication of Bradshaw's interpretation is that whereas priests receive an authority from Christ, deacons receive an authority from the church. Thus, where priests are constitutive of the church, deacons are 'of the church' in such a way that a ministry of care and relief rather than leadership is imposed on them. The conferral of diaconal orders is, in other words, the public authorisation by the church of a charism bestowed by the Holy Spirit.

Cranmer also retained Bucer's emphasis on the deacon's role in relation to the poor, although this was weakened somewhat in the 1552 edition of the Ordinal. The 1552 edition added the words 'in the Churche where he shalbe appoynted' as a condition of the assistance offered by the deacon to the priest, indicating that

1.  Avis, P., 'The Revision of the Ordinal in the Church of England, 1550-2005', *Ecclesiology* 1 (2005), pp. 95-110, at p. 97.
2.  Bradshaw (1998), p. 162.
3.  Bradshaw (1971), pp. 34-5.

deacons were to be licensed to specific parish churches. Deacons were thus bound, to a greater extent than in 1550, to assist a particular priest and thus less free to relieve the poor beyond the church itself. The 1552 Ordinal also placed a greater emphasis on the preaching role of the deacon. Whereas in 1550 the deacon was to preach 'yf he be commaunded by the Bisshop', in 1552 he was to preach 'yf he be admitted thereto by the Bisshop'.[1] In other words, preaching by the deacon had changed from being an occasional event to being a specific ministry expected of any deacon who was duly licensed to do so.

Most importantly of all, the 1552 text appended the condition 'where provision is so made' to the words 'It is his office to searche for the sicke, poore, and impotente people of the parishe'. This addition had a chilling effect on Bucer's original vision of deacons as ministers to the poor for the next 300 years, especially after the 1601 Poor Law institutionalised parish poor relief and removed any vestige of the church congregation's direct involvement. The overall effect of the amendments made to the text in 1552 was to put the deacon firmly back within the four walls of the church building, while not altogether overthrowing Bucer and Cranmer's original theology. The most probable reason for this is that the diaconate remained an apprenticeship for the priesthood in the Edwardian church, and therefore it was considered unfeasible to assign a ministry to deacons radically different from that of priests. On the other hand, there were those prepared to experiment, such as the Bishop of Gloucester (and then Worcester), John Hooper. Hooper, who was amongst the most radical of Edward VI's bishops, applied Bucer's ideas of pastoral care for the poor in his diocese.[2]

Even in Edward VI's brief reign, the stipulation that clergy should remain in deacon's orders for a whole year before being admitted to priest's orders was rarely followed. Mediaeval habits died hard, and the Edwardian church undermined its own reforms by tolerating lay ownership of benefices. The unfinished revision of Canon Law begun by Edward's bishops in 1551, the *Reformatio Legum Ecclesiasticarum* ('Reformation of Ecclesiastical Laws'), provided that laymen could enter into possession of a benefice by taking the Oaths of Supremacy and Allegiance.[3] Although the new

---

1. *The Prayer Book of Queen Elizabeth 1559* (Griffith Farran: London, 1891), p. 166.
2. Van't Spijker (1996), p. 459.
3. *Reformatio Legum Ecclesiasticarum* (London, 1641), p. 66.

canons also required that the layman had to be ordained deacon within six months of appointment, and priest a year after that, because the canons were never promulgated, this did not always happen.[1]

The revised canons stipulated that bishops, priests and deacons were to receive their office and authority by the laying on of hands, 'since there is a mention of it in the Holy Scriptures, and it has been a perpetual custom in the church'.[2] This was hardly an elaborate justification, but it reflected Bucer's conservatism on the issue of orders. Cranmer and Bucer, whilst not necessarily accepting the idea of the apostolic succession of bishops or the idea that ordination conferred a 'sacramental character' on bishops, priests and deacons, believed that the titles of the threefold order of ministry, as well as the relative authority of bishops, priests and deacons, should be preserved. This was in contrast to Calvin's theology of the diaconate where, although the role of deacons was similar to that described by Bucer, deacons were not participants in a threefold ministry with priests and bishops.

In spite of Bradshaw's efforts at interpretation, the service called 'The Form and Manner of Making of Deacons' does not contain a clearly articulated and fully-fledged theology of the diaconate, and this has had important consequences for the development (or underdevelopment) of the diaconate in the Church of England. On the one hand, the deacon of the Edwardian Ordinal is more than just an apprentice priest with limited priestly functions: he has distinct functions in the form of care for the poor. On the other hand, the Ordinal of 1550-52 implies that most, if not all, deacons will proceed to priest's orders, and presents deacons not only as inferior to presbyters but also as being under their authority. The ordaining bishop prays over the deacons:

> [M]ake them we beseche thee, O Lorde, to bee modest, humble, and constant in their ministracion, to have a ready wyl to observe al spiritual discipline, that they havinge alwayes the testimonie of a good conscience, and continuing ever stable

1. For example, in March 1553 the mathematician and astrologer John Dee was appointed Rector of Upton-upon-Severn in Worcestershire without having been ordained deacon or priest; the benefice was in Hooper's diocese. Dee could only keep his benefice under Mary by being ordained deacon and priest (Parry, G., *The Arch-Conjurer of England: John Dee* (Yale University Press: New Haven, CT, 2011), p. 25).
2. *Reformatio Legum Ecclesiasticarum* (1641), p. 30: '... *quoniam illius in sacris Scripturis mentio sit, et perpetuum habuerit usum in Ecclesia.*'

and strong in thy sonne Christ, may so wel use themselves in thys inferior offyce, that they may be found worthi to be called unto the higher ministeries in thy Church.[1]

The Ordinal is perhaps best seen as an unwieldy attempt to fuse a hierarchical model of ministry, essentially unchanged from the pre-Reformation church, with Bucer's proposal that deacons should have a distinct ministry. Not for the last time, the Church of England established a diaconate without sufficient theological consideration beforehand.

## Persecuted deacons

The accession of Mary Tudor in 1553, and the revival of the heresy laws the following year, made the English Prayer Book and the Ordinal illegal texts. The congregations who made use of the English liturgy went underground. In the mid-nineteenth century, when the campaign for a revival of the diaconate was at its height, Charles William Chepmell attempted to popularise Cuthbert Symson, who was burnt as a heretic in March 1558, as the Church of England's first deacon-martyr.[2] In fact, Symson was preceded as a deacon-martyr by the preacher John Bradford (1510-1555), who was burnt at the stake on 1 July 1555. Bradford was a theologian and a fellow of Pembroke College, Cambridge, who was ordained deacon by the Bishop of London, Nicholas Ridley, in the chapel at Fulham Palace on 10 August 1550. Bradford objected to the ordination service, possibly on account of the words 'so help me God, all Saints and the holy Evangelist' in the Oath of Supremacy, which would later be removed in 1552. Ridley agreed to ordain Bradford 'without abuse', gave him a licence to preach and appointed him one of his chaplains.[3]

In August 1551, Bradford was made a prebendary of St Paul's Cathedral, and at the end of the year he was appointed one of six royal chaplains, 'to preach sound doctrine in the remotest parts of the kingdom'. Bradford went on a preaching tour of Lancashire and Cheshire,[4] where he acquired a formidable reputation as a stirring and prophetic preacher. In 1554, John Knox noted that 'Master Bradford . . . spared not the proudest, but boldly declared that God's

1. 'The form and maner of makyng ... Deacons' (1891), p. 281.
2. [Chepmell, C.W.], *Chapters on Deacons* (London, 1849), pp. 252-73.
3. Bradford, J., *The Writings of John Bradford, M.A.*, ed. A. Townshend (Parker Society: Cambridge, 1853), pp. xxii-xxiii.
4. Ibid. p. xxvi.

vengeance should shortly strike those that were then in authority, because they loathed and abhorred the true word of the everlasting God'.[1] Bradford denounced 'ungodly loathsomeness to hear poor men's causes' and bore prophetic witness on behalf of the poor and the oppressed.[2] He was a close of friend of Bucer while the latter was in England, and took a particular interest in Bucer's *De Regno Christi* (1557), with its call for the establishment of social justice.

In contrast to John Bradford, the preaching and prophetic deacon, Cuthbert Symson spent his life in the direct service of the poor of London. John Foxe's account of Symson's arrest, trial and martyrdom gives a unique insight into the role of deacons in London's underground Gospeller congregation during Mary's reign. Foxe's account presents Symson as an organiser, trying to protect the congregation from persecution and providing for their needs:

> This Cutbert Symson was a manne of a faythfull, and zealous hart to Christ and his true flocke, in so much that he neuer ceased labouryng, and Studying most earnestly, not onely how to preserue them without corruption of the Popish religion, but also hys care was euer vigilant, how to keepe them together wythout peryll, or daunger of persecution. The paynes, trauayle, zeale, pacience, and fidelity of this man, in caryng, and prouiding for thys Congregation, as it is not lightly to be expressed.

If Foxe is to be believed, Symson was fulfilling Bucer and Cranmer's diaconal ideal to a greater extent under persecution than had ever been possible during the establishment of the reformed faith. Foxe told how John Rough, the minister of the underground Gospeller congregation, had a prophetic dream in which he foresaw his own and Symson's martyrdom, in which Symson 'had the booke about hym, wherin were written the names of all them which were of the Congregation'.[3] The Ordinal did not require the existence of such a book, which was one of Bucer's recommendations, suggesting that the underground Gospeller congregation was drawing directly on Bucer's diaconal theology and practice as expounded in *De Ordinatione Legitima* (1549) and *De Regno Christi*. Shortly after Rough had dreamt of Symson, Symson entered with the book containing the names of the congregation, and Rough instructed him to stop

1. Ibid. p. xxviii.
2. Ibid. p. xxix.
3. Foxe, J., *Actes and Monuments* (London, 1583), vol. 2, p. 2032.

carrying it around with him – presumably because of the danger of being found in possession of it by the authorities. Symson was reluctant to leave the book with Rough, and in the end he made notes on some of the most crucial information he needed.

On 12 December 1557, the authorities raided the Saracen's Head inn at Islington, where they apprehended John Rough celebrating the Lord's Supper according to the 1552 Prayer Book, 'under the colour of hearing a playe', along with Cuthbert Symson, whom Foxe tells us was a tailor.[1] Admittedly the Gospellers were a persecuted church whose circumstances were hardly normal, but the fact that Symson followed a secular profession (and a lowly one at that) as well as being an ordained deacon may be significant. On 13 December, the Privy Council remanded Symson to the Tower, where he was tortured on the rack in the hope that he would reveal who attended services according to the English Prayer Book. This suggests that the authorities were aware that Symson, as a deacon, knew better than anyone else who was in the congregation.

According to Foxe, Symson was twice racked, then tortured by having an arrow pulled through his bound fingers. Symson left his own account of what happened next:

> Then was I caryed to my lodging agayne, and x. dayes after the Lieuetenant asked me if I would not confesse that, which before they had asked me. I sayd I had sayd as much as I would. Then fiue weekes after, he sent me vnto the high Prieste [i.e. the Bishop of London, Edmund Bonner], where I was greatly assaulted, and at whose hande I receiued the Popes curse, for bearing witnesse of the resurrection of Iesus Christ. And thus I commend you vnto God, and to the worde of his grace, with all them that vnfaynedly call vpon the name of Iesus, desiring God of his endles mercy, through the merites of hys deare sonne Iesus Christe to bringe vs all to hys euerlasting kingdome. Amen. I prayse God for his great mercy shewed vppon vs. Syng Osanna vnto the highest with me Cutbert Simson, God forgeue me my sinnes. I aske all the worlde forgeuenesse, and I doe forgeue all the worlde, and thus I leaue thys world, in hope of a ioyfull resurrection.[2]

Symson was accused of denying the seven sacraments, denying the authority of the Bishop of Rome and denying the real presence of Christ in the eucharist. Only one charge against Symson touched his role as a deacon, however:

---

1. Ibid. p. 2031.
2. Ibid. p. 2032.

Item that thou, contrary to the order of this Realme of Englande, and contrary to the vsage of the holy Churche of this Realme of England, hast at sundry tymes and places, within the Citye and Dioces of London, beene at assemblyes, and conuenticles, where there was a multitude of people gathered together, to heare the Englishe seruice sayed . . . and also to heare, and haue the Communion booke reade, and the Communion ministred, both to the sayd multitude, and also to thy selfe, and thou hast thought, and so thinkest, and hast spoken that the sayd Englishe seruice, and Communion booke, and all thinges conteyned in eyther of them was good and laudable, and for such thou diddest, and doest allowe, and approue eyther of them at this present.[1]

The words 'the Communion ministred, both to the sayd multitude, and also to thy selfe' are a direct reference to the deacon's role in administering the sacrament in the 1552 Prayer Book. However, it remains uncertain whether Symson was an episcopally ordained deacon or whether he was simply commissioned to the office by the congregation during the time of persecution. Symson combined his role of deacon with his work as a tailor, he kept a book containing the names of the congregation (a practice reminiscent of recommendations in the works of Bucer and Calvin) and there is no direct reference to him preaching.

The Gospeller congregations in the reign of Queen Mary were by no means all faithful to the doctrine and practice of the Second Prayer Book of Edward VI, and in the absence of reformed bishops, religious radicals experimented both with doctrine and worship. It would be unhistorical to imagine the persecuted congregations of this era as persecuted Anglicans, and martyrs for the Prayer Book, even if this was often the picture painted by nineteenth-century evangelical Anglicans. Symson may well have thought of himself as a deacon in the sense that Bucer and Calvin advocated, a man chosen by the congregation for his piety who would keep track of the congregation both to admonish them and to distribute alms to the poor. Whatever his status, Symson was burnt at the stake at Smithfield on 28 March 1558, along with two other Gospellers named Foxe and Devenish.[2] He suffered and died to protect the identities of those members of the congregation he had written in his book, in order to relieve their needs in diaconal service.

---

1. Ibid. p. 2033.
2. Ibid. p. 2034.

## Deacons and the Elizabethan Settlement

In November 1558, Mary I was succeeded as Queen by her half-sister Elizabeth. Elizabeth's personal religious convictions are notoriously obscure; her preference was for the First Prayer Book of Edward VI, and even for the Latin liturgy in her own private chapel, but the Act of Settlement of 1559 re-introduced the 1552 Prayer Book with minor amendments. These included the requirement that all officiating clergy wear a surplice, which was not required in Edward's reign. Elizabeth's primary concern was with the outward religious conformity of her subjects, which was widely believed at the time to be a precondition of political and social stability. This policy of conformity alienated the more radical Protestants in Elizabethan England, as well as Roman Catholics, who were the direct victims of the new religious policy.

Elizabeth I's first Archbishop of Canterbury, Matthew Parker, showed scant respect for the Ordinal when he permitted John Scory, the Bishop of Hereford, to ordain ten men deacon and priest on the same day in 1559.[1] However, the church was desperate for new clergy, since many remained loyal to the papacy and were deprived of their benefices. One solution was to rely on lay readers as a temporary measure, although at least some of these readers were later ordained deacon as a means of authorising their ministry and situating it within the church's lawful structures of authority. These were generally men with a grammar school education and therefore some minor knowledge of Latin (then crucial to read the works of the European Reformers), but no university education. One such individual was Thomas Earl, the son of a London draper who received a grammar school education and intended to go to Oxford, but ended up being apprenticed instead to a painter-stainer for ten years. In 1559, Earl became a reader in London, and he was later ordained deacon, receiving the incumbency of St Mildred, Bread Street in 1564.[2]

Parker drew up a set of guidelines for incumbents entrusted with the care of several churches, in which he advised

> The said principal Incumbent to depute, in every such Parish committed to his Care, a Deacon, (if it might be) or some honest, sober, and grave Lay-man: who, as a Reader should read the Order of Service appointed: but such Reader not to intermeddle

1. Strype, J., *Annals of the Reformation* (London, 1709), vol. 1, p. 159.
2. Ibid. p. 178.

to Christen, Marry, or Minister the Holy Communion, or Preach or Prophecy: but only to read the Service of the Day, with the Litany and Homily, as should be prescribed, in the Absence of the principal Pastor.[1]

A deacon was preferable to a lay reader, because he could baptise, marry and assist with the distribution of Holy Communion. However, there is some evidence that congregations of remote chapels-of-ease served by deacons were unhappy that they could only receive the sacrament at infrequent intervals. Edward Haydocke, the deacon who served the Bruera Chapelry in Cheshire in 1628, receiving a stipend of £5, reported that the people had complained that their last incumbent did not celebrate the sacrament, and enthusiastically received the sacrament when he arranged for a minister in priest's orders to celebrate it at Easter.[2]

Part of Elizabeth's drive for conformity involved withholding licences to preach from the majority of the clergy, even priests, who were thereby confined to reading from the approved Book of Homilies. Many radical Protestants were convinced that the Elizabethan Settlement was just a step on the way to a more perfect Reformation. They were consequently unhappy with the continued existence of bishops and cathedrals ('prelacy'), the requirement of wearing the surplice, the use of the sign of the cross in baptism, the widespread ban on preaching and the still hierarchical nature of the church. In 1572, the Puritans Laurence Humphrey and Thomas Sampson wrote an *Admonition to Parliament,* calling on Parliament 'to remove . . . ignorant ministers, to take awai private communions and baptismes, to enjoyne Deacons and Midwives not to meddle in ministers matters, [and] if they doe, to see them sharpelie punished'.[3] The fact that deacons are here coupled with midwives strongly suggests that Humphrey and Sampson's objection was to baptisms conducted by deacons. The Puritans regarded baptism as a form of preaching, which was the proper realm of presbyters rather than deacons. Allowing deacons to baptise implied acceptance of the Catholic doctrine that deacons were partial sharers in the sacramental power conferred upon priests, and that baptism represented an automatic regeneration from sin that could be performed even by a layperson.

---

1. Strype, J., *The Life and Acts of Matthew Parker* (London, 1711), pp. 65-6.
2. Maltby, J., *Prayer Book and People in Elizabethan and Early Stuart England* (Cambridge University Press: Cambridge, 1998), pp. 47-8.
3. Cleugh, H., 'The Prayer Book in Early Stuart Society' in Platten, S. and Woods, C. (eds), *Comfortable Words: Polity, Piety and the Book of Common Prayer* (SCM Press: London, 2012), pp. 35-48, at p. 38.

There were also objections to surviving liturgical manifestations of the diaconate. In 1566, Perceval Wiburn lamented to a Continental Protestant that in the Church of England,

> during prayers, the minister must wear a linen garment, which we call a surplice. And in the larger churches, at the administration of the Lord's Supper, the chief minister must wear a silk garment which they call a cope. And two other ministers, formerly called the deacon and subdeacon, must assist him to read the epistle and gospel.[1]

This was a reference to an ecclesiastical ordinance of 1565-66, later made into canon in the reign of James I, which applied to cathedrals and collegiate churches. This required a gospeller and epistler to assist the main celebrant, recalling the deacon and subdeacon at high mass in previous times. It is unclear whether the gospeller and epistler were ever men in deacon's orders (rather than priests serving as deacons), but there was no reason why they could not be. In the early seventeenth century, Lancelot Andrewes elaborated the liturgical role of the deacon still further, suggesting that he should go in and out of the 'sacrarium' (chancel) to serve the priest during the service, recalling the practice of the deacon going in and out of the holy doors in the iconostasis in the Orthodox Divine Liturgy.[2] Andrewes's emphasis on the deacon's intermediate role between the deacon and the laity, going into but not remaining within the sanctuary, recalled the practice of the early church but also suggested that Andrewes may have expected this liturgical role to have been fulfilled by a deacon rather than a priest performing the deacon's role. Within the context of Andrewes's project to enhance the solemnity of the liturgy, the deacon played a crucial role by demarcating the sanctuary space as sacred and the role of the priest as an especially exalted one.

Puritans were not necessarily opposed to deacons *per se*, or to the idea of diaconal ministry. In 1570, the civic authorities in Norwich appointed two men identified as 'deacons' in each ward to have 'oversight of the poore', with duties that included keeping records of the poor, vagrants, struggling families and newcomers to the city, and ensuring that everyone who could work was put to work. Clearly, these men were not ordained ministers but deacons after

---

1. *Zurich Letters*, ed. H. Robinson (Parker Society: Cambridge, 1846), p. 272.
2. McCullouch, P., 'Absent Presence: Lancelot Andrewes and 1662', in Platten, S. and Woods, C. (eds), *Comfortable Words: Polity, Piety and the Book of Common Prayer* (SCM Press: London, 2012), pp. 49-68, at p. 60.

the Calvinist model.[1] Puritans opposed the idea that the ministerial office could be divided between presbyters and deacons, so that deacons could be delegated to perform some of the functions of presbyters. In 1607, Henry Ainsworth contemptuously listed 'deacons or halfpriests' among the functionaries of the Church of England whom he believed were not authorised by scripture,[2] thereby implying that the Church of England's deacons were not true deacons in the sense that Bucer and Calvin might have intended, but rather mere apprentice priests. On the other hand, other Puritans took advantage of the fact that the requirements for diaconal ordination were lower than those for ordination to the priesthood. The sixteenth-century controversialist Thomas Cartwright (1534/5-1603) was never ordained priest and remained a deacon all his life. Crucially, ordination as a deacon entitled him to seek a bishop's licence to preach.[3] Ironically, Cartwright was a prominent opponent of the very existence of the office of deacon.[4]

The Puritans' assault on the diaconate was, in fact, part of their wider attack on the threefold order of ministry. The man who took up the challenge of defending the Elizabethan church, and therefore the diaconate, was Richard Hooker (1554-1600). In March 1585, Hooker was appointed Master of the Temple Church in London, where he came into conflict with Walter Travers, the Reader of the Temple, who had earlier argued in his *Full and Plaine Declaration of Ecclesiastical Discipline* (1574) that churchwardens and overseers should be converted into elders and deacons on the Calvinist model.[5] Hooker's dispute with Travers over ecclesiastical discipline was one of the principal reasons for his writing *The Laws of Ecclesiastical Polity*, first published in 1594, which provided a systematic defence of the government of the Church of England.

In his *Laws*, Hooker argued that bishops, priests and deacons represented three degrees of power in the church but only two categories of ministry: priest-bishops and deacons.[6] In Hooker's

---

1. Griffiths, P., 'Inhabitants' in Rawcliffe, C. and Wilson, R. (eds), *Norwich since 1550* (Hambledon: London, 2004), pp. 63-89, at p. 67.
2. Ainsworth, H., *The Confession of Faith of certayn English People living in Exile* (n. p., 1607), p. 47.
3. Collinson, P., 'Cartright, Thomas' in *ODNB*, vol. 10, pp. 409-13.
4. Strype (1725), vol. 1, p. 627.
5. Gibbs, L.W., 'Life of Hooker' in Kirby, T. (ed.), *A Companion to Richard Hooker* (Brill: Leiden, 2008), pp. 1-26, at p. 11.
6. Simut, C.C., 'Orders of Ministry' in Kirby, *A Companion to Richard Hooker*, pp. 403-34, at p. 415.

view, the fundamental difference between deacons and presbyters was that, while the former were elected by Christ before his ascension, the deacons were appointed by the Apostles after the ascension. The primary purpose of both presbyters and deacons was to preach the Gospel, and Hooker did not devote much consideration to deacons' work in relation to the poor.[1] He was critical of the Presbyterian view that a deacon was 'one which hath charge of the alms-box, and of nothing else'.[2] Hooker's *Laws* picked up on a theme in mediaeval ecclesiology by identifying bishops with the High Priest of Solomon's Temple, priests with the Aaronic priests and deacons with the Levites:

> Priests in the Law had authority to do greater things than Levites; the high priest greater than inferior priests might do, therefore Levites were beneath priests, and priests inferior to the high priest. . . . In like sort, presbyters having a weightier and worthier charge than deacons had, the deacon was in this sort the presbyter's inferior.[3]

Hooker argued that Stephen and the other early 'deacons' in Acts were not made deacons by their choice by the Apostles or their acclamation by the people. Rather, it was the imposition of hands from the Apostles 'which gave them their very being; all other things besides were only preparations unto this'.[4] Hooker acknowledged that the role of deacons had evolved in the church; they were originally 'stewards of the church, unto whom at first was committed the distribution of church-goods, the care of providing therewith for the poor, and the charge to see that all things of expence might be religiously and faithfully dealt in'. Now, however, the role of the deacon had expanded to include preaching. Hooker attacked those 'to whom it seemeth a thing so monstrous that deacons should sometime be licensed to preach' and responded to Puritan critics with a powerful defence of the role of deacons as teachers of the faithful:

> To charge them for this [i.e. preaching] as men not contented with their own vocations, and as breakers into that which appertaineth unto others, is very hard. For when they are thereunto once admitted, it is part of their own vocation, it

---

1. Ibid. pp. 413-14.
2. Hooker, R., *Of the Lawes of Ecclesiastical Politie* (London, 1723), p. lxviii.
3. Ibid. p. 353.
4. Ibid. p. 370.

appertaineth now unto them as well as others; neither is it intrusion for them to do it, being in such sort called, but rather in us it were temerity to blame them for doing it. Suppose we the office of teaching to be so repugnant unto the office of deaconship, that they cannot concur in one and the same person? What was there done in the church by deacons, which the apostles did not first discharge, being teachers? . . . Now tract of time having clean worn out those first occasions for which the deaconship was then most necessary, it might the better be afterwards extended to other services, and so remain, as at this present day, a degree in the clergy of God which the apostles of Christ did institute.[1]

In Hooker's view, the original deacons were only ever individuals to whom the Apostles delegated one of their original ministries – that of caring for the poor and serving at tables. Therefore, it made sense that in the contemporary church, other needful functions, such as preaching, could also be delegated to deacons. Hooker's argument defended the diaconate, but at the expense of relegating deacons' traditional role of relieving the poor to the past. It seems likely that it was a direct consequence of Hooker's approach that, for the next two centuries, lifelong and long-term deacons would serve primarily as curates and schoolmasters.

James I, who succeeded Queen Elizabeth in 1603, was a cautious Protestant conservative who was determined to uphold the authority of bishops, convinced that it underpinned his own authority. One of the early achievements of James's bishops was the revision of the canons, a process begun in 1551 but not completed until 1604. Four of the Canons of 1604 had an important bearing on deacons. Canon 34 laid down a minimum ordination age of twenty-three for deacons and twenty-four for priests, and Canon 32 outlawed the practice of ordaining candidates deacon and priest on the same day.[2] This ban had limited effect, and Gianetta Hayes has compared the ordination practices of Welsh bishops in the sixteenth century to conclude that the stipulations of the Ordinal were rarely followed. The length of time between orders was an indication both of 'clerical quality' and 'episcopal conscientiousness' – the one potentially cancelling out the other, if bishops were so lax as to waive the diaconal period for almost all candidates.[3] Bishops continued to flout the Ordinal

1. Ibid. pp. 281-2.
2. *Canons 1604*, p. 35.
3. Hayes (2005), p. 720.

and Canon 32 even as late as the eighteenth century, but Canon 32 represented the beginning of a trend towards a longer interval between diaconal and priestly ordinations.

Canon 76 required that 'No man being admitted a Deacon or Minister shall . . . afterward use himself in the course of his life as a layman, upon pain of excommunication'.[1] This was generally interpreted to mean that priests could not engage in trade, although it was not generally applied to deacons, and a law of 1529 specifically permitted the clergy to farm and sell corn or cattle if their glebe lands were insufficient to support them.[2] Finally, Canon 24 formalised the ordinance of 1565-66 by instructing that the celebrant of Holy Communion in a cathedral church was to be assisted by a gospeller and epistler.[3] Deacons were thus guaranteed a liturgical role in the larger collegiate and cathedral churches.

## Diaconal ordinations in the Reformation period

Little analysis of ordinations to the diaconate (and indeed the priesthood) during the Reformation period has been undertaken by historians. Two notable exceptions are Kenneth Fincham's study of the ordination practices of Jacobean bishops and Gianetta Hayes's study of ordinations in Wales and the Marches between 1540 and 1640. Both Fincham and Hayes relied on ordination registers specific to individual dioceses, highly suitable for a case-study approach, but the best sources for a broader overview of ordinations during the period are alumni lists for Oxford and Cambridge, where most (but by no means all) candidates for ordination were educated. Unfortunately, the standard list of Oxford alumni (Joseph Foster's *Alumni Oxonienses* of 1888) does not contain sufficient detail, but John and John Archibald Venn's thorough *Alumni Cantabrigienses* (1922-54) contains the dates of individuals' diaconal and priestly ordinations where these were available to Venn and his son.[4]

Venn's *Alumni* is in three parts: matriculations up to 1500, matriculations between 1500 and 1751, and matriculations between 1751 and 1900. For the purpose of this analysis, I have taken the first 155 alumni on the list whose diaconal ordination is recorded between

1. *Canons 1604*, p. 75.
2. Vaughan (1987), pp. 9-10.
3. *Canons 1604*, p. 25.
4. The Clergy of the Church of England Database (CCEd) contains information on ordinations, but it is not currently possible to search the database by ordination (http://theclergydatabase.org.uk).

1560 and 1642 (surnames under the letter 'A', Abbes to Ayscough; see Appendix A). 1560 was the year from which the English Ordinal was consistently used, following the Act of Uniformity which came into effect on 24 June 1559. 1642 was the year in which the outbreak of Civil War plunged the Church of England into a fight for survival that lasted until the Restoration of the monarchy in 1660. There are a number of potential limitations to this sample. Until the 1660s, a lower standard of education than an Oxford or Cambridge degree was sometimes accepted as sufficient for ordination, especially to the diaconate, and therefore there can be no certainty that Cambridge-educated deacons were representative of deacons as a whole. Secondly, accurate records of ordinations do not always survive, and if they did, they were not always available to Venn. Thirdly, in the sixteenth and seventeenth centuries, Cambridge was very much the local university for the south east of England, and most alumni were ordained in the dioceses of Ely, Peterborough, Norwich and London.

A sample of clerical Cambridge alumni does not necessarily constitute a representative sample of the clergy as a whole. As Fincham has demonstrated, the education levels of the clergy varied greatly from region to region. Only 49 per cent of ordinands in the Diocese of Bangor between 1617 and 1625 were graduates, and a similar situation obtained in other Welsh dioceses. In Durham, 51 per cent of men ordained after 1617 did not have a degree; the figure was 73 per cent in Carlisle. Fincham argued that whereas almost all ordinands in the south-east quadrant of England had a university degree, only 60-70 per cent of clergy in the Midlands and West Country were university men. In Wales and the Province of York, graduates were in the minority.[1] However, even with the proviso that Cambridge-educated ordinands represented the upper echelon of the clergy, Venn's *Alumni* remains the only collection of data that can provide a broader picture than the individual ordination registers. Furthermore, Venn's list is based on matriculations (admissions to colleges) at Cambridge, rather than graduations. In the sixteenth and seventeenth centuries, many men went up to university but did not graduate, with potentially limiting consequences for their career prospects in the church.

Of the 155 Cambridge alumni in the sample ordained between 1560 and 1642, 47 have a diaconal ordination recorded, but no record of their admission to priest's orders. Most of these men were probably ordained priest, albeit no record of their ordination survives, since they went on to hold benefices as rectors. Although it was legally possible for a deacon

---

1.  Fincham (1990), p. 183.

to hold a benefice until 1661, the higher the status of an individual within the church, the less likely it was that he would remain a deacon. An analysis of the 47 individuals for whom no priestly ordination is recorded reveals 13 rectors, while no information on subsequent careers is available for 17 individuals. The remaining 19 pursued more lowly careers and may, therefore, have remained in deacon's orders only.

**Table 1: Ordained Cambridge alumni, 1560-1642, Abbes-Ayscough**

| Category | Number |
|---|---|
| Deacons ordained priest | 108 |
| Deacons probably ordained priest | 28 |
| Deacons probably not ordained priest | 19 |
| Total | 155 |

**Table 2: Analysis of probable lifelong deacons in Table 1**

| Type of Ministry | Number |
|---|---|
| Vicar | 6 |
| Curate | 5 |
| Schoolmaster | 4 |
| Perpetual curate | 1 |
| Suspended from benefice | 1 |
| Died before priestly ordination | 1 |

The first group of probable lifelong deacons contains vicars, curates and perpetual curates. Thomas Adams of St John's College (ordained 20 September 1628) was successively perpetual curate of chapels at Rushton and Blurton in the Diocese of Lichfield. The fact that Adams was never involved in normal parish ministry would argue in favour of his having remained a deacon for the rest of his life. Perpetual curates and chaplains usually had no need to be ordained priest, since they were employed to preach rather than to administer the sacrament. Peter Amies, Vicar of Bradfield in Essex, was ordained deacon on 6 April 1600 at the age of thirty-five. This was an advanced age at which to enter the ministry and Adams was unlikely to have gained further

preferment, suggesting that he may well not have progressed beyond
the diaconate, because he would have been unable to obtain a title
for priest's orders. John Anthony, ordained deacon in March 1562,
'learned his grammar at Cambridge', a phrase suggesting that he did
not complete his degree. Grammar (meaning the Latin language) was
the basic prerequisite for university studies. If Anthony was no more
than literate in Latin, it is likely that he remained a deacon. Ordination
registers of this period often recorded whether a candidate was
*literatus* or *illiteratus* in the Latin language; an *illiteratus* was far more
likely to be expected to remain a deacon only.

Benjamin Nightingale's 1911 study of clergy in Cumberland and
Westmoreland deprived (ejected from office) under the 1662 Act
of Uniformity provides considerable insight into the lives of these
perpetual deacon-curates. In the dioceses of Chester and Carlisle,
where many parishes covered vast areas, perpetual curates in
deacon's orders were widely deployed. Of the clergy mentioned by
Nightingale, fifty-six were ordained priest, while twenty-seven seem
to have been in deacon's orders only.[1] It does not seem unreasonable
to imagine that just under half of the clergy of Cumberland and
Westmoreland were lifelong deacons, given their generally poor
standard of education. In 1676, George Messenger, the deacon-
curate of Embleton, hinted at common problems that accompanied
deacon curates when he reported that

> Our Chappel yard is well fenced for keeping out swine &c.
> Neither is there any encroach[en]t made thereon, nor any
> Excommunicate p[er]son buryed therein. Our Minister being

1. Nightingale, B., *The Ejected of 1662 in Cumberland and Westmoreland*
   (Manchester, 1911). The deacons were: William Addison (ordained 1670)
   (p. 186), William Ardrey (ordained 1624) (p. 673), Giles Ashpool (ordained
   1685) (p. 557), Thomas Bewley (ordained 1684) (p. 187), John Calvert
   (ordained 1685) (p. 269), James Carlile (ordained before 1583) (p. 554), John
   Collier (ordained 1622) (p. 201), Nicholas Deane (ordained 1622) (p. 228),
   John Gosling (ordained 1684) (p. 284), Francis Gregson (ordained 1662)
   (p. 736), Thomas Holme (ordained 1691) (pp. 529-530), George Hume
   (ordained 1684) (p. 221), George Lowthion (ordained 1668) (p. 345), George
   Messenger (ordained 1674) (p. 677),Thomas Milburn (ordained 1671) (p.
   205), George Moon (ordained 1684) (p. 448), Richard Murthwaite (ordained
   1674) (p. 734), Robert Raylton (ordained 1611) (p. 210), Thomas Robinson
   (ordained 1618) (p. 220), William Sanderson (ordained 1680) (p. 740), John
   Sharples (ordained 1663) (p. 505), Gabriel Smallwood (ordained 1673) (p.
   214), John Todd (ordained 1673) (p. 675), Robert Troutbeck (ordained 1622)
   (p. 451), Thomas Warwick (ordained 1623) (p. 251), Anthony Wharton
   (ordained 1622) (p. 723) and Thomas Wilson (ordained 1622) (p. 290).

but Deacon always p[ro]cures a minister in full Orders to Administer the holy Sacram[en]t. And he baptizes none but with God fathers & God mothers. . . . [H]e is of a good life, is allowed by the Bishopp, his allowance is but 5li 7s. per Annum & he is Episcopally ordained.[1]

The fact that Messenger took the trouble to say these things suggests that in some other places, churchyards were overrun with farmyard animals, and excommunicated persons, such as suicides, were regularly buried there. Some deacons, less scrupulous than Messenger, may have taken it upon themselves to celebrate Holy Communion, and some may have performed baptisms without godparents. Furthermore, some deacons may not have been episcopally ordained and were perhaps survivors of Commonwealth-era presbyteries. At least some deacons were former schoolmasters. One schoolmaster, having been ordained deacon and instituted as curate, refused to live any longer in the schoolmaster's humble lodgings.[2]

One incentive for ordaining a less educated man as a deacon, especially in cash-strapped dioceses, was that he would be cheaper than a university-educated priest. In 1630, Bishop Bayly of Bangor confessed that 'I was sometimes compelled to make some few ministers that were but country scholars to serve poor Welsh chapels where the stipend is not sufficient to maintain a university man'.[3] It seems almost certain that Bayly ordained these 'country scholars' as deacons only. Bayly's critics accused him of ordaining a sexton and an alehouse-keeper, amongst others. In 1636, Bishop Barnaby Porter of Carlisle was forced to ordain 'mean scholars' – the alternative was to license lay readers, who could neither preach nor solemnise marriages.[4] Conditions were placed on these half-educated deacon-curates; Thomas Bewley, ordained by the Bishop of Chester in 1684, 'promis'd my L[or]d never to aim at priest's orders; nor to take a Cure', presumably on account of his inferior education.[5]

The second significant group in the list of Cambridge alumni are the deacon-schoolmasters. These include Thomas Allen of Corpus Christi College (ordained 24 February 1605), who was a schoolmaster at Hough in Lincolnshire in 1607; the Danish national Christian Alpinas (ordained 19 December 1563), who returned to

1. Nightingale (1911), p. 678.
2. Ibid. p. 273.
3. Fincham (1990), p. 181.
4. Ibid. pp. 182-3.
5. Ibid. p. 187.

run the royal school at Sora near Copenhagen; Henry Alston of Christ's College (ordained 25 March 1601), who was Master of the Grammar School at King's Lynn 1608-12; and John Anderson of Emmanuel College (ordained 24 December 1609), who was Master of Kimbolton School in 1611. A total of fifty-six Cambridge graduates ordained deacon (but not priest) between 1560 and 1642 served as schoolmasters. Schoolmasters, like perpetual curates, had no need to be ordained priest because they had no need to administer the sacrament. At the same time, however, teaching was seen as a task preferably to be undertaken by a minister, and by an appropriately qualified layman only where no minister was available. Schoolmasters were licensed by the bishop, just like clergy, which ensured that the education of young men remained under the watchful eye of the Elizabethan and Jacobean church. Deacon-schoolmasters were not confined to obscure provincial schools. Thomas Browne, who was ordained deacon on 18 October 1561, served as Headmaster of Westminster School 1564-70, and Nicholas Goldisborough, ordained deacon on 28 September 1577, was Headmaster of the King's School, Canterbury, 1580-84. Elijah Corlett, ordained deacon on 22 September 1633, served first as Master of Halstead Grammar School in Essex before emigrating to the Massachusetts colony, where he became the first Master of the Grammar School at Harvard, which prepared students for Harvard College, between 1641 and 1687. Corlett is considered a founding figure of American education.

The Elizabethan and Jacobean church was plagued by the problem of unbeneficed clergy, men who had been ordained but never managed to gain legitimate clerical employment, and instead wandered from place to place, using their education to cause trouble. Usually these men would spend time as schoolmasters, tutors and, occasionally, unlicensed preachers. Although it is difficult to say with certainty, because unbeneficed clergy were often referred to only as 'ministers', it seems highly likely that most of these individuals were deacons. It was easier to obtain deacon's than priest's orders, although some men seem to have been extremely anxious about this; one student of Magdalen College, Oxford, committed suicide at Christmas in 1632 because his ordination as a deacon was delayed.[1] By way of contrast, another Oxford scholar, Edmund Campion, felt so guilty about receiving deacon's orders

---

1. Porter, S., 'University and Society', in Tyacke, C. (ed.), *Seventeenth-century Oxford* (Oxford University Press: Oxford, 1997), pp. 25-104, at p. 97.

in the established church in 1569 that he fled to Ireland and later became a Jesuit priest.[1] However, a small proportion of graduates found themselves trapped in a 'twilight zone' of their clerical careers, ordained deacon but unable to proceed, through lack of education or patronage, to priesthood and its attendant benefits. On occasion, men seem to have been ordained deacon in order to undertake specific non-priestly ministries within the church. For instance, John Amner (d. 1641), who served as organist of Ely Cathedral, was an ordained deacon.[2] There was no particular reason why an organist should have needed to be in holy orders, except for the fact that it gave Amner the opportunity to supplement his income through a stipend for serving a church or chapel, or even for serving as gospeller or epistler in Ely Cathedral, where he was a minor canon.

Of the 108 men in the sample who were ordained priest, just under a third (31 per cent) were ordained to the diaconate and priesthood on the same day, while 58 per cent were ordained priest either on the same day or the next day following. Nevertheless, the average interval between diaconal and priestly ordination was 239 days (just under 8 months), largely because certain individuals in the sample spent a long time in deacon's orders before proceeding to the priesthood. John Abell of Queens' College, ordained deacon on 17 December 1615, was not ordained priest until almost 9 years later. The poet Robert Anton, ordained deacon on 23 December 1610, waited almost 8 years, and seems to have served as curate of Shalford in Surrey in the interim. Thomas Archer of Trinity College, ordained deacon on 18 December 1641, was not ordained priest until February 1646, although it is possible that the religious upheaval of the Civil War era intervened in this case. John Ashley, Rector of Elmsett in Suffolk (ordained 23 May 1624), remained in deacon's order for just under 3 years, while John Atkinson of Christ's College (ordained in September 1620) waited almost 6 years.

These long-term deacons were unusual exceptions. An analysis of the average interval between diaconal and priestly ordination over the nearly 80 years between 1560 and 1639 reveals that the interval disappeared altogether in the 1590s, when almost all the clergy in the sample were ordained deacon and priest on the same day. Perhaps in light of the promulgation of Canon 32 in 1604, the decade 1610-

1. Childs, J., *God's Traitors: Terror and Faith in Elizabethan England* (Bodley Head: London, 2014), pp. 25-6.
2. Morehen, J., 'Amner, John' in *ODNB*, vol. 1, pp. 964-5.

19 saw the interval between ordinations increase to ten months. If Canon 32 did have any impact, it was short-lived, and in the 1620s 87 per cent of clergy were ordained deacon on the same or the next day. It was only in the 1630s that 80 per cent of clergy were ordained priest after an interval of more than a few days, and in 70 per cent of cases after more than a year. Likely reasons for this development include the more rigorous examinations of ordination candidates imposed by many bishops during the era of the Laudian reform, the more rigorous enforcement of the canonical age of ordination and a dwindling pool of available benefices as the professional clergy expanded.

**Table 3: Average intervals between diaconal and priestly ordinations by decade, 1560-1639**

| Decade | Number of clergy in sample | Average interval between diaconal and priestly ordinations |
|---|---|---|
| 1560-1569 | 6 | 144 days (4 months) |
| 1570-1579 | 7 | 319 days (10 months) |
| 1580-1589 | 9 | 165 days (5 months) |
| 1590-1599 | 8 | Same day |
| 1600-1609 | 13 | 125 days (4 months) |
| 1610-1619 | 26 | 323 days (10 months) |
| 1620-1629 | 23 | 147 days (4 months) |
| 1630-1639 | 10 | 403 days (1 year 1 month) |

## Nicholas Ferrar the deacon

Nicholas Ferrar (1592-1637) is without doubt the best known of all post-Reformation English deacons, and the only one commemorated by the Church of England (on 4 December). Ferrar was a successful businessman, and a member of the Virginia Company, until his sudden withdrawal from public life in 1624. He purchased an estate at Little Gidding in Huntingdonshire, where he, his family and some close friends established the closest approximation to a religious community that had officially existed in England since the

Reformation.[1] Ferrar re-established the idea of religious life within the Church of England, even if his experiment at Little Gidding was cut short by the Parliamentarian government in 1646, and he provided direct inspiration to the nineteenth-century revivals of religious life that followed in the wake of the Oxford Movement.

In 1626, after his establishment of the Little Gidding community, Ferrar was ordained deacon by William Laud (1573-1645), then Bishop of St Davids. He made a public and conscious decision not to seek ordination as a priest. He was, therefore, arguably one of the Church of England's first distinctive deacons. However, Ferrar's significance to the history of the diaconate, like his significance to the history of Anglican religious life, remains unclear. Ferrar may have been inspired to seek ordination to the diaconate by his close friend, the poet George Herbert, who was ordained deacon in 1625 or 1626, without any clear idea about whether he wanted to be ordained priest (Herbert was eventually ordained priest in 1630). For both Herbert and Ferrar, ordination to the diaconate seems to have been a decision of profound spiritual importance that represented their letting go of the possibility of worldly preferment; shortly before his ordination, Herbert had embarked on a career as a Member of Parliament.

Late in 1624, while he was on a leave of absence from Cambridge University, Herbert wrote to the Archbishop of Canterbury, George Abbott, to request a dispensation from the requirement laid down by the Bishop of Lincoln, John Williams, that Herbert should wait a year before receiving deacon's orders. It is unclear how general this requirement was, or whether Williams was simply being a stickler for order. Given that the minimum age of ordination was twenty-three, and most men completed their university studies before the age of twenty-one, a 'probationary year' was implied – even if not strictly required – by the canons. Herbert, as a thirty-one year old man contemplating a career change, was an unusual case. Furthermore, the opening question of 'The Form and Manner of Making of Deacons', 'Do you trust that you are inwardly moved by the Holy Ghost to take upon you this office and ministration?',[2] suggests that some period of reflection ought to have been required of potential deacons.

---

1. On Ferrar see Cranfield, N.W.S., 'Ferrar, Nicholas' in *ODNB*, vol. 19, pp. 417-19; Muir, L.R. and White, L.J., *Materials for the Life of Nicholas Ferrar* (Leeds Philosophical and Literary Society: Leeds, 1996); Blackstone, R. (ed.), *The Ferrar Papers: containing a life of Nicholas Ferrar* (Cambridge University Press: Cambridge, 1938).
2. 'The form and maner of makyng ... Deacons' (1891), p. 280.

Abbot granted Herbert a dispensation on 3 November 1624, allowing him to be ordained deacon at any time.[1] Herbert was accordingly ordained at some point in 1625, although he does not seem to have abandoned his secular life until he was ordained priest in 1630. According to his biographer, Izaak Walton, on that occasion Herbert finally 'chang'd his sword and silk Cloaths into a Canonical Coat', and declared to his wife 'You are now a Ministers Wife'.[2] This suggests that Herbert regarded his diaconal status before 1630 as something intermediate between the lay and clerical states; a renunciation of worldly preferment, perhaps, but not yet the assumption of the full duties of ministry or the adoption of a self-consciously clerical lifestyle.

Both Herbert and Ferrar were members of a close-knit group of high church enthusiasts, led by Laud, Archbishop of Canterbury from 1633, and Richard Neile (1562-1640), Archbishop of York from 1631. Laud has lent his name to a movement in the Church of England that was in reality much wider than his own personal influence extended, and began late in the reign of Elizabeth I, as the Queen's drive for conformity began to crystallise as a distinct theology and spirituality of its own. Peter Lake and others have called this new theology and spirituality '*avant-garde* conformity'.[3] It was a form of 'radical orthodoxy' (to borrow a late-twentieth century term), placing great stress on the inherited doctrine of the church and its dignity as an institution, as opposed to the theology of the reformers. Outwardly conservative, *avant-garde* conformists nevertheless devised innovative means of expressing their conformist ideology. The *avant-garde* conformists emphatically denied the need for further reform of the Church of England and regarded the Elizabethan Settlement as having established the most perfect form of ecclesiastical government in Christendom, yet at the same time they pressed for the church to have restored to it some of the privileges it had lost at the Reformation.

Lake's *avant-garde* conformists were traditionally interpreted as crypto-Catholics or proto-Anglo-Catholics, but this is to read the conditions of the nineteenth century back on to the seventeenth, as

1. Charles, A.M., 'George Herbert, Deacon', *Modern Philology* 72 (1975), pp. 272-6, at pp. 272-3.
2. Walton, I., *The Life of Mr George Herbert* (London, 1670), p. 65.
3. See Lake, P., 'Lancelot Andrewes, John Buckeridge and *Avant-Garde* Conformity at the Court of James I' in Peck, L.L. (ed.), *The Mental World of the Jacobean Court* (Cambridge University Press: Cambridge, 1991), pp. 113-33.

if the Laudians were simply Victorian Tractarians wearing pointy beards and Bishop Andrewes caps. Laudians did not act out of sympathy with Rome (whatever their Puritan antagonists may have suspected), but rather out of the conviction that that the Church of England as an institution enjoyed legal continuity with the pre-Reformation church. Thus they made a distinction between the pre-Reformation abuses that were legitimately suppressed by royal authority (such as indulgences and clerical celibacy) and illegitimate exercises of royal power (such as the confiscation of church property, suppression of the monasteries as charitable institutions and the authority given to Parliament over the church).

The ordinations of George Herbert and Nicholas Ferrar are hardly sufficient evidence that there was widespread enthusiasm for the diaconate amongst high church Laudians, but the men's actions were certainly in keeping with the aims of the Laudian movement. High churchmen wanted to see the church's original offices, and therefore the threefold order of ministry, restored to their primitive importance. So, for instance, Laudians adopted an exalted view of the authority of bishops over both clergy and laity, and insisted on the spiritual authority of the clergy. At the same time, they were uneasy about lay intrusions into the church, such as the right of laymen to present to benefices, lay ownership of church lands and the power given to laymen in Parliament to legislate with regard to the church.

The significance of the diaconate to Laudians was that, as the lowest rank of the clergy, it provided a means of authorising and 'clericalising' individuals and their work on behalf of the church. Laudian theology was, in other words, open to the idea of administrators and officials in deacon's orders, after the model of the early and mediaeval church. Laud's personal support for this idea is suggested by the fact that he agreed to conduct a private ordination of Nicholas Ferrar, with no expectation that Ferrar would proceed to the priesthood. As the many offers of patronage that followed Ferrar's ordination show, most people (perhaps including Laud) expected that Ferrar would now use the administrative gifts that had benefitted the Virginia Company for the benefit of the church.

John Ferrar, in his biography of his brother, is rather obscure when it comes to the reasons why Nicholas chose to be ordained deacon, merely telling us that at Pentecost 1626 he 'grew to a full resolution and determination of that thing and course of life he had so often wished for, and longingly desired'. Ferrar approached his tutor, Dean Linsell, about being admitted to holy orders, and Linsell accordingly reached a private arrangement with Laud that Ferrar should be privately ordained deacon in 'Westminster Chapel' (presumably St Stephen's Chapel, within the Palace of Westminster) on Trinity Sunday. Ferrar told his tutor that 'he durst not presume to step one inch higher or further. So a deacon he was made'.[1] There is no indication that Ferrar was ordained with a title to a curacy, but Laud may have set aside this canonical requirement on account of his great admiration for Ferrar. Owen Cummings has interpreted Ferrar's decision to be ordained deacon as a form of dedication to God, rather than the beginning of a career of ministry.[2] Ferrar refused all of the livings offered to him by the members of the Virginia Company and returned to the community he had already set up at Little Gidding.[3] In the absence of any form of monastic life in the Church of England, Ferrar's ordination took the place of a solemn profession and religious vows. In contrast to Cummings's view, Jill Pinnock saw Ferrar as being in the tradition of deacon-administrators.[4]

The only direct evidence for the nature of Ferrar's diaconal ministry at Little Gidding is a problematic source, because it was written by one of his Puritan detractors. The anonymous pamphlet *The Arminian Nunnery* (1641) purported to describe a visit to Little Gidding, which the author portrayed as mimicking Roman Catholic religious communities. The visitor described Ferrar as the 'prolocutor' of the community, and noted that he had been ordained deacon:

> Now I was invited by this Deacon to goe with him into the Chappell to their devotion, at the entrance whereof this Priestlike deft Deacon made a low obeysance, a few paces farther lower, and comming to the half-pace which is at the East end where the altered [sic.] Table stood, hee bowed and prostrated himselfe to the ground, then he went up into a faire large reading place. . . . We being all placed before the Deacon (for now so we must call him) with a very loud and shrill voyce began and trolled out the Letanie, and read divers other Prayers and Collects in Book of Common Prayer and Athanasius his Creed; and concluded with the forme of words, of, The peace of God, &c.[5]

1. [Ferrar, J.], *Life of Nicholas Ferrar* in *Nicholas Ferrar: Two Lives*, ed. J.E.B. Mayor (Cambridge University Press: Cambridge, 1855), pp. 24-5.
2. Cummings, O.F., *Deacons and the Church* (Paulist Press: Mahwah, NJ, 2004), pp. 63-9.
3. Ferrar (1855), pp. 26-7.
4. Pinnock (1991), p. 21.
5. *The Arminian Nunnery: or, A Briefe Description and Relation of the late erected Monasticall Place, called the Arminian Nunnery at Little Gidding in Huntington-Shire* (London, 1641), pp. 5-6.

The level of detail included by the anonymous visitor would seem to indicate that he really visited the community; and indeed there is no reason to suspect that he did not, since Little Gidding received many visitors. However, the author rather puzzlingly claimed that Ferrar consecrated the bread and wine at Holy Communion, an accusation that hardly fits with the rest of the content of *The Arminian Nunnery*, which labours to portray Ferrar as a Romanist. The view that deacons could preside at Holy Communion was widely held amongst Puritans, since they held that ordination was to a single indivisible ministry; indeed, this was the reason why Puritans opposed the institutions of the diaconate and episcopacy altogether, preferring a single presbyterate. On the face of things, it seems unlikely that Ferrar, a highly educated man who paid much attention to the immemorial customs of the church, would have overstepped his authority as a deacon by presiding at Holy Communion. On the other hand, the church at Little Gidding was essentially the private chapel of the community, and what took place there was private rather than public worship. It is possible that Ferrar followed Bucer's reasoning that the offices of bishop, presbyter and deacon were three aspects of a single ministry. Having been ordained as a deacon, Ferrar was authorised only to exercise this ministry publicly, but in private he exercised a presbyteral ministry as needed. On the other hand, the author of *The Arminian Nunnery* may simply have been in error.

The author acknowledged that the members of the Little Gidding community 'pretend to be very charitable to the poore, but as it is verily thought in a meritorious way' (in other words, he thought that they did good works to gain merit with God). Furthermore, the Little Gidding community was engaged in catechesis in the wider community: 'They also take upon them to be Catechisers and to task many poore people with Catechisticall questions: Which when they come and can make answere thereunto, they are rewarded with money and their dinners, and so they pretend they feed the poores bodies and soules'.[1]

In spite of the author of *The Arminian Nunnery*'s hostility to Ferrar's theology, three important aspects of diaconal ministry are nevertheless recognisable in the book's account of the Little Gidding community: Ferrar's liturgical role in reading prayers, his role in relieving the poor and his role in catechesis. Ferrar thus presented a holistic model of diaconal ministry that drew on the traditional

---

1.  Ibid. pp. 8-9.

conception of the deacon as a partial substitute for a priest in the liturgy, but also drew on the instructions of the Ordinal and the example provided by Cuthbert Symson of the deacon as servant of the poor. Richard Hooker's conception of the deacon as teacher and catechist, embodied for instance in John Bradford, completed the picture. Had Ferrar lived longer, and had the existence of his community not been cut short by the Civil War, it is possible that he could have established a coherent theology of the diaconate in the Church of England and inspired the ordination of other men. He certainly provided a spiritual inspiration to others. A late seventeenth-century manuscript commonplace book compiled by a priest of pronounced high church sympathies, now in Cambridge University Library, consists largely of extracts copied from John Ferrar's life of his brother and *The Arminian Nunnery*.[1] As things stand, however, the most that can be said of Nicholas Ferrar the deacon was that he became the first of several solitary examples of lifelong deacons in the Anglican tradition, providing an inspiration to contemporary deacons but hardly the founder of any recognisable movement in his own lifetime.

---

1. Cambridge University Library, Add. MS 4484. The author's high church sympathies are suggested by a series of Latin quotations copied from the Roman missal.

# 2

# *Deacons from Restoration to Reform, 1660-1832*

Between the Restoration of the Monarchy in 1660 and the Great Reform Act of 1832, England's political, judicial and ecclesiastical institutions remained essentially intact and nominally unchallenged. This apparent stability masked profound changes, such as the Revolution of 1688 and the Hanoverian succession in 1714, but the legitimation of these events depended on their presentation as something other than change. What was true of the British constitution was true also of the Church of England: on the surface, the church was quiescent (even stagnant) between the Act of Uniformity and the 1830s, when the relationship between church and state underwent a radical reorientation. Beneath the surface, however, tensions created by the 1689 Toleration Act, the schism of the Non-Jurors and the Methodist movement disrupted the otherwise complacent life of the established church.

In the 1660s, the church's priority was reconstruction and consolidation after the suppression of the Prayer Book and episcopal government during the Commonwealth period. The Restoration of Charles II in May 1660 was welcomed enthusiastically by most people in England, not so much because they were loyal Royalists or churchmen, but because the Protectorate had made itself so unpopular. There was also a sense that the return of the King meant the restoration of the order of nature which had been overthrown by the Puritans; the personal qualities of the King himself were incidental. Charles was passionate in his support for episcopacy, and his father Charles I was posthumously constructed as a martyr for episcopal government and thereby, implicitly, the threefold order of ministry.

Between 1646 and 1660, ordinations were carried out by the laying on of hands by groups of ministers (presbyteries), some of whom were deacons as well as priests. The Commonwealth church made no distinction between orders of ministry. At the Restoration, all incumbent ministers who refused to accept the Church of England's doctrine of orders were deprived of their benefices. Some Presbyterians conformed, of course; others had never liked the Parliamentarian changes anyway; still others continued their ministry by leaving the established church and setting up dissenting congregations, which were then classed as illegal conventicles. The reign of Charles II saw the last sustained attempt to impose a national religion on England in more than just a symbolic sense, through the enforcement of compulsory church attendance and the universal authority of the church courts. It was a losing battle, since the momentum created in Protestant dissent during the eleven years of the interregnum made it an unstoppable force.

Charles II's Roman Catholic brother, James II, saw Protestant dissenters as potential allies in the cause of religious toleration when he came to the throne in 1685. However, his attempt to grant toleration to dissenters by a royal 'Declaration of Indulgence' (as a prelude to granting toleration to Roman Catholics) was received by contemporaries as an attack on the established Church of England. The 'Seven Bishops' willingly faced imprisonment to defend the church, but they were placed in an awkward position when the Convention Parliament of 1689 offered the crown to William of Orange and James's daughter Mary. Most clergy passionately supported the idea of a Protestant monarchy, but a significant proportion of them found that they could not, in conscience, swear the Oath of Allegiance to William and Mary while James II was still living. These men, who were led by the deposed Archbishop of Canterbury, William Sancroft, became known as the Non-Jurors. Over time, they would develop their own distinctive interpretation of the high church tradition.

Recognising that the support of dissenters for James II represented a potential threat, the new government sought to neutralise the dissenters first by attempting a revision of the Prayer Book in 1689, in which the sign of the cross in baptism and wedding rings were made optional. These two 'relics of popery' in the Anglican liturgy had been a major cause of contention between high churchmen and Puritans in the 1630s and earlier. However, as far as the dissenters were concerned, these concessions were too little, too late. The 1689 revision of the Prayer Book failed, and Parliament eventually passed the 1689 Act of Toleration instead, which allowed dissenters to worship in public without fear of arrest. From this point onwards, the established church was forced to defend itself by the pen of the apologist rather than the sword of the magistrate.

The Non-Juror William Law's *Serious Call to a Devout and Holy Life* (1729) provided the inspiration for the young John Wesley to form his 'Holy Club', and although Wesley and the early Methodists never shared the Non-Jurors' political convictions, they certainly identified with the Non-Jurors' spiritual priorities. Until the 1780s, the term 'Methodist' referred to a particular brand of 'enthusiastic' churchmanship rather than a distinct denomination. It would be inaccurate to use the term 'evangelical' to describe Methodists, since it carries connotations of Calvinist theology. Whilst George Whitefield was a Calvinist, the Wesleys were Arminians, but both Whitefield and the Wesleys shared a belief in the need for charismatic preaching and spiritual revival, unfettered by the usual restrictions of parish and diocesan structures.

To a certain extent, the Church of England adapted to this new movement, permitting the establishment of proprietary chapels staffed by enthusiastic preachers, but ultimately, the Methodists' unwillingness to submit to episcopal government, and their adoption of a Presbyterian system of ordinations by other ministers, led to their separation from the body of the established church. This traumatic secession and the growing influence of Protestant dissent would have important consequences for Anglican thought on the diaconate in the nineteenth century. The 1801 Act of Union saw the amalgamation of the Church of England and the Church of Ireland as the 'United Church of England and Ireland', but on the whole the church made little attempt to respond creatively to the challenge of dissent, allying itself closely with the Tory party and opposing any moves towards Roman Catholic emancipation. The eventual success of emancipation in 1829 allowed Roman Catholics to sit in Parliament and marked the final extinction of any pretensions that the Church of England had to be a truly national church of all the people, as opposed to the official religion of the political establishment.

## The late Stuart church

The Restoration church was a socially divided institution. On the one hand, the sons of the aristocracy were guaranteed a relatively smooth journey to the better rewarded offices: bishoprics, deaneries, prebends and wealthy benefices. On the other hand, many of the clergy were men of humble birth, the sons of tradesmen and even labourers who had been fortunate enough to be sponsored through a grammar school education, and had then worked their way through an Oxford or Cambridge degree as 'sizars' or college servants. Since most advowsons (the right to present to a benefice) were owned by secular patrons (local gentry or civic corporations), obtaining an incumbency depended almost entirely on obtaining a patron. A few of the poorer clergy managed this by becoming popular preachers or indispensable advisers to the elite, but the majority found themselves working as curates or chaplains for absentee incumbents, many of whom held several benefices in plurality and whose income vastly exceeded that of the working clergy.

Contemporary perceptions of the supply of clergy in the late seventeenth-century church differed considerably. Gilbert Burnet, Bishop of Salisbury 1689-1715, believed that there was a shortage of clergy and attempted to set up a theological college in Salisbury. His plans were opposed by Oxford University, and the college was never built.[1] Burnet was a Whig, a reformer and a strong supporter of William of Orange, whereas Oxford remained a stronghold of sympathy for James II, and these political differences may partly explain the opposition. Conservative high churchmen claimed that the church was suffering from a surfeit of ministers, and in 1679 John Eachard, the Master of Catharine Hall in Cambridge, complained that this was because men were seeking ordination for the wrong reasons:

> That which increases the unprovided-for number of clergy, is people posting into orders, before they know their message or business, only out of a certain kind of pride and ambition. Thus some are hugely in love with the mere title of priest, or deacon: never considering how they shall live, or what good they are likely to do in their office: but only they have a fancy that a cassock, if it be made long, is a very handsome garment, thought it be never paid for: and that the desk is clearly the best, and the pulpit the highest seat in all the parish; and they shall take place of most but esquires and right worshipfuls.[2]

However, the Stuart church remained, as in the Middle Ages, one of the very few vehicles of social mobility in a rigidly hierarchical society. The son of a labourer would never be an earl, a duke, a judge or a Minister of the Crown, but it was not inconceivable that, under

---

1. Marshall (2009), p. 165.
2. Eachard, J., *The Grounds and Occasions of the Contempt of the Clergy* (1679) in *The Works of John Eachard* (London, 1772), vol. 1, pp. 102-3.

the right circumstances, he could rise to be a bishop one day. Eachard acknowledged this reality to a certain extent when he identified a group of men who sought ordination in the church as 'a place of refuge':

> Thus we have many turn priest and deacons, either for want of employment in their profession of law, physic, or the like: or having been unfortunate in their trade: or having broken a leg or an arm, and so disabled from following their former calling: or, having had the pleasure of spending their estate, or being . . . disappointed of their inheritance.[1]

Eachard's use of the phrase 'priests or deacons' (at a time when the terms 'minister' or 'clerk' were more common) suggests that he was aware of individuals who were able to obtain ordination to the diaconate but did not proceed to the priesthood because they were unable to obtain a title for ordination. Men who remained deacons for a lengthy period of time, or even for life, were most likely to be found at the lower social end of the clergy. Furthermore, deacons, unlike priests, were permitted to continue in a secular profession, and the lawyers or doctors whom Eachard claimed sought ordination 'for want of employment' may well have hoped to carry on their practice in holy orders. Ordination to the diaconate, in other words, provided additional social status (if not income) while they continued in their chosen profession.

It seems likely that Burnet and Eachard were both partly right: there were too few clergy to serve the population in real terms, but the meagre income available to the clergy made it seem as if there were too many. Put simply, the church's income was concentrated in the hands of too few privileged individuals. The government of Queen Anne finally acted to assist the poor clergy in 1704, when Queen Anne's Bounty was established. This was a commission that received the income from the first year of a new incumbent's benefice (annates), which since 1532 had gone directly to the Crown. The commissioners of Queen Anne's Bounty assigned this income to pay the stipends of the unbeneficed clergy, the curates and chaplains who were struggling to minister to ordinary people in the parishes. The moving spirit behind the Bounty, in addition to the Queen herself, was none other than Burnet, who was motivated not only by a desire to restore the reputation of the clergy, but also by the need to combat religious dissent in the aftermath of the Toleration Act.[2]

---

1. Ibid. p. 104.
2. See Savidge, A., *The Origins and Foundation of Queen Anne's Bounty* (SPCK: London, 1955), pp. 4-30.

Queen Anne's Bounty finally recognised the contribution of the 'working clergy', as opposed to the wealthy beneficed absentees, and marked the beginning of a progressive improvement in clerical standards that continued throughout the eighteenth century. By the middle of the century, the educational standards expected of ordinands were higher and more uniform, and it was unusual for clergy to be ordained priest after less than a year in deacon's orders. The prescriptions of the Ordinal were followed more consistently, and a small number of lifelong and long-term deacons flourished, primarily as schoolmasters, but also as college fellows, perpetual curates, preachers and chaplains. It also seems to have been the case that, as Mary Tanner suggested, some incumbents were in contravention of Canon Law by remaining deacons for years, 'either because of the fees involved [in priestly ordination] or because they feared an examination by the bishop's chaplains'.[1]

## Defending the diaconate

At the Savoy Conference in 1661, which was an attempt to reconcile the conflicting views of Presbyterians and Episcopalians in the aftermath of the Restoration, the episcopal party defended the continued existence of the diaconate on the grounds that the Ordinal conferred a power of preaching on the deacon, but an additional power of absolution on the priest. For this reason, it was necessary for the Prayer Book to use the word 'priest' to identify the minister of absolution, rather than the generic term, 'minister', for which the Puritans were pressing:

> It is not reasonable that the word Minister should be only used in the Liturgy. For since some parts of the Liturgy may be performed by a Deacon, others by none under the order of a Priest, viz., absolution and consecration, it is fit that some word, as priest, should be used for these offices, and not minister, which signifies at large everyone that ministers in that holy office, of what order soever he be.[2]

A similar reasoning, based on the need to refute Presbyterian errors, lay behind the suggestion of Matthew Wren, Bishop of Ely, that the title of the Ordinal should be changed to 'The Manner of Ordering,

---

1. *DMC*, p. 15.
2. Quoted in Cooke, W., *The Power of the Priesthood in Absolution, and a few Remarks on Confession* (John Henry and James Parker: London, 1858), p. 72.

Making and Consecrating Bishops, Priests, and Deacons'. Wren, who made his revisions while imprisoned in the Tower of London during the Interregnum, intended 'ordering', 'making' and 'consecrating' to be treated as synonyms, so that Puritans would not be able to argue that by applying the word 'consecration' to bishops, the Church of England was approaching too close to Rome. Likewise, by making it clear that 'making' was the same as ordering and consecrating, they would not be able to claim that the diaconate was 'in itself nothing else but a Laicall Faculty, that thereby they may give a little more colour to their Lay Presbytery'.[1] William Sancroft, later Archbishop of Canterbury, picked up on this change of title in his revisions,[2] but in the form in which the Ordinal was confirmed by Convocation in 1661, 'consecrating', 'ordering' and 'making' referred to the three orders of bishop, priest and deacon.[3] It would seem perverse to claim that this meant the Restoration church did not regard the service for making deacons as an ordination; it clearly was an ordination, but the use of the plainer word 'making' suggested that the occasion was to be attended with less solemnity than the ordination of priests and bishops (just as Bucer had suggested over a century earlier). One consequence of the Restoration re-assertion of the doctrine of the threefold order of ministry and the need for ordination was that some individuals, who had received a Presbyterian 'laying on of hands' in the Interregnum, had to be ordained as deacons before they could serve in any official capacity in the Restoration church. For example, Joseph Brown, a preacher and schoolmaster in Essex who had been 'ordained' in 1649, had to be ordained deacon by the Bishop of London on 8 June 1661.

References to the diaconate in the theological literature of the eighteenth century are few and far between, and generally occur in the context of more general defences of the threefold order of ministry. Little theological thought, it seems, was devoted to the meaning and significance of the diaconate in the mainstream of the established church. In 1713, Thomas Brett argued that there was a scriptural warrant for baptism by deacons, because Phillip was a deacon when he baptised the Ethiopian eunuch.[4] Brett argued that bishops or priests should baptise if present, but that deacons could baptise too:

---

1. Bradshaw (1971), pp. 87-8.
2. Ibid. pp. 89-91.
3. Ibid. p. 93.
4. Brett, T., *An Enquiry into the Judgment and Practice of the Primitive Church, In Relation to Persons being Baptized by Lay-men* (London, 1713), p. 5.

Where the Bishop could do it conveniently himself, the
Presbyters did not Minister it but in particular Cases, and where
a Presbyter could be procured for this Ministration, a Deacon
ought not to intrude. But it does not therefore follow that
Deacons were not esteemed by them as the ordinary Ministers
of Baptism, as well as Priests.[1]

Brett argued that the authority of both priests and deacons derived
from that of the bishop, quoting St Jerome with approval: 'Without
the Chrism and Command of the Bishop, neither Priest nor Deacon
have a Right to baptize'.[2]

In 1708, Samuel Hill approvingly quoted St Jerome that 'a deacon
is able to ordain no cleric, for it is not the church if it does not have a
priest', adding acidly, 'let foreign Societies look to this'.[3] This seems
to have been a reference to the Society for the Propagation of the
Gospel, founded in 1701 to evangelise England's American colonies,
which often relied on lay readers and catechists when no ordained
clergy were available. The Society intended that schoolmasters
should be ordained deacon, but this soon proved impractical.[4]
The idea of the SPG appointing lay readers and catechists without
episcopal authority approached too close to Presbyterianism for the
comfort of high church commentators. Hill followed Hooker's view
that there was no essential difference between bishops and priests,
but insisted that there was an important difference between priests
and deacons analogous to the difference between priests and Levites
in the Old Testament:

> The Comparison [between Priests and Levites] is not design'd
> between Bishops and Presbyters as the two Opposites, but
> between Presbyters, (who enjoy the Priesthood with the Bishops)
> and Deacons, who have no share in such Consecration, but are
> meer subservient Ministers, as the Levites of the Priests.[5]

Hill made these observations in the context of a commentary on a
letter of St Jerome, in which the Church Father complained that some
deacons were claiming an authority above their station. He reported

---

1.  Ibid. p. 13.
2.  Ibid. p. 31.
3.  Hill, S., *A Thorough Examination of the False Principles and Fallacious
    Arguments, advanc'd against the Christian Church, Priest-hood, and Religion*
    (London, 1708), p. 238.
4.  O'Connor, D., *Three Centuries of Mission: The United Society for the
    Propagation of the Gospel 1701-2000* (Continuum: London, 2000), p. 27.
5.  Hill (1708), p. 241.

that another contemporary theologian, Dr Lowth, considered that Jerome's letter was necessary because the deacons, as the bishop's attendants, were beginning to treat the presbyters charged with the running of local churches with contempt.[1] Whilst there was no direct danger of this occurring in the church of Queen Anne, high churchmen were keen to invoke the authority of the Church Fathers against innovations in church government such as the foreign missionary societies. However, denigration of the authority of deacons was accompanied by an insistence that a diaconate was necessary, and one commentator noted in 1733 that 'When the diaconate is faithfully discharged, 'tis by no means a contemptible office'.[2] Such a choice of words seems to imply that the diaconate was regarded with contempt by most of the clergy, most of the time.

Yet deacons had their uses in the eighteenth-century church. Diaconal ordination was a welcome solution to irregularities, as the Bishops of Carlisle and Chester discovered in the reign of George II. Both of these dioceses contained vast, straggling rural parishes whose parish churches could not possibly serve all the communities within their boundaries, and as a consequence, laymen acting as readers served chapels-of-ease in remote parts of the parish. This was a relic of the Elizabethan church, as indeed were the Bibles in the chapels, which were often still the Geneva Bible of 1560 rather than the Authorised Version of 1611. The bishops resolved that 'no one should officiate who was not in deacon's orders'. They therefore ordained a clogger, tailor and butter-print-maker to the diaconate without any examination, and these men continued to pursue their secular professions alongside their new ministry.[3] The deacon-curates who served remote parishes in the north of England were the true workforce of the Church of England, ensuring that regular worship continued, even in the most inaccessible places. Isaac Whykes, who remained in deacon's orders for ten years, served the parishes of Lockton and Levisham in the Rydale Deanery of the Diocese of York between 1752 and 1762. The parishes are located in a valley so steep, with gradients of 1:2 in places, that Whykes could not use a horse and would have had to walk. Somehow he managed to lead a service at Lockton and Levisham every Sunday while remaining the curate of nearby Ebberston and Allerston as well.[4]

1. Ibid. pp. 246-7.
2. *A Paraphrase and Notes on St. Paul's Ist Epistle to Timothy: in imitation of Mr. Locke's manner* (London, 1733), p. 67.
3. Ferguson, R.S., *Carlisle* (SPCK: London, 1889), pp. 173-4.
4. Jago (1997), pp. 95-6.

It was amongst the Non-Jurors that an appreciation of the liturgical and pastoral importance of deacons was rediscovered in the first half of the eighteenth century. This was largely because the Non-Jurors, who prided themselves on their patristic scholarship, were keen to revive early forms of the liturgy. Anxious to defend themselves against the accusations of popery that their pronounced high churchmanship and support for the Jacobite cause attracted, the Non-Jurors turned to the Greek Fathers to assure their critics that their liturgical innovations were derived, not from mimicking Rome, but from the practice of the early church. At first, the Non-Jurors adopted the liturgy of the First Prayer Book of King Edward VI (1549), but some of them subsequently moved beyond this to abandon the Prayer Book liturgy altogether.

Thomas Deacon (1697-1753), a Manchester physician, was consecrated a bishop by Archibald Campbell, Bishop of Aberdeen, in 1733, and in 1734 he published his *Clementine Liturgy*. Deacon's *Holy Liturgy*, based on the 1549 Prayer Book, with components added from the Liturgies of St Basil the Great and St John Chrysostom, required the deacon to call the congregation to prayer at specific points in the service (although Deacon acknowledged that a priest might have to serve in this role in the absence of a deacon).[1] Deacon's service of ordination for deacons required the congregation to elect 'a proper person', who was then to be presented to the bishop by two deacons. Deacon also required anyone being ordained deacon to be twenty-five years old or above, in contrast to Canon Law, which set a minimum age of twenty-three.[2] His description of the office of a deacon, whilst clearly dependent on the Ordinal, added several new elements:

> It appertaineth to the office of a Deacon, to be subservient to the Bishop or Priest in Divine Service, and especially in the Service of the Altar; to take care of the Holy Table, and of all the ornaments and utensils belonging thereto; to read Holy Scriptures and Homilies in the Church, and to instruct the Catechumens and the youth; to distribute the Eucharist, and to baptize in cases of necessity, where no Priest is to be had; to bid prayers in the Congregation, and to preach with the Bishop's License; to correct and rebuke men who behave themselves irregularly at church; to attend upon the Bishop, and to inform him or the Priest of the misdemeanours of the People; to search

1. Deacon, T., *A Book of Common Prayer or Clementine Liturgy* (London, 1734), pp. 74-101.
2. Ibid. p. 232.

for the orphans, and the sick and poor people of the parish, to intimate their estates, names, and places where they dwell, and to distribute to them such charities as shall be delivered to him by the Bishop or Priest towards their relief and assistance.[1]

Deacon portrayed the deacon as 'subservient', in contrast to the Ordinal, where the deacon 'assists' the priest, in line with the Non-Jurors' exalted conception of priesthood. Deacon specified that the deacon was 'to take care of the Holy Table, and of all the ornaments and utensils belonging thereto' as well as assisting the priest in the distribution of Holy Communion. Again, this pointed to the more elaborate ceremonial in Thomas Deacon's church. The deacon was 'to bid prayers in the Congregation', a practice borrowed from the Liturgy of St John Chrysostom, while Deacon tightened the Ordinal's provision for baptism by deacons. Whereas the Ordinal has the deacon baptise 'in the absence of the Priest', Deacon's deacons could baptise only 'in cases of necessity, where no Priest is to be had'. Roger Laurence had already denied the validity of baptism by anyone but a priest or deacon in 1710, supported by George Hickes, the leading Non-Juror of the time.[2]

Thomas Deacon seems to have been drawing on the traditions of the eastern church once again when he instructed that deacons should 'correct and rebuke men who behave themselves irregularly at church'. However, this may simply have reflected the fact that Deacon's chapel did not have the churchwardens whose task this was in parish churches. Deacon seems to have imagined deacons as direct assistants to the bishop, although the requirement that they should 'inform him or the Priest of the misdemeanours of the People' suggests that he may have been excessively concerned about controlling the behaviour of his flock. When it came to the deacon's involvement with the poor, however, Deacon removed the Ordinal's condition 'where provision is so made' and insisted that it was of the essence of the deacon's ministry to visit the sick and poor.

## A sample of deacons

As I observed in the Introduction above, the few attempts to tell the story of the diaconate in the Church of England that have been made have been dismissive of the eighteenth century, treating it as a time

1. Ibid. p. 237.
2. Laurence, R., *Lay Baptism Invalid* (London, 1710), pp. 36-7. Laurence argued that the priest's authority to baptise derived from his authority to forgive sins, making baptism by a deacon less than satisfactory.

when the diaconate practically ceased to exist as anything more than a technical prerequisite for priestly ordination, which followed a few days later. None of the authors who have put forward this view have supported their case with evidence. However, such evidence is available in Venn's *Alumni Cantabrigienses* and the expanded online ACAD database based on Venn's work. The analysis of deacons in this chapter is drawn from Cambridge alumni ordained between 1660 and 1758, covered by the central four volumes of Venn's work, with surnames under the letter 'A', from Abbott to Ayscough (see Appendix B). Of these, details of diaconal ordination were available for 201 individuals.

**Table 4: Ordained Cambridge alumni, 1660-1758, Abbott-Ayscough**

| Category | Number |
|---|---|
| Deacons ordained priest | 155 |
| Deacons probably ordained priest | 29 |
| Deacons probably not ordained priest | 17 |
| Total | 201 |

These 201 men do not represent the total number of all Cambridge graduates ordained between 1660 and 1758; a small number of graduates are known to have been clergy, but either no details of their ordination survive, or only the date of their ordination to the priesthood is known. I have excluded these from the sample, since nothing is known of the interval between their diaconal and priestly ordinations. Of the 201 whose diaconal ordination is recorded, 46 have no surviving record of a priestly ordination, leaving 155 men who are known to have proceeded to the priesthood. However, this should not be taken as evidence that 23 per cent of clergy remained deacons for life during this period. In the majority of cases, it is clear that these clergy *did* proceed to priest's orders, since they are known to have been appointed as rectors (which required priestly ordination after 1661); it is simply that evidence of their priestly ordination does not survive.

## *Lifelong deacons*

Within the 201 clergy in the sample, there are a small number of individuals who did not proceed to incumbencies, and therefore may have remained in deacon's orders. I have identified 17 of these, who make up 8.5 per cent of the total. On the assumption that Cambridge-educated clergy with surnames beginning with the first letter of the alphabet are a reasonably representative sample of men ordained during the period, it seems likely that the proportion of the clergy who remained deacons for life in the eighteenth century was a little under 10 per cent. If this figure is accurate, it would indicate that lifelong deacons were a much more significant group in the Church of England than has previously been recognised. There were certainly more deacons than the 'tiny number' suggested by Mary Tanner, and the diversity of ministries undertaken by these deacons challenges Jill Pinnock's picture of a 'greatly attenuated version of a permanent diaconate' in the pre-twentieth-century Church of England.[1]

**Table 5: Analysis of probable lifelong deacons in Table 4**

| Type of Ministry | Number |
|---|---|
| Schoolmaster | 4 |
| Chaplain | 2 |
| College fellow | 2 |
| Lecturer/perpetual curate | 2 |
| Baronet | 1 |
| Canon lawyer | 1 |
| Deprived under 1662 Act of Settlement | 1 |
| Incumbent | 1 |
| Non-Juror | 1 |
| Unknown | 1 |
| Died before priestly ordination | 1 |

As observed in Chapter 1 above, a major reason for clergy to remain in deacon's orders was their involvement in education. However, contrary to the assertions of Pinnock and Tanner that most lifelong

1. *DMC*, p. 16; Pinnock (1991), pp. 9-10.

deacons in the eighteenth century were college fellows, there are only two such individuals who can be identified from the sample selected. John Amyas, ordained deacon in May 1706, was a fellow of both Emmanuel and Gonville and Caius Colleges, and there is no evidence that he ever proceeded to priest's orders. William Andrews, ordained deacon in September of the same year, was Chaplain of Trinity College 1706-20. Tanner rightly pointed out that the Holy Communion was so rarely celebrated in college chapels (usually once a term) that there was no need for fellows (or even chaplains) to be priests. College statutes nevertheless required them to be in holy orders, but it would seem that comparatively few remained deacons for life. There were two main interconnected reasons for this: until the late nineteenth century, the statutes of Cambridge colleges required fellows to be celibate, meaning that any fellow who wished to marry was compelled to resign his fellowship. This in turn required him to find an alternative source of income, usually a living in the gift of the college. To become an incumbent, a former fellow in deacon's orders was compelled to seek priest's orders. Pinnock and Tanner were, however, partially correct: fellows of colleges remained in deacon's orders for much longer than average, a phenomenon that will be examined further below.

In theory, it was possible after 1661 for deacons to be invested with ecclesiastical dignities that did not constitute a cure of souls. This meant that deacons could be prebendaries, canons and even deans of collegiate and cathedral foundations. John Massey (1651-1715), who was appointed Dean of Christchurch, Oxford, under James II's royal prerogative in October 1686, is a case in point. Massey had received deacon's orders but, owing to his interest in Roman Catholicism, had not been ordained a priest in the Church of England. It is probable that James fully expected Massey to become a Roman Catholic once he became Dean, and Massey publicly declared that he was a Roman Catholic in March 1687. He was forced to flee Oxford in November 1688 and was finally ordained as a Roman Catholic priest in 1695.[1]

Anthony Aggas, ordained deacon in 1670, received a dispensation from the Archbishop of Canterbury to become Rector of Rushbrook in Suffolk in 1681. Since no record of priestly ordination for Aggas survives, the most likely reason for this dispensation was that Aggas remained a deacon, contrary to the 1662 Act of Uniformity that restricted incumbencies to men in priest's orders. However,

---

1. Bedard, A.C., 'James II and the Catholic Challenge', in Tyacke, C. (ed.), *Seventeenth-century Oxford* (Oxford University Press: Oxford, 1997), pp. 907-54, at pp. 933-4.

there were certainly cases of individuals who flouted this rule, such as George Atton, who was appointed Rector of Willingham in Cambridgeshire in 1722. Atton was ordained deacon in January 1721 but did not proceed to priest's orders until September 1724, two years after becoming Rector. This provides some support for Tanner's suggestion that a minority of incumbents avoided ordination to the priesthood for years, for fear of the fees or examinations that might be involved.

A further reason for a clergyman to remain a deacon was that he took up a position that did not legally require him to proceed to priest's orders, such as a chaplaincy or lectureship. Thomas Alexander, ordained deacon in June 1674, was Lecturer at Ipswich, and there is no record of his priestly ordination. Lectureships usually existed in large towns with a Puritan tradition, and they were ministers licensed to preach by the bishop but not incumbents; there was consequently no need for them to be priests. Another deacon, John Audley, was perpetual curate of St Katherine Cree in London from 1672 until his ejection as a Non-Juror in 1692. Again, Audley may well have been a priest, but perpetual curacies did not come with incumbent status, and thus there was no legal reason for him to be in priest's orders. Marmaduke Allenson, ordained deacon in June 1684, was chaplain to Bishop Nathaniel Crewe of Durham, and Benjamin Archer, ordained deacon in May 1719, was chaplain to the Countess of Winchelsea. At the time, most chaplains served rather like private secretaries, in contrast to mediaeval private chaplains, who celebrated mass and heard the confessions of their patrons.[1]

Deacons continued to practise as canon lawyers in the late seventeenth and early eighteenth centuries, as they had done for centuries. William Arundell, who was called to the bar at the Middle Temple on 24 August 1698, was ordained deacon on 23 May 1700. Rather than a change of profession, it is likely that Arundell's ordination was intended to allow him to practise as a canon lawyer. After the break with Rome, there was no specific training available for canon lawyers in England, and most trained as barristers before proceeding to an examination in Canon Law at the Court of Arches. However, it was considerably easier for an ordained minister to practise as a canon lawyer than a layman at

---

1. This was not always true, and in 1674, Edward Lewis of Cherbury, who had served as a deacon-curate in several Herefordshire parishes, wrote to a relative that he needed to be ordained priest, since he was required to administer the sacrament in his new role as chaplain to a Mr Jones living between Montgomery and Beriew (Marshall (2009), p. 166).

this period, since other clergy were more likely to respect the legal opinion of a fellow clergyman. However, by the mid-eighteenth century it had become more difficult for deacons to practise as both canon and civil lawyers. On 5 July 1794, a committee of benchers of the Inns of Courts decided that deacons should not be called to the bar and serve as barristers,[1] but it remained less clear whether a deacon could still practise as a civil lawyer. In 1764, one deacon applied to Archbishop Thomas Secker for a licence to practise the civil law at Doctors' Commons and was rejected. This incident was brought up in the House of Commons on 10 August 1807, when the MP William Smith read a petition to the House from Nathaniel Highmore of Jesus College, Cambridge, a Doctor of Canon Law. Highmore, who was in deacon's orders, had applied for a licence to practise at Doctors' Commons, which was originally granted, but later withdrawn when the Archbishop discovered that Highmore was a deacon.

Smith rejected the idea that being a deacon should be a bar on practising the law: 'Even if allowing to this he was to be considered a spiritual person, it was not a reason why he should not practise in a court of civil and ecclesiastical law, and more especially since the practice was, till the 37th of Henry the 8th, entirely confined to spiritual persons'.[2] Furthermore, Smith noted that the chancellors of the dioceses were all in holy orders. There was no legal precedent or legislation that forbade deacons from practising in a civil court. However, Smith believed that the real reason why Doctors' Commons did not want to admit a deacon was because they wanted to limit the number of new members joining the society, which acted as a kind of professional association for civil lawyers. Since both ecclesiastical and civil cases were heard in Doctors' Commons, this made it difficult for deacons to continue practising Canon Law. It may be that this was an inevitable result of the increasing professionalisation of the law in eighteenth-century England, but it went against a long tradition of deacon-lawyers.

Some men remained deacons on account of their continued involvement in civic life. It was only in the early nineteenth century that deacons came under the same general exclusion from politics and secular employment as priests. Marmaduke Allenson, Bishop Crewe's chaplain, served as Mayor of Durham 1684-85, an honour that would have been closed to a priest but was acceptable for a

---

1. *Reports from Commissioners* (London, 1834), vol. 26, p. 59.
2. *The Parliamentary Debates from the Year 1803 to the Present Time*, ed. T.C. Hansard (London, 1812), vol. 9, p. 1155.

deacon. A few more individuals in the sample never proceeded to priest's orders owing to changed circumstances, political misfortune or premature death: Thomas Scargill Allen, ordained deacon in September 1679, 'died insane' soon after, and Peter Austin, ordained in December 1660, was ejected from the living of Castle Ashby before he could be ordained priest, presumably for his failure to conform to the Prayer Book. John Amy, ordained deacon in May 1694, became a Non-Juror soon after and seems never to have been ordained priest. Only one of the Non-Juring bishops, William Lloyd of Norwich, was prepared to conduct ordinations, and since, as a Non-Juror, John Amy was unable to receive any preferment in the Church of England, there was little reason for him to be ordained priest anyway. Christopher Armitage, who resigned his fellowship at Peterhouse in 1690 and was described as 'in Holy Orders', may have been in a similar position. John Audley, the perpetual curate of St Katherine Cree, was likewise a Non-Juror.

More fortunate circumstances might also lead a clergyman to forgo priestly ordination. William Anderson, ordained deacon in May 1743, succeeded as Baronet of Kilnwick in Yorkshire in 1765, and was probably never ordained priest. In an age when second sons of the gentry seeking a career in the church often inherited estates through the unexpected deaths of close relatives, there was a convincing case for aristocratic clergy remaining deacons, since they would never need to hold a benefice. Canon Law forbade priests from engaging in large-scale farming or commercial activity and, although dispensations from these canons could be obtained, it was easier to remain in deacon's orders after inheriting an estate. Clergy from wealthier backgrounds could also afford to do this.[1]

Deacon-schoolmasters may have been the single largest group of lifelong deacons. Two men named Edward Abbott, ordained as deacons in 1699 and 1725, both served as schoolmasters, along with John Alcock, Master of Tatershall School in Lincolnshire, who was ordained deacon in 1662. The career of Thomas Atcherly, a graduate of Peterhouse ordained deacon in 1753, was typical of the deacon-schoolmaster. Atcherly was appointed a minor canon of Ely Cathedral in 1764 and served as minister of Chettisham Chapel, a chapel-of-ease just north of Ely. In 1767, he was appointed Under Master at the Ely Cathedral Grammar School, but resigned the office the following year in order to serve as Curate of Stuntney.

---

1. Another likely deacon was Stephen Aldhouse, who never seems to have held a benefice and was described simply as a 'clerk' when he died at Thwaite in Norfolk in 1735.

However, since no one could be found to replace him as Under Master, Atcherley continued in this role until 1775. However, he remained a minor canon and died in the College at Ely in 1800.

At Ely there was an expectation that any schoolmaster at the Cathedral Grammar School should be in holy orders, since in 1718 the Chapter (which governed the Grammar School) had instructed that the office of epistler (subdeacon) should be joined to that of Under Master.[1] The epistler assisted with the distribution of Holy Communion, so the Under Master had to be in holy orders, but there was no reason for him to be a priest. Masters were also expected to take on pastoral duties in addition to their teaching, and just as Atcherley had looked after the churches at Chettisham and Stuntney, so his successor Mr Stevens was appointed Curate in the parish of Holy Trinity, Ely. The number of students in the school was so small at this point that the Chapter did not consider it burdensome to add extra duties.

A total of 107 men ordained deacon (and not subsequently priest) between 1660 and 1760 and educated at Cambridge served as schoolmasters. Assuming that at least as many Oxford graduates followed the same path, there were over 200 graduates who served as deacon-schoolmasters during the period. However, we know from other evidence that many (perhaps most) country schoolmasters were not university graduates, and at least some of these were in deacon's orders. There were also many schoolmasters in priest's orders. The early eighteenth century saw intense competition between the Church of England and the dissenters in setting up local schools, which required nothing but a room, a teacher and a few books. In 1723, there were 268 schools in the Diocese of Lincoln alone.[2] However, the majority of these church schools provided only primary education, and teachers in holy orders would have been confined to those schools providing secondary education. According to a law of 1647, a grammar school was supposed to exist in every town of more than 100 households, but by the eighteenth century many had dwindled to a tiny number of pupils or closed completely. Even at a conservative estimate of the number of schoolmasters, graduate deacon-schoolmasters can only have made up a tiny minority of schoolmasters (and schoolmasters

1. Owen, D.M. and Thurley, D. (eds), *The King's School Ely: A Collection of Documents relating to the History of the School and its Scholars* (Cambridge Antiquarian Society: Cambridge, 1982), pp. 72-4.

2. Jones, M.G., *The Charity School Movement: A Study of Eighteenth Century Puritanism in Action* (Cambridge University Press: Cambridge, 1938), p. 65.

in holy orders) during the eighteenth century. The total number of deacon-schoolmasters, including those who were Oxford and Cambridge graduates, is unlikely to have been fewer than 500 during the whole century.

In general, clergy in deacon's orders during this period do not seem to have to have served as headmasters of the oldest and most important schools, although there were exceptions. Edward Abbot, ordained in June 1699, was Master of Repton School 1705-13; John Gaylard, ordained 15 June 1712, was Headmaster of Sherborne School 1733-43; Thomas Horne, ordained 22 September 1667, was a Fellow of Eton College from 1682, and Vice-Provost 1697-1708; and Richard Lloyd, ordained in February 1686, was Headmaster of Shrewsbury School 1687-1722. The majority of deacon-schoolmasters served as under masters or second and third masters at the great public schools, and as headmasters of small provincial grammar schools. The taking of holy orders by teachers was encouraged, and assisted by the fact that a man could obtain a title to ordination by being a schoolmaster, without attachment to a particular parish church.

A final reason for a man to remain in deacon's orders without proceeding to priestly ordination was disrepute. It was generally easier to obtain ordination to the diaconate than to the priesthood, meaning that some undesirable individuals slipped through the net. Communication between dioceses was a problem, and in the case of Walter Edwards, an alumnus of St John's College, Cambridge, the system did not altogether work as it should have done. Edwards, who had stolen silver from his college, applied to Lord James Beauclerk, Bishop of Hereford, for ordination to the diaconate in June 1763, but Beauclerk deemed Edwards 'far from qualified' and declined to ordain him. Edwards then went to the Diocese of St Davids, where he managed to obtain deacon's orders, but Beauclerk alerted the Archbishop of Canterbury, Thomas Secker, who sent out a general alert to the bishops not to admit Edwards to priest's orders.[1]

## Interval after diaconal ordination

The cross-section of eighteenth-century lifelong deacons examined here has revealed deacon-fellows, deacon-schoolmasters, deacon-preachers, deacon-chaplains and deacon-administrators. However, lifelong deacons were the exception rather than the norm in the

1. Jago, J., *Aspects of the Georgian Church: Visitation Studies of the Diocese of York, 1761-1776* (Associated University Press: Cranbury, NJ, 1997), pp. 244-5.

eighteenth-century church, and a far more significant group of clergy were long-term deacons, men who remained deacons for considerably more than the 1 year laid down by the Ordinal. The average length of time that the clergy in the sample remained deacons was 704 days, which equates to a little under 2 years. This was longer than was required by the Ordinal or Canon 34, which stipulated a minimum ordination age of 23 for deacons and 24 for priests.

Of the 155 clergy in the sample whose diaconal and priestly ordinations are recorded, 37 per cent waited for less than a year to be ordained priest, and only 13 were ordained priest within less than a month. Just under a third waited for between 1 and 2 years; 18 per cent waited for between 2 and 3 years; and a further 14 per cent waited for three years or more before proceeding to priest's orders. These men were certainly long-term deacons, like Henry Forrest, curate of Loweswater in Westmoreland, who was ordained deacon in 1708 and priest in 1730.[1] One important piece of information missing from Venn's *Alumni Cantabrigienses* is the ages of the Cambridge alumni at the time of their ordinations to the diaconate. Tanner suggested that one reason for an interval of more than 1 year between a man's ordination to the diaconate and priesthood could be his relatively young age. This may well be true, but it hardly explains the 14 per cent who remained deacons for 3 years or more.

Five of the long-term deacons were college fellows before proceeding to incumbencies: John Abbott (four years and five months), John Alsop (five years), Andrew Alvis (five years), George Ashby (four years and five months) and Daniel Austin (three years and seven months). One man, George Arnot (three years and five months), came from Edinburgh, and was incorporated a Master of Arts of Cambridge University in 1728. It would make sense that a bishop would want to ensure that a man educated in Scotland had the same level of education as an Oxford or Cambridge graduate. The remaining seventeen long-term deacons had otherwise unremarkable careers, proceeding to hold incumbencies after their priestly ordinations. What they were doing as deacons is not recorded by Venn, but since they were not college fellows, it seems likely that they were serving as curates and chaplains. Worsopp Atkinson of Peterhouse, ordained deacon on 21 December 1712, did not receive priest's orders until 9 June 1723, eight and a half years later. Atkinson then proceeded to a benefice, and was Rector of Pitchcott in Buckinghamshire from 1727 until his death in 1762.

---

1. Nightingale (1911), vol. 2, p. 744.

**Table 6: Average interval between diaconal and priestly ordinations by decade, 1660-1758**

| Decade | Number of clergy in sample | Average interval between diaconal and priestly ordinations |
|--------|---------------------------|-----------------------------------------------------------|
| 1660-1669 | 17 | 288 days |
| 1670-1679 | 14 | 434 days |
| 1680-1689 | 6 | 474 days |
| 1690-1699 | 10 | 845 days |
| 1700-1709 | 13 | 582 days |
| 1710-1719 | 27 | 979 days |
| 1720-1729 | 24 | 585 days |
| 1730-1739 | 19 | 741 days |
| 1740-1749 | 16 | 672 days |
| After 1750 | 9 | 539 days |

A decade-by-decade analysis of the intervals between diaconal and priestly ordination reveals that the longest intervals occurred in the 1690s, 1710s and 1730s, when a deacon might expect to wait two years or more before being ordained priest. The shortest interval (ten months) was in the 1660s, as might be expected at a time when the church was trying to replenish the clergy quickly after the chaos of the Interregnum. Although there was not a simple decade-by-decade increase in the interval between diaconal and priestly ordination, this was the general trend, with the interval in the Georgian era averaging out at a year and nine months, as opposed to a year and five months between 1660 and 1709.

It seems unlikely that many clergy deliberately chose to remain in the diaconate for a lengthy period of time, since this limited their career prospects. One possible reason for the gradually lengthening interval was an increase in the number of clergy relative to the number of incumbencies available, at a time when the creation of new parishes was a very infrequent event indeed, even in response to a growing population (new parishes could be created only by Act of Parliament). Another possible reason was the application of stricter standards of examination of candidates for ordination by the bishops, who were concerned about the reputation of the clergy, as well as the expansion of the number of fellowships available at Oxford and Cambridge and positions as schoolmasters. These last two factors allowed more men to gain a livelihood whilst remaining deacons. The translator and journalist Percival Stockdale (1736-1811) was in deacon's orders for twenty-three years, serving as a tutor and raising money from his writing.[1] Others chose to remain in deacon's orders for more perverse reasons, such as the radical preacher Thomas Manton (c. 1620-77), who was ordained deacon in 1660 but made no move to obtain priest's orders because he believed that the ministerial office could not be divided.[2] Robert Aitken (1800-1873), ordained deacon in 1823, was unable to proceed to priest's orders owing to a dispute with the Bishop of Sodor and Man.[3]

Many men seem to have remained in deacon's orders because their education was insufficient to allow them to proceed to priest's orders, and this is a group absent, for obvious reasons, from the sample of Cambridge alumni examined in this chapter. Bishop Richard Reynolds of Lincoln reported to William Wake (Archbishop of Canterbury 1716-37) that one candidate for the priesthood, who had been a deacon for twelve years, could 'just read a verse or two in the Greek Testament, and turn an article out of Latin into English. . . . But what is still worse, he is utterly ignorant of everything that relates to the doctrines of the Articles and of every branch of Divinity'. However, because the candidate was 'modest, sober and well-behaved', and his mother was presenting him to a living in succession to his father, Reynolds agreed to ordain him priest.[4] In March 1671, Thomas Adney, the Rector of Rusbury, wrote to Bishop Croft of Hereford's chaplain in support of a schoolmaster named Woode, who was seeking ordination to the diaconate:

> He is no university man, and therefore I hope you will not put him upon any philosophical questions – but I assure you he is an ingenious and industrious person and one that is like to make a profitable instrument of much good in the church.[5]

---

1.  Sherbo, A., 'Stockdale, Percival' in *ODNB*, vol. 52, pp. 824-5.
2.  Vernon, E.C., 'Manton, Thomas' in *ODNB*, vol. 36, pp. 565-8.
3.  Courtney, W.P., 'Aitken, Robert' in *ODNB*, vol. 1, pp. 536-7.
4.  Jacob, W.M., 'Reynolds, Richard, Bishop of Lincoln' in *ODNB*, vol. 46, pp. 569-70.
5.  Marshall (2009), pp. 165-6.

However, attitudes seemed to have hardened later: in 1753, the sponsor of John Bromwich, the Master of Bridgenorth School who was seeking deacon's orders, expressed concern about his learning and the appropriateness of ordaining an older man.[1]

By far the greatest challenge for the newly ordained deacon in the eighteenth-century church was finding a patron. Obtaining a title for diaconal ordination and a curacy was one thing, but obtaining an incumbency, unless it was a college living, required an individual or corporate patron. George Whitefield (1714-1770), ordained deacon by Bishop Martin Benson in Gloucester Cathedral on 20 June 1736, was an example of a graduate from a humble background who could not obtain a title for priestly ordination. Instead of serving an ordinary curacy, Whitefield sailed for Georgia, where he eventually managed to gain the support of the trustees of the orphanage he had founded there, who obtained the title for him.[2] He was ordained priest on 14 January 1739, having spent eighteen months as a deacon.

John Wesley was a deacon for almost three years, between 25 September 1725 and his priestly ordination on 22 September 1728. In Wesley's case, the gap between his diaconal and priestly ordinations can be explained by his status as a college fellow. However, there may have been theological reasons for Whitefield's two-and-a-half-year stint as a deacon. Called primarily to preaching, Whitefield gave his first sermon on the day after his diaconal ordination, and as a deacon, Whitefield was able to do what he loved most. Furthermore, Whitefield did not want to exercise a parochial ministry, and it was unlikely, given his evangelical theological convictions, that he would secure patronage to do so. He eventually became a private chaplain to Selina, Countess of Huntingdon. There was hardly any urgency, therefore, in his being ordained priest in order to celebrate the parish communion.

George Whitefield was a preaching deacon, but he also belonged to another important category of deacon within the eighteenth-century church: the missionary deacon. These were young men who, instead of serving curacies in England, sought employment in the American colonies, where the Church of England was making efforts both to convert the indigenous people to Christianity and to strengthen the position of the church against dissenters. One such man was Thomas Hatton, the son of a town clerk from Shrewsbury who was ordained deacon on 21 May 1758, shortly

1.  Ibid. p. 166.
2.  Schlenther, B.S., 'Whitefield, George' in *ODNB*, vol. 58, pp. 640-49.

after he graduated with a Bachelor of Arts degree from St John's College, Cambridge. Hatton found a job as Usher (second-in-charge) at the grammar school attached to William and Mary College in Williamsburg, Virginia. He arrived in America on 29 September 1758 and remained in Williamsburg until the summer of 1760, when he returned to England and was ordained priest on 21 September the same year.[1]

Writing home to his friend George Ashby, a fellow of St John's, Hatton observed with distaste that the clergy in Virginia were paid in tobacco, and therefore had to engage in trade in order to sell it:

> The clergyman's salary is 16000 lb weight of tobacco, with a glebe of 200 acres, and a house upon it. . . . And though this may seem a handsome maintenance, yet it will barely support him, according to the exorbitant price goods sell at, unless he adds to it by an advantageous marriage, or has an estate independent of it. Several of the clergy deal in the mercantile way, besides what their tobacco obliges them, and I myself know one, who has set up a common brew house.[2]

Although it was a moot point whether the Canon Law of the Church of England applied in the colonies (John Wesley later famously exploited this loophole to ordain men to the ministry), Canon 76 was generally interpreted to mean that priests could not engage in trade. The rule was not usually applied to deacons, which gave a good reason for clergy working in the colonies to remain in this order. The diaconate, in other words, enabled frontier ministry, as the Anglican church in the United States would subsequently discover.[3] Ironically, native Virginians who entered the church were more likely to be ordained priest and deacon in quick succession, in recognition of the fact that a journey to England was expensive and hazardous.[4] Virginians could only be ordained in England, since there was no bishop in the American colonies, which were under the jurisdiction of the Bishop of London.

1. Venn, J., *Alumni Cantabrigienses, Part II* (Cambridge University Press: Cambridge, 1922-55), vol. 3, p. 287.
2. Thomas Hatton to George Ashby, 18 December 1758, Suffolk Records Office, Bury St Edmunds, E2/22/1.
3. Plater, O., *Many Servants: An Introduction to Deacons* (Cowley Publications: Boston, MA, 1991), pp. 41-6.
4. Nelson, J.K., *A Blessed Company: Parishes, Parsons and Parishioners in Anglican Virginia, 1690-1776* (University of North Carolina Press: Chapel Hill, NC, 2001), pp. 120-21.

## John Wesley's deacons

Just as the Non-Jurors experimented with the Ordinal in the early eighteenth century, so by the end of the century, John Wesley was adapting the Ordinal to meet the needs of the Methodist connexion. To the end of his days, Wesley insisted that he was not a separatist from the Church of England, and was acting within the Anglican tradition. However, Wesley's most dramatic departure from historic Anglican norms was his personal ordination of ministers for mission in North America, without the involvement of a bishop. Wesley's views on orders had been changing since the 1740s. In 1738, he declared his belief that bishops, deacons and priests were 'of divine appointment', but in 1746, his reading convinced him that although the orders of bishop, priest and deacon were described in scripture, they were not binding on all churches. In 1747, the Methodist Conference concluded that the three orders of ministry were described in the New Testament, and had existed in the early church, but denied that 'God designed the same plan should obtain in all Churches throughout the world'.[1]

On 1 September 1784, Wesley ordained Richard Whatcoat and Thomas Vasey deacons, using an adapted form of the service for the ordering of deacons from the Ordinal. Wesley made only the changes that were necessary to remove any reference to the parish structures of authority mentioned in the Ordinal, but he added nothing new. The collect remained identical, but Wesley shortened the description of the office of deacon:

It appertaineth to the office of a Deacon, to assist the elder in Divine Service, and especially when he ministereth the holy Communion, to help him in the distribution thereof, and to read and expound the holy Scriptures; to instruct the youth, and in the absence of the elder to baptise. And furthermore, it is his office, to search for the sick, poor and impotent, that they may be visited and relieved.[2]

As in the Ordinal, the deacon was ordained by the imposition of hands by the Superintendant alone, but he was to be presented with the whole Bible rather than just the New Testament.

---

1. Bowmer, G.C., *The Sacrament of the Lord's Supper in Early Methodism* (Dacre Press: London, 1951), pp. 156-7.
2. Burdon, A., *Authority and Order: John Wesley and his Preachers* (Ashgate: Aldershot, 2005), pp. 87-8.

Adrian Burdon has argued that Wesley did not intend to confer Anglican orders on Whatcoat and Vasey, since he remained faithful to the doctrine of apostolic succession in some form.[1] Thus, Wesley subsequently ordained Whatcoat and Vasey as elders rather than priests, and ordained Thomas Coke as a superintendant rather than a bishop. 'Deacon' was the only ministerial term used by Wesley that came directly from the Ordinal, and one explanation for this is that Wesley may have believed that a presbyter had the power to confer diaconal ordination.[2] Alternatively, Wesley may have believed that the ordination of deacons was not a true ordination at all, but merely an appointment to an office, in contrast to the ordination of priests and bishops. However, if Wesley believed that he was not really ordaining Whatcoat and Vasey to the priesthood, it is unclear why he should have followed the practice of the established church by ordaining them deacons first – direct ordination to the presbyterate as elders would have sufficed.

Wesley was not necessarily acting as far outside of the Anglican tradition as might first appear when, as a mere presbyter, he ordained deacons contrary to the Church of England's Canon Law and ancient practice. Richard Hooker argued that the difference between a priest and a bishop was a difference of authority rather than sacramental character; it was only deacons who differed in character from priest-bishops, since the power to absolve and consecrate was shared equally by priests and bishops, but not by deacons.[3] Wesley had, in effect, been forced into assuming the position of 'scriptural bishop' over the Methodist connexion by the Church of England's intransigence in meeting their pastoral needs. He was adamant that the ministers ordained by him could serve only outside England, since within England an episcopal government of the church prevailed. Thus, for Wesley in the 1780s, episcopacy was primarily a matter of authority rather than apostolic succession or sacramental character. Burdon has argued that Wesley saw himself as an *episkopos* or 'scriptural bishop' and viewed the ordination of deacons not as a conferral of orders but as the appointment of direct assistants, after the practice of the early church.[4]

Wesley ordained Whatcoat and Vasey elders the day after their diaconal ordination, thereby deviating from the Ordinal and, indeed, late eighteenth-century Anglican practice. There is no evidence that

1. Ibid. pp. 60-62.
2. Ibid. p. 82.
3. Simut (2008), p. 415.
4. Burdon (2005), p. 27.

any of the early Methodist ministers remained deacons only, and after Wesley's death, ordination of ministers by the imposition of hands fell into abeyance in the Methodist connexion, except for overseas ministry. Reception into full connexion took the place of ordination until 1836, although Wesley's adaptation of the Ordinal retained official authority within Methodism. In 1846, a new rite of ordination merged elements of the rites for the ordination of deacons, elders and superintendents into a single text, effectively ending any vestiges of a threefold order of ministry in Methodism. It was not until 1993 that the Methodist Conference recognised deacons as an order of ministry (rather than a ministry of the laity) and revived the Methodist Diaconal Order.[1]

In 1817, John Brewster composed a series of reflections for newly ordained deacons that gives a sense of how the diaconate was regarded in the pre-Victorian church. Brewster noted that 'The office of a Deacon occupies but a small portion of the life of a Minister of the Gospel in the Established Church'.[2] Comparing the deacons of the New Testament to the deacons of the Regency era, he acknowledged that 'the alteration of times has indeed made a considerable change in the profession of a Deacon; but the Church very wisely considers his situation as a state of probation'. Curiously, Brewster did not consider deacon's orders 'indelible', like priest's orders, even though in statute a deacon was considered just as much a cleric and a 'spiritual person' as a priest. However, he did emphasise the doctrine of cumulative ordination: '[Priestly ordination] does not supersede, but perfect and confirm my former obligations'.[3]

Brewster made no attempt to pretend that the deacon was still called upon to minister to the poor and sick: 'Though I am not now called upon, as a Deacon to search for the sick, the poor and the impotent, and to intimate their cases to the superior minister, or officiating curate; yet am I solemnly required to do this, and much more, for *myself*'.[4] Brewster argued that the conferral of the diaconate by the imposition of hands by the bishop did not constitute a conferral of grace, but was rather 'only a symbol of the power which confers the office, and of those ordinary graces, which

1. Westerfield-Tucker, K.B., 'Ordination: Methodist' in Bradshaw, P.F. (ed.), *The New SCM Dictionary of Liturgy and Worship* (SCM Press: London, 2005), pp. 352-3.
2. Brewster, J., *Practical Reflections on the Ordination Services for Deacons and Priests, in the United Church of England and Ireland* (London, 1817), p. 94.
3. Ibid. pp. 95-6.
4. Ibid. p. 96.

are to be obtained by prayer'.[1] This suggests that Brewster regarded the diaconate primarily as an *office*, rather than a sacred character. The diaconate was 'the first opening of an ecclesiastical life', which 'brought with it a succession of holy duties'.[2] At the beginning of the nineteenth century, the diaconate was at one of its lowest ebbs; men who remained permanently in deacon's orders had largely disappeared, and a prevailing low theology of holy orders regarded the diaconate as nothing more than a 'charge of probation'. But society was changing, and within a few years, the idea of reviving the original purpose of deacons would re-emerge with a vengeance.

---

1. Ibid. p. 104.
2. Ibid. p. 106.

# 3

# *The Victorian Call for Deacons,*
# *1839-1901*

In the early 1830s, the Church of England was plunged into a period of profound soul-searching by the wide-ranging reforms instigated by the Whig government. The Duke of Wellington's failure to prevent Roman Catholic emancipation, which was finally approved by Parliament in 1829, spelled the final defeat of the traditional alliance of the Church of England and the Tory party. Although the Whig government's primary concern was the reform of Parliament and the electoral system, its attention also turned to the church. The church was divided over the question of reform, with some 'latitudinarian' bishops and clergy supporting it, while high churchmen opposed it. In 1835, the newly appointed Church Commissioners recommended the creation of new dioceses, a reduction to the income of existing dioceses, and smaller cathedral chapters, with the revenues of canonries and prebendaries directed to the poorer parishes. Tithes were rationalised and in 1838, the Pluralities Act outlawed the holding of more than one benefice.[1]

Taken individually, these were not particularly radical changes, but together they re-established Parliament's authority over the church in a way that had not been seen for at least a century. The sense that the church's national position was threatened by interference from liberal parliamentarians was the origin of John Keble's 1833 sermon on 'National Apostasy', traditionally regarded as the birth of the Oxford Movement. Keble and his friends elaborated their principles in the *Tracts for the Times* published between 1833 and 1841, developing a novel form of *avant-garde* high

---

1. Woodward, L., *The Age of Reform*, 2nd edn (Clarendon: Oxford, 1962), pp. 509-11.

churchmanship that looked for inspiration beyond Laud and the Non-Jurors to the pre-Reformation church. It proved an extremely divisive development. The conversion of John Henry Newman to Roman Catholicism in 1845 convinced many that the Oxford Movement was a Trojan horse for Romanism in the Church of England, while the Tractarians themselves made strenuous efforts to identify themselves with the pre-Reformation English church as 'Anglo-Catholics' rather than Roman Catholics. As the legality of the ritual innovations introduced by the Oxford Movement was challenged, the Church of England became polarised between those who regarded it as a branch of the Catholic Church and those who insisted on its Protestant character.

Anglo-Catholics and evangelicals were united, however, in the belief that greater professionalism was needed amongst the clergy. Part of the process of 'professionalisation' was the Pluralities Act, which made it illegal 'for any spiritual person, beneficed or performing ecclesiastical duty' to engage in trade or commerce.[1] This represented a formalisation of Canon 76 of 1604, which forbade a clergyman 'to use himself . . . as a layman'.[2] 'Any spiritual person' included deacons, and the Pluralities Act thus removed the possibility of part-time clergy. However, the call for a more professional clergy was balanced by pressure for more clergy to serve England's expanding towns and cities, which were growing faster than the church could build new churches and the government could erect new parishes. The call for more clergy and the call for a better, more professional clergy were, to all appearances, at odds with one another.

## *Thomas Arnold's proposal and the 'Lay Address' of 1844*

The mid-nineteenth-century call for the renewal of the diaconate as an active order of ministry emerged from concerns about the speed of population growth in the cities and the inadequacy of the parish system as an effective model of ministry and pastoral care. The Poor Law system, which saw the poor committed to workhouses paid for by parish rates, was widely regarded as inhumane, and the church was accused of conniving at the mistreatment of the poor. In December 1835, the editor of *The Times* observed that although the needs of the poor were committed to 'no higher order than deacons' in the early church, this did not 'necessarily imply that

1. 1 and 2 Victoria, cap. 106, s. 29.
2. *Canons 1604*, p. 75.

their wants were to be treated of with derision, insult, and deceit, after the approved modern model of any gowned and banded orator who might choose to curry favour with the higher powers'. It would be absurd to imagine, the editorial continued, that 'the primitive deacons were a parish board for starving the infirm and destitute in a suitable residence for the purpose'.[1] The implication was that the church needed to recover a sense of what the real role of those 'primitive deacons' was, and perhaps restore the order of deacons as well.

In the 1970s, David Roberts argued that origins of the campaign for a revived diaconate lay within the Tory periodicals, which consistently demanded an enlargement of the clergy. Editorials in these periodicals proposed that the resources to address the needs of an industrial society lay within the ancient structure of the church, without the need for legal reform and the establishment of new structures. The revival of the diaconate and the restoration of the offertory to its proper place within the life and worship of the church represented a radically traditional solution to contemporary social problems:

> They not only wanted more bishops, priests, and cathedral institutions, but collegiate institutions, hospitals, houses of mercy, female penitentiaries, sisters of charity, and monasteries. . . . For the Tory reviewers the Church of England, divinely ordained and apostolic, had a place in it for a diaconate which, under a bishop's superintendence, could manage schools and almshouses and guarantee an effective use of the offertory.[2]

In Roberts's view, this high church vision foundered on its failure to include, or even acknowledge the existence of, the dissenters. However, Roberts's portrayal of the call for a revived diaconate as a largely high church phenomenon is not the whole truth, and the first articulate proposal came from a liberal, Thomas Arnold (1795-1842), the reforming Headmaster of Rugby School. Arnold first mooted the idea of a revived diaconate in a letter to A.P. Stanley in February 1839, and he preached on the issue in Rugby's parish church that December.[3] In May 1841, Arnold published a pamphlet entitled *Order of Deacons*, in which he suggested that the church should repeal the canons that prevented deacons from being in secular employment.

1. *The Times*, 3 December 1835, p. 4A.
2. Roberts, D., 'The Social Conscience of Tory Periodicals', *Victorian Periodicals Newsletter* 10 (1977), pp. 154-69, at p. 159.
3. Vaughan (1987), p. 28.

For Arnold, the main benefit of reviving the diaconate would be to introduce an intermediate order between clergy and laity that would broaden people's conception of what the church meant:

> A link would be formed between the clergy and the laity, by the existence of an order partaking of the character of both. The confusion of confining the term Church to the clergy would be greatly dispelled: inasmuch, as there would be not only members but even ministers of the Church who did not belong to the clergy considered as a profession.

Arnold was expressing an anxiety shared by many at the time, including his high church opponents, that the secular 'profession' of clergyman was overshadowing the sacred order of priesthood. The early nineteenth-century clergy thought of their authority in terms of their possession of an incumbency as an item of property, or their appointment to a specific office. The legal authority of bishops mattered far more than their sacred authority, and the idea that bishops and priests held a divine commission as well as a remunerative office was a rallying cry that attracted adherents from beyond the confines of the Oxford Movement.

Arnold was concerned that the church had become the exclusive preserve of the highly educated, who were, in the main, also the wealthy. By reviving the order of deacons, 'The ministry of the Church would . . . be most safely and beneficially opened to persons of inferior rank and fortune, who cannot afford the expense of a University education'. Arnold noted the popularity of various forms of Protestant dissent among the lower middle classes, and suggested that many men who had chosen to become dissenting ministers only did so because ministry in the Church of England was closed to anyone without a university degree and knowledge of ancient languages.[1] In Arnold's view, a deacon was 'half a layman',[2] and the church had made a mistake in rejecting this intermediate state.

Arnold's proposal was both more sensitive than many that followed and more enduring in its appeal. His idea of expanding people's conception of 'the church' to include the laity anticipated Vatican II's constitution *Lumen Gentium* (1964) by more than a century. Others were inspired by Arnold to submit a 'Lay Address to the Archbishop of Canterbury' in 1844, which proposed 'the

---

1. Arnold, T., 'Order of Deacons', reprinted in Mackenzie, H., *The Fuller Restoration of the Diaconate, a Means of strengthening the Church* (Smith, Elder and Co: London, 1845), pp. 20-22.
2. Vaughan (1987), p. 31.

expediency of increasing largely the number of the third order of our clergy – the deacons'. Like Arnold, the authors of the 'Lay Address' saw the diaconate as an opportunity to involve the less educated in ministry, and they recommended

> admitting, on such condition as will maintain the order and discipline of our Church, persons who have not the means of proceeding to a university degree, but who are found competently trained for the service of the sanctuary; their advancement to the higher order of ministry being made contingent upon a faithful discharge, during a lengthened period, of the office of a Deacon.

The 'Lay Address' also proposed the creation of 'a class of laymen, who, without altogether abandoning their worldly callings, might be set apart under episcopal authority, to act as visitors of the sick, Scripture readers, catechists, and the like, in parishes where their introduction should be approved by the parochial clergy'.[1] By the end of the 1840s, licensed 'scripture readers', who had never entirely died out since their institution by Archbishop Matthew Parker in the 1560s, had appeared in churches throughout the country.

At the same time that Arnold was pressing for deacons for social and ecclesiological reasons, elsewhere in the church, a parallel movement existed for deacon-schoolmasters. This can be traced back to the foundation of the National Society for Promoting the Education of the Poor in the Principles of the Established Church in 1811. By the late 1830s, several members of the National Society's central committee, led by the barrister Samuel Francis Wood, felt that it was desirable for teachers trained by the Society to be in deacon's orders. Wood shared this vision with John Henry Newman and Henry Edward Manning, then still Anglican clergymen (but both future Roman Catholic cardinals). In 1841, St Mark's College was founded in Chelsea to train teachers for church schools, and the college's principal, Derwent Coleridge, supported the idea of some teachers being lifelong deacons. The plans of Wood and Coleridge were vociferously opposed in the press, partly because Coleridge was suspected of Tractarian sympathies. His contact with Newman, who converted to Rome in 1845, made the scheme especially controversial.[2]

On 12 April 1845, Henry Mackenzie, Perpetual Curate of Great Yarmouth, preached a visitation sermon before the Bishop of Norwich. He took as his text Acts 6:2-4, the Apostles' appointment

---

1. Quoted in Mackenzie (1845), p. 18.
2. Nicholas (2010), pp. 321-3.

of men to 'serve at tables', and used the opportunity to argue for the revival of the diaconate. Mackenzie portrayed the revival of deacons as a natural consequence of respect for the hierarchy of the church, as properly constituted, and believed that evil consequences had followed the abandonment of the order of deacons as a meaningful ministry:

> In the neglect we have shown with reference to the Order of Deacons, I much fear the sin of Faithlessness rests upon us: and in the evils that have followed that neglect, I cannot but trace the effects of faithlessness visited on our Church. The Church, as I apprehend it, forms a kind of moral pyramid in every Diocese; the base and chief bulk being composed of its Lay Members, the Deacons ministering among them, the Presbyters forming a smaller body over them; the Bishop himself, in the awful dignity of Christ's Representative, forming the apex, through whom, beneath the shadow of the cross, are derived the spiritual powers and functions exercised by the inferior priesthood. Now, if this view be the true one, it is manifest that any interference with the arrangement intended, must interfere with the intended harmony of the entire fabric. And this I apprehend to have really been the case in our National Church, wherein the Diaconate has not (for some centuries at least) been fully realized.[1]

Mackenzie's rigidly hierarchical conception of the church as a social pyramid was in tune with conservative Victorian conceptions of society, and he insisted that 'the Deacons were to be ministering servants to the Order, or rather Orders, over them: it was of the Accident of their office to preach and baptize, but of its Essence to serve'. Deacons would remain, in other words, 'an inferior office'.

Mackenzie deplored the decline of the diaconate, becoming as it had 'a mere brief apprenticeship to the Priesthood', and he believed that the sin of 'separation' (religious dissent) was directly attributable to neglect of the possibilities of diaconal ministry within the Church of England. Mackenzie's evangelical sympathies are suggested by his belief that the church should have done more to respond to the 'spirit of revival' in the eighteenth century, and he blamed the church's 'coldness' for its failure to win back the dissenters.[2] Indeed, Mackenzie's vision of deacons made them sound like an Anglican version of Methodist lay preachers:

1. Mackenzie (1845), pp. 6-7.
2. Ibid. pp. 8-9.

We want men like the early Deacons . . . to labour among our masses from house to house, teaching everywhere that men should repent and turn unto the Lord Jesus Christ – We want men who shall supply the ministrations of the Gospel, and carry the realities of The Church to the houses of the whole as well as the sick – We want men in sufficient numbers to visit every house, in every parish, with the offer of the Gospel.[1]

The ministry of Mackenzie's deacons would be primarily evangelistic, but he declared that he did not want deacons who were qualified for the priesthood by a university education, who were licensed to preach in church or who felt 'entitled' to go on to priestly ordination. Deacons were to be subordinate to local incumbents, and until there was one priest for every thousand people, the church should expect priests to 'raise their cry and call for Deacons to be placed under them, while they may give themselves "continually to Prayer and to the Ministry of the Word"'. Mackenzie's deacons were, in other words, to be parish deacons and pastoral assistants, although he also suggested that licensed schoolmasters could also be deacons. Historically, many had been, but this was comparatively rare by the middle of the nineteenth century.

Mackenzie gave a number of reasons to justify his proposal. He insisted that 'No change of ordinance, no Act of Parliament, no innovation of any kind would be needed' in order to bring his scheme about.[2] This was because his deacons would be full-time ministers, in contrast to Arnold's suggestion that working men should serve as deacons. Mackenzie pointed out, quite correctly, that Arnold's proposal would require the repeal of the Pluralities Act, and Parliament was unlikely to be willing to devote its time to such a matter. Most importantly, however, the existence of a renewed order of deacons would 'establish a sympathy between the church and the lower section of the middle class'.[3]

The argument for deacons based on class would prove to be a recurring theme of nineteenth-century calls for the renewal of the diaconate. The Church of England was beginning to wake up to the fact that it still largely commanded the loyalty of the aristocracy, gentry and rural poor, but the dissenting congregations held the hearts and minds of the rapidly expanding commercial middle class, and the Roman Catholic Church was influential amongst the industrial poor

1. Ibid. pp. 9-10.
2. Ibid. p. 11.
3. Ibid. p. 12.

in the northern cities. Given that Victorian society was increasingly being shaped by middle class moral ideals, the established church was in grave danger of being left behind in a Georgian time warp unless it made itself relevant to middle class concerns.

Mackenzie called Arnold's proposed deacons 'lay-deacons' (because they were following a secular profession, rather than because they were not ordained), and accused Arnold of advocating a return to 'regular' and 'secular' clergy, as in the Roman Catholic Church. However, Mackenzie was also convinced that his own plan would not be divisive: 'Party need not exist in the restoration of the Diaconate: the man of the extremest views on the one side of the church, could not deny that it was a Church Ordinance; or of the extremest on the other, that it was a Gospel Ordinance'.[1] Mackenzie was responsible for drafting a petition for more deacons to the Bishop of Norwich. The petition opposed the proposal for lay readers contained in the petition to Canterbury, on the grounds that moderate churchmen feared innovation, high churchmen objected to 'lay agency' and evangelicals objected that episcopal licensing of lay readers interfered with their existing freedom to appoint lay assistants without interference from the bishop.[2]

The editor of *The Times* in 1844 opposed the petition to Canterbury, describing it as 'at best but a fresh experiment upon our present state and system of ecclesiastical discipline', because deacons 'would themselves object to remaining subordinates beyond the usual period'.[3] The newspaper painted a vivid picture of future deacons:

> Imagine . . . a set of men, ill-paid, ill-disciplined, meanly apparelled, and poorly fed – still occupied in mechanical or commercial labours – just as distant as before from the society and standing of the clergy, and quite convinced that no efforts of their own will ever emancipate them from the inferiority of their position; trusted and encouraged to follow their spiritual task, but ever regarded and remunerated as subordinates of the lowest order in the church.[4]

J. Osmond Dakeyne, Rector of South Hykeham in Lincolnshire, expressed his disapproval of the petition, arguing that deacons would be so resentful of being forbidden to advance to the priesthood that they would leave the Church of England altogether, and thus 'we

---

1. Ibid. p. 25.
2. Ibid. pp. 25-7.
3. *The Times*, 4 December 1844, p. 4C.
4. *The Times*, 6 December 1844, p. 4B.

should be rearing up a strong body of Dissenting ministers having episcopal ordination'.[1] Another correspondent observed that there was no shortage of university graduates who wanted careers in the church, but the meagreness of clergy stipends prevented them from seeking ordination.[2]

After being circulated amongst the clergy, the petition for an increase in deacons, catechists and scripture readers was finally presented to the Archbishop of Canterbury in July 1845 by Viscount Sandon, Sir Robert Inglis and Henry Kingscote. The Archbishop replied that he would be only too happy to see an increase in the number of curates, but only if there were a corresponding increase in stipends and if the usual educational standards were maintained.[3] Supporters of the diaconate were undeterred, however, and later that year an anonymous priest took Mackenzie's class-based arguments a stage further. He noted that while the purpose of the bishops was to evangelise the higher aristocracy, priests evangelised the gentry. What was missing was an order of clergy to evangelise the lower middle class. The author lamented, 'We have no deacons – at least such as are taken from what seems to be their natural rank – the class of the commonalty'.[4] Distinctive deacons were necessary because 'The delicate and sensitive tone nurtured in a young clergyman by his university education' made it difficult for him to relate to the lower orders.[5] Deacons were the 'natural ministers' to the lower orders, and this was probably why God had provided this third order of the clergy in the first place.[6]

These arguments reveal a less attractive feature of the campaign for deacons than its concern to advance social justice: the possibility that the revival of deacons could be a way of strengthening the class system within the clergy. However, the author's overarching intention was that, by evangelising the lower orders, deacons would make the Church of England a national church once again.[7] In his 1846 pamphlet on increasing the efficiency of the church, James Akroyd Beaumont emphasised the problems that priests were experiencing on account of their much reduced incomes, combined with a much

1. Letter to *The Times*, 14 December 1844, p. 5G.
2. 'A Country Churchgoer', letter to *The Times*, 14 December 1844, p. 5G.
3. *The Times*, 30 July 1845, p. 4E.
4. A Presbyter of the Church of England, *Reasons for the Restoration of the Order of Deacons* (Francis and John Rivington: London, 1845), pp. 7-8.
5. Ibid. p. 11.
6. Ibid. p. 37.
7. Ibid. pp. 82-3.

increased workload, especially in urban areas. He advocated the creation of many more dioceses and parishes, along with extension of the diaconate, so that priests were relieved from the 'harassing cares' of their office. The church's increasing involvement in education required priests to sit on innumerable committees, never mind the business of dealing with the parish clerk, poor law officials and various charitable organisations.[1]

In April 1847, *The Times* estimated that there were 2,678 men in deacon's orders who would not go on to be ordained priest.[2] This seems an improbably high number, given the continued insistence of apologists for the diaconate that there were no lifelong deacons. It seems likely that neither *The Times* nor the apologists were right. F.W.B. Bullock calculated that between 1834 and 1843, 5,350 men were ordained deacon, of whom 565 were described as 'literates' or trained elsewhere than Oxford, Cambridge, Durham and Trinity College, Dublin.[3] 'Literate' meant that they had some knowledge of Latin but did not hold a university degree. These were the men most likely to remain in deacon's orders without proceeding to the presbyterate. Men in deacon's orders continued to serve as schoolmasters and fellows of colleges in the mid-nineteenth century, even if only in the low hundreds. Deacons continued to be closely associated with education, and in 1847 the Bishop of St Davids noted that a pamphlet in Welsh was warning Welsh dissenters that the government was planning to train 15,000 schoolmasters who would also be ordained deacons in the established church, seducing Welsh children from the principles of dissent. As the editor of *The Times* jested, under the proposals in the petition to Canterbury, 'we must inevitably become a priest-ridden, or at least a deacon-ridden people'.[4]

However, concern from dissenters about a plan for more deacons that never came about had serious consequences. Under the terms of the 1847 Education Act, which provided local schools with grants

---

1. Beaumont, J.A., *More Bishops, More Priests, More Deacons: How to increase the efficiency of the church* (Rivington: London, 1846), p. 12-14.
2. According to *The Times* of 9 April 1847, p. 4A, of 2 million children currently in school, 80,000 would become 'stipendiaries'. Of these, 40,000 would become pupil-teachers. Of the male pupil teachers, 'fifteen sixteenths' (18,750) would become clergy of the Church of England, and 'of those [ordained] Deacons six-sevenths at least will ultimately pass on to the degree of Priest'.
3. Bullock, F.W.B., *A History of Training for the Ministry of the Church of England . . . from 1800 to 1874* (Budd & Gillatt: St Leonards-on-Sea, 1955), p. 74, quoted in Nicholas (2007), p. 26.
4. *The Times*, 6 June 1847, p. 5C.

from the government to pay teachers, and was a precursor of the 1870 Education Act (which provided for universal primary education), primary schools run by a clergyman were excluded from receiving grants. This policy effectively brought an end to the tradition of local deacon-schoolmasters, and thereafter clerical schoolmasters were confined to the established public schools.

Up until the end of the 1840s, the advocates of the revived diaconate showed no conspicuous influence from the Oxford Movement. This was fortunate for them, since involvement with such a controversial cause would doubtless have further strengthened opposition to the call for deacons. However, in 1849, an anonymous 'Parish Priest' published *The Diaconate and the Poor*, a pamphlet strongly influenced by the 'Christian socialism' that often accompanied ritualist ideals. The author praised the authors of the Ordinal of 1550, who 'wished to restore to the Diaconate those functions which had been distributed amongst subdeacons and the minor orders', but lamented that 'we, by our neglect, have allowed them all to pass away from the Deacon into the unsanctified hands of those anomalous and ungovernable functionaries – parish clerks and relieving officers'.[1] The crucial point was that deacons, unlike parish clerks, were 'sanctified' to their administrative duties and their office of relieving the poor. Yet the sermon on the duty and office of deacons specified by the Ordinal was never preached, and so the original function of the diaconate had been lost.[2]

In spite of opposition, the movement for lifelong deacons picked up pace in the late 1840s. In 1847, Herbert Smith went so far as to found an entire journal dedicated to the revival of the diaconate. The first number of *The Advocate for the Restoration of the Order of Deacons in the Church of England* appeared in May 1847, although there was only one more issue.[3] On 18 June 1848, the Bishop of London, Charles Blomfield, ordained one of the schoolmasters at St Mark's College, Henry Cuttill Stubbs, to the diaconate.[4] In 1849, the most remarkable product of the mid-nineteenth century interest in the diaconate, Charles William Chepmell's *Chapters on Deacons*, was published. This was the first book dedicated to the diaconate in the Church of England, and it presented the lives of fourteen

1. A Parish Priest, *The Diaconate and the Poor: the duty of the laity of England briefly considered with reference to the above two objects* (J. Ollivier: London, 1849), p. 10.
2. Ibid. p. 11.
3. Nicholas (2007), pp. 26-7.
4. Ibid. p. 159.

deacons of the early church as exemplars to contemporary deacons. These were accompanied by lives of Alcuin, the Reformation martyr Cuthbert Symson, and Nicholas Ferrar.[1] The appearance of Symson in Chepmell's book was somewhat incongruous, given the author's unabashed references to 'the sacrifice of the mass'. Chepmell was unambiguously Tractarian in belief, and declared that the function of the deacon was to stand in for and represent the people of God in the liturgy: 'The Deacon is as the hand of the people stretched out to receive the blessing, and as their ear attentive to hear what God the Lord will say, and as their mouth to answer with them, Amen'.[2] Chepmell's book took the form of a devotional collection of lives of deacons, and his intention seems to have been to promote devotion to the memory of 'deacon saints' within the Church of England.

## The Convocation of 1861

In spite of the particular Tractarian enthusiasm for the campaign for deacons, it remained a mainstream issue within the church as a whole, commanding support from all quarters. In 1850, the cause was taken up by a proponent almost as distinguished as Arnold, the Archdeacon of London, William Hale Hale (1795-1870). Hale was also the Master of Charterhouse School, and his advocacy was all the more powerful for the fact that he was known to be an opponent of ecclesiastical reform. In *Duties of the Deacons and Priests in the Church of England compared* (1850), Hale noted that the Greek word *diakonos* was best translated as 'minister', and could therefore be applied to both priests and deacons. Nevertheless, in his years as a bishop's chaplain and archdeacon he had come to understand that the functions of deacons and priests were indeed more different than was usually supposed.[3] Bishop's chaplains at the time were the officials who had the primary task of selecting and examining candidates for ordination. Hale explained that he considered deacons to be partly 'in the world' in a way that priests were not:

> The distinction between the Diaconate and the Presbyterate of our Church appears to me to be as strongly marked as that between the secular and religious of the Church of Rome; the

---

1. [Chepmell, C.W.], *Chapters on Deacons* (London, 1849), pp. 252-73 (Cuthbert Symson), 274-303 (Nicholas Ferrar).
2. Ibid. p. xiii.
3. Hale, W.H., *Duties of the Deacons and Priests in the Church of England compared* (Rivington: London, 1850), pp. 9-10. On Hale's argument see Vaughan (1987), pp. 26-32.

Deacon is permitted to perform the ordinary duties of life, but the Presbyter bids adieu to wordly employments, and makes the duties of the Ministry his all-absorbing thought and care.[1]

For Archdeacon Hale, the revival of the order of deacons seems to have been as much a means of drawing attention to the exalted nature of the priesthood as having deacons for their own sake. Hale was opposed to the use of lay scripture readers, whom he noted already existed in populous parishes,[2] on the grounds that they represented an innovation in the government of the church. Most priests, he claimed, would prefer to have the assistance of an ordained deacon rather than a scripture reader. Indeed, Hale believed that many readers were themselves troubled in conscience that they were taking upon themselves a clerical function without proper authorisation. Hale was more open to the idea of ordained subdeacons,[3] and on 24 May 1852 he delivered a charge to the clergy of the Archdeaconry of London on the subject.[4]

Hale did not have sufficient authority, as an archdeacon, to revive the orders of deacon and subdeacon himself, but he enjoyed considerable influence. He was neither a reformer nor a supporter of the Oxford Movement, but an old-fashioned high churchman whose priority was the suppression of innovation. The attraction of the diaconate to such a man was the fact that it was a dormant ancient institution rather than a new one. The latitudinarian Arnold, the Anglo-Catholic Chepmell and the old-fashioned high churchman Hale were all in favour of deacons: indeed, the only voice in the Church of England not speaking out for revival was that of the evangelicals. In June 1851, Exeter's Diocesan Synod discussed 'the increase of authorized teachers or permanent deacons by a diminution of the expenses of ecclesiastical education',[5] and other diocesan bodies may well have followed suit. In Leeds, the pioneering vicar Walter Farquhar Hook seized on the idea of ordaining less educated men as deacons as a solution to his problem of ministering to a large city that was a single parish; Hook published his own set of proposals for training in 1852.[6]

---

1. Hale (1850), p. 15.
2. Ibid. p. 5.
3. Ibid. p. 31.
4. Hale, W.H., *Suggestions for the Extension of the Ministry and the Revival of the Order of Sub-deacons* (Rivington: London, 1852).
5. *The Times*, 12 August 1851, p. 4E.
6. Vaughan (1987), pp. 37-9.

The stage was set for the call for deacons to reach the church at large, and the man who led the fight was Francis Charles Massingberd (1800-1872), the Chancellor of the Diocese of Lincoln and a leading figure in the revival of the Convocation of Canterbury. Massingberd had called for the revival of Convocation as early as 1833, and in 1854 it met briefly. The first major session of Convocation, however, did not take place until 1861. Massingberd drafted a 'memorial' calling for the revival of the diaconate, which was signed by a number of ruridecanal synods (the ancestors of today's Deanery Synods) in January 1862. The memorial was then submitted to the Lower House of Convocation, which represented the ordinary clergy.

According to W.P.S. Bingham, the Rector of West Pinchbeck in Lincolnshire, 'The result of the debate [in Convocation] was rather to elicit objections to all plans proposed, than to strike out one which should be free from all inconvenience'.[1] These objections were threefold. In the first place, there were grave doubts about the possibility of being able to pay the new deacons; secondly, there was a concern that the reputation of the clergy could be endangered by admitting men without a university education to holy orders; and thirdly, there was concern that 'permanent' deacons would look on their fellow 'transitional' deacons with jealousy and question why they were unable to proceed to the priesthood. Nevertheless, on 12 February 1862, the Lower House agreed to a address a representation to the Upper House of Convocation (the bishops), 'that whatever increase may take place in the number of persons admitted to the Diaconate, a supplemental agency is also required, which shall be in accordance with our Ecclesiastical system'.[2] The choice of words was diplomatic: no assumption was made that there would be distinctive deacons, but even if there were, 'a fourth agency' (subdeacons or scripture readers) would also be required.

Bingham himself opposed the appointment of scripture readers, on the grounds that they could not perform a range of functions sufficient to liberate the time that priests so desperately needed for prayer and study. Bingham blamed the tendency of Anglo-Catholic clergy to convert to Roman Catholicism on inadequate learning, the consequence of 'want of leisure for study' amongst the clergy.[3] He thereby made the revival of the diaconate seem a solution to what was considered the church's chief problem at the time – the danger

1. Bingham, W.P.S., *The Extension of the Diaconate: A Paper read before the Spalding Clerical Association* (Joseph Masters: London, 1862), p. 5.
2. Ibid. pp. 14-15.
3. Ibid. pp. 6-7.

of clergy defecting to Rome. Bingham's model of the diaconate, like most other proposals, put the deacons under the direct control of the local incumbent:

> To these men might be committed, under the superintendence of the Parish Priest, the care of Schools, visitation of the poor and sick, funerals and those secular duties which are felt by clergymen to be so great an encroachment on their time, such, for instance, as searching registers, collecting subscriptions, keeping accounts of parochial charities and receiving money for coal and clothing clubs and penny banks.[1]

Bingham also suggested that individuals already engaged in 'diaconal' service, such as parish clerks and schoolmasters, could be ordained deacon. However, he noted that the rules of the Privy Council's Committee on Education made it impossible for schools with a master in holy orders to receive funding from the government. Whilst it was common for the heads of fee-paying schools to be clergymen, this was rare for schoolmasters of free schools. Bingham regretted this development, and believed that including schoolmasters in the clergy would guarantee the Church of England's hold over the education system as a whole. He was also in favour of deacons pursuing a secular profession other than teaching: 'The example of S. Paul in following his occupation as a tent-maker affords a precedent for deacons spending some portion of their time in secular employments'.[2]

The Convocation of Canterbury's misgivings about full-time deacons are understandable, given the difficulties of paying existing clergy. Allowing men in secular employment to be deacons would have required the repeal of the 1838 Pluralities Act, and Convocation was reluctant to involve itself in a lengthy tussle with Parliament. On the other hand, the anxiety expressed over jealous deacons eyeing their clerical colleagues seems to have been the result of a 'commodification' of clerical office that went back to the eighteenth century. Priestly ordination meant an incumbency, and therefore a better income, and Convocation was loath to introduce yet another level of the class system into the clergy. The obvious response to the difficulty of reviving the diaconate, and the manifest need to assist the clergy, was the establishment of a 'fourth order' of ministry, and the arguments of the 1860s and '70s were largely about the nature of this proposed lay order.

---

1. Ibid. p. 11.
2. Ibid. p. 13.

In addition to deacons, deaconesses were also on the agenda of the Convocation of 1861-62. Already in 1849, Chepmell had imagined a revived diaconate of both men and women, including 'a sisterhood devote / To works of mercy' in the poem that prefaced his *Chapters on Deacons* (1849). However, Elizabeth Catherine Ferard (1825-1883), the first Anglican deaconess, was inspired by the German Lutheran deaconesses at Kaiserswerth rather than pre-Reformation or Roman Catholic models. Ferard was licensed by the Bishop of London on 18 July 1862. In 1869, the Bishop of Ely, Harold Browne, ordained Fanny Elizabeth Eagles using an adapted form of the service for the ordination of deacons. The ordination service for deaconesses was adapted from the ordination service for deacons, although local practice varied from diocese to diocese. However, 'any implication that the status of the deaconess was equal to that of the deacon was swiftly repudiated'.[1]

In the Lower House of Convocation on 12 February 1862, Henry Mackenzie successfully moved an objection to 'committing the Church of England to the recognition of Orders as conferred upon Deaconesses in the same sense as that in which they are conferred upon Deacons'.[2] It is likely that Mackenzie objected because he feared that any perception that women were being ordained as deacons could bring the diaconate that he was trying so hard to revive into disrepute. By the end of the nineteenth century, however, deaconesses were often treated just like deacons, and an 1896 report noted that 'The position our Deaconess holds in the diocese is the same as that of the Deacon, she is licensed to the parish, receives her own stipend, and is entirely independent of the Head Deaconess, but she is responsible to her Vicar and her Bishop'.[3] This was a best-case scenario for deaconesses, however, and in other dioceses they were treated as laywomen in all respects; indeed, confusion as to the exact nature and identity of deaconesses was to persist until 1987.

1.  Knight, F., *The Nineteenth-Century Church and English Society* (Cambridge University Press: Cambridge, 1995), p. 197. In the chapel of the Bishop's Palace in Ely, where the ordination took place, there is a stained glass window installed by Bishop James Woodford (1873-1885) depicting an Apostle laying hands on a woman, which may have been intended to commemorate this event or refer to the community of deaconesses in the diocese.
2.  Blackmore, H., *The Beginning of Women's Ministry: The Revival of the Deaconess in the 19th-century Church of England*, Church of England Record Society 14 (Church of England Record Society: London, 2007), pp. xxii-xxiii.
3.  Quoted in ibid. p. xxxiii.

## *Deacons, subdeacons and scripture readers, 1861-1888*

In 1865, William Baird published an open letter to the Bishop of London asking for the establishment of a subdiaconate, as well as the revival of the order of deacons. Baird, who declared that 'nothing save the power of absolving and of celebrating the Holy Communion . . . separated [the diaconate] from the second Order of Christian Ministry',[1] seems to have been motivated to write his letter by a petition addressed to the Archbishop of Canterbury by the Church of England Young Men's Society. The Society asked the Archbishop that

> either by instituting a lower or special Order, or by reviving the true character of the Diaconate, according to its primitive intention . . . there be added to the existing Clergy a large body of earnest-hearted men to carry on the work of the Church in its more secular and subordinate departments, and also peculiarly adapted to the evangelization of the Mechanic Classes, and other sections of the community as yet but little reached by ordinary ministration.

Baird claimed that 'a Society is in course of formation, which will have for its object the establishment of such Orders'.[2] Whether this society ever came into existence is unclear, but by 1864 at least ·12 deacon-schoolmasters trained at St Mark's College were in post leading teacher training in their own right,[3] and a total of 117 graduates of St Mark's had received holy orders.[4] It is noteworthy that in the aftermath of the Convocation of 1861-62, proponents of the diaconate had changed the terms of their argument to request either the diaconate or a fourth order. In 1866, J.E. Dibb finally added an evangelical voice to the debate when he delivered an address to the Church of England Clerical and Lay Association for the Maintenance of Evangelical Principles. Dibb opposed extension of ordained clergy on the grounds of lack of funds and the danger of allowing 'mere literates' to be admitted to holy orders.[5]

The question of help for the clergy was starting to divide the church on party lines, with high churchmen more likely to argue for deacons and liberals and evangelicals generally favouring the

1. Baird, W., *A Plea for the Extension of the Ministerial Office* (Rivingtons: London, 1865), p. 5.
2. Ibid. pp. 19-20.
3. Nicholas (2007), pp. 168-9.
4. Ibid. p. 191.
5. Dibb, J.E., *The Sub-diaconate* (William MacIntosh: London, 1866), p. 6.

commissioning of laymen as subdeacons or scripture readers. In 1864, the issue of deacons came up once more at the Convocation of Canterbury, coupled with a request for the more general licensing of readers.[1] Accordingly, on Ascension Day, 1866, the bishops reached an agreement that Readers could be licensed in all dioceses to lead prayers and preach in the absence of a clergyman,[2] although scripture readers had already been operating in some areas for decades. The 1866 decision removed the ambiguity of Readers' canonical status and established them as a para-clerical 'order of ministry'.

There was a backlash from some clergy, however, against the perceived innovation of lay ministry. In 1868, Henry Almack, the Rector of Fawley in Buckinghamshire, lamented that nothing was being done to address the clergy's demands for aid apart from commissioning an odd assortment of laymen:

> Catechists, Scripture-readers, lay helpers, have been resorted to, and in some quarters sub-Deacons have been commissioned; but nothing seems to be attempted, in real earnest, to provide a staff of men equal to our wants, of that order in the Church which is so ancient, and coming to us with the highest sanctions.[3]

Almack proposed that each diocese should establish its own training college for deacons,[4] and came back to Bingham's ideas that parish clerks and schoolmasters could be ordained.[5] He proposed just one year's training for deacons,[6] as opposed to the three years of a university education, but insisted that deacons should not normally be granted a licence to preach, as these should be confined to clergy with knowledge of Latin and Greek.[7] By this time, however, Almack seemed to be out of touch with the reality of church life. Few dioceses had the resources to establish training colleges for priests, let alone deacons. At a church congress in Liverpool in October 1869, there was a call for the canonical age of ordination for deacons to be lowered from twenty-three to twenty-one, since men were finishing university at twenty-one and then

---

1. *The Times*, 20 April 1864, p. 8D.
2. Wallwork, C.N.R., 'Lay Ministries' in Bradshaw, P.F. (ed.) *The New SCM Dictionary of Liturgy and Worship* (SCM Press: London, 2005), p. 273.
3. Almack, H., *A Plea for Deacons* (Rivingtons: London, 1868), p. 5.
4. Ibid. p. 10.
5. Ibid. p. 13.
6. Ibid. p. 14.
7. Ibid. p. 16.

having to support themselves for two years before ordination.[1] This concern indicated a greater willingness to consider the needs of poorer individuals seeking a career in the church.

At the Convocation of Canterbury in 1870, the Bishop of Llandaff declared that he had been following a policy of ordaining less educated men as long-term or lifelong deacons for seventeen years:

> [F]or, from the circumstances of his diocese, it was necessary to draw some of the candidates for orders from the Welsh farming classes, and they had not received so good an education as the English clergy had received. He was thus obliged to ordain inferior men, whom he certainly would not ordain if he had a selection.[2]

The Bishop informed these candidates that if they agreed to attend St David's College in Lampeter when the examiners visited from Oxford and Cambridge, he would waive the requirement that they would have to remain deacons for at least five years. Nevertheless, most of the candidates still spent five years or even longer in deacon's orders.

In 1875, George Wingate Pearse, the Rector of Walton in Buckinghamshire, suggested that there were insufficient grounds in tradition for the appointment of subdeacons, and favoured more deacons instead.[3] He noted that the Ordinal did not require deacons to give up a secular profession, and noted that amongst professionals with university degrees, doctors were particularly well-placed to arrange their surgery hours so that they could also serve as deacons.[4] Pearse differed from previous proponents of the diaconate by insisting on a higher level of education for deacons, thereby undercutting the class-based arguments put forward in the 1840s.[5] Pearse's deacons were not so much a group of Anglican lay preachers drawn from the lower middle class as a group of professional men who gave up their free time to serve the church. They were, in other words, non-stipendiary clergy.

The debate rumbled on, and *The Times* reported that there was a committee of Convocation sitting on the subject of the diaconate in May 1876.[6] Lay voices, which had largely fallen silent in the 1860s, began to re-emerge in the 1870s. An anonymous layman ('A Layman')

1. *The Times*, 7 October 1869, p. 7F.
2. *The Times*, 7 July 1870, p. 8A.
3. Pearse, G.W., *Opening of the Diaconate to Persons engaged in Professions and Trades* (Rivingtons: London, 1875), p. 6.
4. Ibid. p. 8.
5. Ibid. p. 10.
6. *The Times*, 11 May 1876, p. 11A.

published a pamphlet on the subject of the diaconate in 1877. 'A Layman' saw the role of a revived diaconate as being 'to evangelise the masses and to teach the illiterate',[1] although the author recognised the difficulty of paying deacons a small stipend when they had no prospect of advancement in the church's hierarchy. This, in his view, was an argument for allowing deacons to remain in secular employment.[2]

In 1878, the second Lambeth Conference, a gathering of bishops from America and the British colonies, considered the question of whether the church in the West Indies should be allowed to ordain lifelong deacons. The Bishop of Kingston, Reginald Courtenay, had already ordained an Irish doctor named Hugh Croskerry on 17 September 1871, and argued in a sermon on the occasion that it was possible for a man to serve as a deacon and continue in a profession.[3] The Conference expressed concerns about the fact that the proposed West Indian deacons would not go on to be ordained priest (which was hardly a legitimate theological concern, given that lifelong deacons already existed in England), that the deacons would have to engage in secular employment and that their level of education would be below that of the rest of the clergy.

It is very likely that these concerns masked the bishops' real concern: the proposed deacons would be black West Indians.[4] In fact, the 1878 Lambeth Conference was not the first time that the issue of deacons elsewhere in the Anglican communion had arisen; William Hale Hale had proposed to Bishop Broughton of Sydney as early as the 1830s that 'some of the local magistrates and chief owners of property might act as Deacons' in order to serve remote communities in Australia,[5] and in the 1860s, J.H. Nicolls, a Canadian priest, had taken up the cause of deacons.[6] In 1880, the Canadian church introduced a canon that specifically permitted deacons to continue in secular employment.[7] The ordination of Hugh Croskerry in Jamaica was followed by similar experiments in the Windward Islands, but Vaughan has argued

1. A Layman, *The Restoration of the Diaconate the only way to increase the supply of ministers in the Church of England* (Edward Stanford: London, 1877), p. 11.
2. Ibid. pp. 12-13.
3. Vaughan (1987), p. 42.
4. Redmond Curtis, W., *The Lambeth Conferences: The Solution for Pan-Anglican Organization* (Columbia University Press: New York, 1942), p. 255.
5. Vaughan (1987), p. 33.
6. Nicolls, J.H., *Essay on the Subject of the Restoration of the Diaconate* (J. Lovell: Montreal, 1863).
7. Vaughan (1987), p. 51.

that it was the very charisma of the leaders involved that meant the experiment had no lasting consequences: 'The development collapsed after a change of episcopal leadership and when the sense of crisis and missed opportunity was evaporating, because of an increased flow of ordinands for the traditional ministry'.[1]

While the distinctive diaconate was taking shape elsewhere in the Anglican world, the Church of England was dragging its feet. The Convocation of Canterbury's committee produced no report, and in 1881 *The Times* noted that the Convocation of York had yet to form its own committee on the extension of the diaconate.[2] At the Convocation of Canterbury of 1884, the focus of some bishops was almost exclusively on Readers,[3] although the Bishops of Winchester and Exeter successfully tabled a motion calling for men of private means, or in the professions, to be admitted to the diaconate (this circumvented the 1838 Pluralities Act).[4] Meanwhile, the possibility of men without university degrees being admitted to the diaconate was removed in 1884, when a standard academic examination for admission to deacon's orders was introduced.[5]

By 1887, the term 'diaconate' had become semantically diluted in Convocation debates, and was being used to refer to any assistance, clerical or lay, that could be offered to priests.[6] In his speech to Convocation, Henry Twells frankly admitted that the church could not afford to pay deacons, and therefore the church had to face the fact that deacons would need to be in secular employment.[7] Twells was wary of readers and subdeacons on the grounds that deacons wanted 'the definite authority which shall justify them, in their own eyes, and in the eyes of others, in assuming their position'.[8] He pointed out that the law prohibited 'those who deal in goods, wares and merchandise' from entering holy orders, but this still allowed barristers, solicitors, doctors and surgeons to become deacons since they were educated professionals rather than tradesmen.[9]

---

1. Ibid. p. 46.
2. *The Times*, 2 May 1881, p. 6B.
3. *The Times*, 17 May 1884, p. 6E
4. Vaughan (1987), p. 52.
5. Dowland, D., *Nineteenth-Century Anglican Theological Training: The Redbrick Challenge* (Oxford University Press: Oxford, 1997), p. 61.
6. *The Times*, 10 February 1887, p. 13A.
7. Twells, H., *Extension of the Diaconate: A Speech delivered in the Lower House of the Convocation of Canterbury on Friday, July 8, 1887* (Rivington: London, 1887), p. 17.
8. Ibid. p. 21.
9. Ibid. p. 25.

The Convocation of 1884 produced a resolution that called for the ordination of men without university degrees to the diaconate, who would serve for at least four years before being examined for admission to the priesthood. Convocation's concern was not so much to create a viable order of deacons but rather to use an extended diaconate as a gateway to priesthood for these less educated men. The Convocation of 1887 went further, and suggested that men engaged in commerce or trade should be admitted to the diaconate (and eventually the priesthood) as well, a motion sponsored by the Bishops of Llandaff and Winchester.[1] In January 1887, the MP Sydney Gedge introduced the Deacons (Church of England) Bill to the House of Commons, which was intended to repeal the 1838 Pluralities Act insofar as it prevented deacons from following a secular trade, but it failed to obtain a second reading. Although Gedge repeatedly reintroduced it, he finally withdrew it in 1889.[2]

The bishops spoke in favour of a renewed diaconate again in February 1888,[3] but the Lower House of Convocation insisted that no one should be ordained deacon who was not prepared to dedicate himself entirely to spiritual work. The deadlock was insurmountable, and as a consequence, the issue was not raised again in the 1890s.[4] When the issue of pastoral aid for the clergy was discussed again at Convocation in 1900, all talk was of Readers and subdeacons, and deacons were not even mentioned.[5] Nevertheless, there is some evidence that a handful of lifelong deacons were ordained after 1884. George Harwood (1845-1912), a graduate of London University and chairman of a cotton spinning company in Bolton, was ordained deacon by the Bishop of Manchester in 1886 and licensed as a curate at St Anne's Church in the city between 1886 and 1889. Harwood exercised a successful preaching ministry, especially to the business community, but in 1892 he successfully applied to be returned to lay status. In 1895, he was elected MP for Bolton. Had he remained a deacon he would not, of course, have been able to stand for Parliament.[6]

---

1. *The Times*, 12 May 1887 p. 7F.
2. Vaughan (1987), pp. 52-3.
3. *The Times*, 29 February 1888, p. 5E.
4. Vaughan (1987), p. 55. In Vaughan's view it was the widely publicised arguments of Canon William Bright that swayed opinion against deacons in 1888 (ibid. pp. 57-60).
5. *The Times*, 7 February 1900, p. 4F.
6. Vaughan (1987), p. 56.

## Deacons in the liturgy

Before the late nineteenth century, deacons were virtually invisible in the liturgy. Deacons wore exactly the same choir dress as priests: a surplice and black preaching scarf. However, as preaching scarves began to give way to stoles in the liturgical colour of the season under the influence of the Oxford Movement, deacons and priests became distinguishable. Deacons were wearing stoles over one shoulder as early as 1887, even outside avowedly ritualist churches.[1] In Anglo-Catholic churches themselves, even those where no deacon was serving as curate, priests regularly appeared at the altar as deacons and subdeacons, vested in dalmatics or tunicles, at celebrations of high mass that followed pre-Reformation or Roman rubrics.

The question of how much of the service a deacon could lead was confused by the rubrics of the 1662 Prayer Book and the Act of Uniformity. Whereas a strict interpretation of the rubrics of the Prayer Book led some to conclude that a deacon could read only the litany (and not the orders of morning and evening prayer), Canon Law required both priests and deacons to read morning and evening prayer daily in public or in private. Richard Mant's 1820 commentary on the Prayer Book cited numerous divines who argued that it was not permissible for a deacon to pronounce the absolution, although he acknowledged that a proposal from the ecclesiastical commissioners in 1691 that absolution should be explicitly limited to priests was never put into effect.[2] In February 1824, a correspondent in *The Christian Observer* noted that the Prayer Book's use of the term 'priest' in the rubrics was ambiguous, and could mean either a man in priest's orders or the minister (whether priest or deacon) leading the service.

Debate concerning absolution by deacons rumbled on into the Victorian era. William Cooke insisted in 1858 that the absence of a specific permission to remit sins from the service for the ordering of deacons meant that deacons could not absolve. Whereas deacons were given authority 'to read the Gospel, and to preach', priests were told that 'whose sins thou dost forgive, they are forgiven; and whose sins thou dost retain, they are retained'.[3] Richard Paul Blakeney, by contrast, argued that deacons could pronounce the absolution. The

---

1. Twells (1887), p. 9.
2. Mant, R. (ed.), *The Book of Common Prayer, and Administration of the Sacraments* (W. Baxter: Oxford, 1820), p. 12.
3. 'H.G.', 'Reply to X.X. on Deacons officiating', *The Christian Observer* 24 (1824), pp. 85-7.

words of absolution declared that 'God hath given power to his ministers to declare and pronounce to his people, being penitent, the absolution and remission of their sins', and Blakeney interpreted 'ministers' as including both priests and deacons. He classified the absolution as a prayer, thereby making it possible for deacons to pronounce it. Furthermore, the Act of Uniformity explicitly forbade deacons from celebrating the eucharist and holding a benefice, but it did not forbid deacons to absolve: Blakeney took this as an argument from silence that constituted permission for deacons to pronounce the absolution. Finally, Blakeney pointed out that deacons were able to baptise, and baptism was a form of absolution – it was therefore theologically inconsistent to maintain that deacons could not absolve.[1]

Blakeney's view of absolution as a form of prayer and preaching rather than 'an actual conveyance of pardon' was in contrast to the high church (and Tractarian) view that priestly absolution was necessary, and it would seem that Blakeney was arguing from a low church perspective. Two views existed in the nineteenth-century Church of England, then, on the lawfulness of absolution by a deacon, and the current canons remain unclear on this point. Canon B11 forbids a layperson to read the absolution, and Canon B29 limits the ministry of absolution to priests, but this clearly refers to a ministry exercised with respect to individual persons seeking forgiveness, and not to the general absolution pronounced at morning or evening prayer. Stephen Platten noted that Cyprian (*Letters* 18.1) permitted a deacon topronounce absolution and reconcile penitents in an emergency,[2] suggesting that deacons have the power to absolve but do not ordinarily exercise it.

The Victorian Church of England's inactivity against the odds in response to the ongoing demand for distinctive deacons from both the clergy and laity might be seen as one of the great missed opportunities of Anglican history, like the church's failure to accommodate the Methodist movement or William Booth's Salvation Army. The nineteenth-century Anglican literature on the diaconate is very extensive, speculative and repetitive; many authors do not seem to have been aware that they were not the first person to have the brilliant idea of reviving deacons. On one reading, the call for deacons was an attempt by a pampered clergy to shirk their social responsibilities by trying to insinuate a mirror-image of the

---

1. Blakeney, R.P., *The Book of Common Prayer in its History and Interpretation* (James Miller: London, 1870), pp. 322-5.
2. *DMC*, p. 86.

Victorian class system into the structure of the church's ministry. A more sympathetic interpretation would see the call for deacons as a visionary measure anticipating the non-stipendiary clergy of today. What is certain is that the desire for deacons arose partly out of a recognition that the church needed to reconnect with the poor and conduct its own outreach to the marginalised, separate from the increasingly impersonal apparatus of the state.

The more or less complete failure of the Victorian project of reviving the diaconate (with the exception of the deacon-schoolmasters of St Mark's College) can be attributed, at least in part, to the very small size of the constituency of men who could be ordained under the existing legislative situation: professionals, schoolmasters and gentlemen of private means with the time and inclination to serve their local churches on a non-stipendiary basis. Those few who were ordained to a ministry other than teaching belonged to a minority so tiny that it struggled to find any kind of identity, with the result that they either sought ordination to the priesthood or a return to the lay state. The issue of deacons did not go away at the end of the nineteenth century, but as so often in church debates of that era (and indeed today), the intransigence of the bishops, the Convocations and the law itself obstructed the creativity of individual enthusiasts, so that their arguments burnt themselves out in frustration.

# 4

# *Deacons in the Twentieth Century*

The campaign for a revived diaconate as a solution for a shortage of clergy limped on into the twentieth century, but without the enthusiasm that had surrounded the issue up to the Convocation of 1888. A tiny number of individuals were ordained as lifelong or long-term deacons as experiments, but until the Second Vatican Council's reorientation of the theology of the church and ministry, the prospects for a revived diaconate, either in Roman Catholicism or Anglicanism, were bleak indeed. The indirect effect of Vatican II on the Church of England, combined with a growing recognition that the ministry of women should develop beyond lay roles, led some to suggest that the diaconate could be a catch-all ministry used to subsume existing lay ministries – deaconesses, lay workers, Church Army officers and so on. However, the Church of England's relatively sudden conversion to the idea of a lifelong or distinctive diaconate came in the 1980s, as a consequence of the need to accommodate women's aspirations to ordained ministry. Yet less than ten years after the momentous decision to admit women to deacon's orders, the distinctive diaconate was brought to the brink of extinction as the majority of women deacons sought ordination as priests.

This chapter will consider the theological development of the idea of the diaconate in the Church of England before and after the admission of women to deacon's order in 1987, as well as the impact of liturgical reform in the 1980s and the gradual influence of a developing theology of the diaconate in the 1990s. With the benefit of hindsight, it is easy to see the eventual revival of the diaconate in 1987 for women as a politically motivated compromise on the way to the ordination of women to the priesthood, and there is no doubt much truth in this analysis. However, subsequent developments in women's ministry ought not to be allowed to obscure the potential value of the theological thought on the diaconate that was stimulated before and after 1987, and formed the foundation for further work on the diaconate in the twenty-first century.

The first half of the twentieth century was a challenging time for the Church of England, as the church was obliged to balance its historic status as the mother church of the British Empire with the need to offer pastoral care to a nation left in ruins by two world wars. The Church of England, and the Anglican Communion as a whole, was obliged to come to terms with the consequences of decolonisation, as well as the dwindling size of congregations. With the disestablishment of the Church in Wales in 1920, the established church became one small part of a wider Anglican Communion, in which overseas churches sometimes seemed more vibrant and full of missionary opportunities than the mother church herself. The Church of England was forced to contend at times with negative public perceptions of the church as an enabler of government propaganda during the First World War, while the church itself remained mired in internal controversy in the 1920s, most notably over the 1928 revision of the Prayer Book, which ultimately came to nothing but absorbed much parliamentary time. The twentieth-century church struggled to navigate a middle course between acting as the nation's conscience and acting as its 'master of ceremonies', as it remained intimately tied to the institutions of the state.

Twentieth-century urbanisation continued to present a challenge to the church's traditional models of parish ministry, although in the second half of the twentieth century, urbanisation began to affect large and medium-sized towns as well as the larger cities as post-war governments pursued a policy of relocating 'overspill' populations. Many new parishes were created, and the Synodical Government Measure of 1969 created a much more effective system of internal governance for the church than the old Convocations of York and Canterbury. At the same time, however, the parochial model of priestly ministry remained the central, and indeed almost exclusive, model of ministry within the Church of England. The sense that the Church of England needed more priests was reinforced by the Welsby Report of 1968, which recommended that the shortfall could be made up by non-stipendiary, part-time clergy. The idea of the priest as the central enabler of worship was further reinforced by the development of the parish communion as the main, and often exclusive, act of Sunday worship in almost all Anglican churches, irrespective of churchmanship. This represented a major victory for the Oxford Movement, since before the First World War, weekly communion services had primarily been a feature of Anglo-Catholic churches. However, the extension of communion and the conscious mirroring of Roman Catholic sacramental practice that took hold in the Church of England in the aftermath of the Second Vatican Council had the effect of creating the expectation of weekly communion amongst congregations. This expectation was one factor that marginalised the idea of deacons.

## Before Vatican II

In 1909, John James Lias, the Chancellor of Llandaff Cathedral, looked back wistfully on the innumerable failed attempts to revive the diaconate in the nineteenth century, and concluded that 'the whole question has been allowed to sleep for at least a generation' because there were not enough English and Welsh bishops to give the issue the attention it deserved.[1] This was a reflection of the disproportionate responsibility shouldered by the Upper House of Convocation before the Synodical Government Measure of 1969. The Church of England was too mired in bureaucracy to make any progress, and Lias suspected that it would be the colonial bishops, if anyone, who might be expected to take up the idea of the revived diaconate.

However, in addition to criticising the church for its excessively bureaucratic approach, Lias also hinted at the kind of reasons that prejudiced English bishops against the revival of the diaconate. He recounted two cases that, he claimed, had turned the Anglican episcopate as a whole against the idea of distinctive deacons. In the first case, a man was ordained as a distinctive deacon in England, but wanted to progress to the priesthood. This suggests that at least one bishop in the Church of England was prepared to act on the demand for deacons without the agreement of Convocation. None of the English bishops would accept the man for priestly ordination because he lacked the required level of education, so he went to several British colonies until he found a bishop willing to ordain him priest, and then returned home. This behaviour clearly undermined the authority of the English episcopate, who were obliged to honour the man's priestly ordination conferred abroad, even though they had originally rejected him for priest's orders.

1.  Lias, J.J., *The Extension of the Diaconate* (J.S. Nicholas: Bristol, 1909), p. 5.

In another case,

A gentleman in the Civil Service of a certain Colony was admitted to the permanent diaconate by his Bishop. He straightway donned priestly attire, put 'Rev.' on his cards, and continued his services to the State in the department to which he had previously belonged. The very natural result was a series of squabbles with his brother members of the Civil Service, who refused to regard him as a 'clergyman' while he continued to perform his civil functions. The Bishop, at once, ceased to ordain permanent deacons, a kind of mental Marconigram instantly thrilled through the Anglican Episcopate, and one of the most useful reforms of our Anglican method of working was peremptorily, but, let us hope, not finally, dropped.[1]

Lias proposed that 'non-preaching deacons' (distinctive deacons) should be sharply distinguished from 'preaching deacons' (transitional deacons) by not being allowed to adopt clerical dress or use the title of 'Reverend'. Such restrictions raise the question of what the difference would have been between Lias's 'non-preaching deacons' and Readers. It would have been an ironic situation for a clerk in holy orders to be forbidden from preaching in a church where preaching lay Readers were now a common sight. Lias's proposal for a two-tier diaconate, in which distinctive deacons know their place below transitional deacons, seems class-conscious even for the Edwardian period, and it was also out of step with the spirit of those nineteenth-century arguments that maintained that the revival of the diaconate was the restoration of an ancient order rather than an innovation.

In the immediate aftermath of the First World War, there was a brief flurry of enthusiasm for a restored diaconate, and the nineteenth-century arguments were recycled by E.W.J. MacConnel in *A Plea for a Proper Diaconate* (1919) as well as in a report produced by the Diocesan Synod of the Diocese of Southwark. The latter was the first report to suggest that deacons could be trained part-time.[2] However, the emphasis of the argument for voluntary clergy had moved from a discussion of deacons to a debate about part-time priests, and the issue of deacons receded into the background in England. In other parts of the Anglican Communion, the momentum continued, and the Bishop of Melbourne in Australia reported that he was about to ordain a Reader as a lifelong deacon in 1925.[3] However, the case for

1. Ibid. pp. 12-14.
2. Vaughan (1987), pp. 98-9.
3. Ibid. p. 109.

deacons was made again at the Convocation of Canterbury in 1929 and supported by the Upper House.[1] More deacons were ordained in England in 1930 than in any year since 1914, but it seems likely that few (if any) of them remained in deacon's orders only.[2] However, the proposed Prayer Book of 1928 seems to have been preparing for the possibility of a distinctive diaconate. The revised service for the ordination of deacons omitted the prayer 'Almighty God, giver of all good things . . .', containing a reference to 'this inferior office', and replaced it with another:

> Fill [these deacons], we beseech thee, with the Holy Ghost, that, enabled by the sevenfold gift of his grace, they may be faithful to their promises, modest, humble, and constant in their ministration, and may have a ready will to observe all spiritual discipline; that, having always the testimony of a good conscience, they may continue ever stable and strong in thy Son Christ.[3]

Alternatively, it is possible that the reference to deacons proceeding to the priesthood was removed from the 1928 Prayer Book because some considered that the service for the ordination of deacons, or an adaptation of it, could be used to 'ordain' deaconesses.

By the middle of the twentieth century, it was becoming increasingly apparent that the church could not survive without supplementary or voluntary clergy. At the same time, as a consequence of the Oxford Movement, eucharistic worship had become established as the norm for Sunday services. The most vocal advocates of voluntary clergy were now calling for the extension of the priesthood rather than the diaconate. A few conservatives, concerned about the possible attenuation of the priesthood if 'volunteer clergy' were admitted, still clung to the idea of a lifelong diaconate as a compromise measure for solving the shortage of clergy; this was the view of J.O. Cobham in an article published in 1953.[4] However, the 1950s also saw an attempt to extend the 'worker priest' movement, which began in the Roman Catholic Church in France, to the Church of England in the form of 'worker deacons'. A Cambridge undergraduate named Michael Jackson visited the founder of the worker priest movement, the

1. Ibid. p. 130.
2. Ibid. p. 126.
3. 'The Form and Manner of Making of Deacons' in *The Book of Common Prayer with the additions and deviations proposed in 1928* (Cambridge University Press: Cambridge, 1928), pp. 619-24, at p. 623.
4. Ibid. p. 160.

Abbé Godin, in 1949, and went to work in a Sheffield factory on his return to England. In 1955, he was ordained deacon and continued to work as a non-stipendiary deacon (licensed as Curate of Tinsley) until 1957, when he withdrew from his unusual industrial ministry and was ordained priest.[1] Jackson judged the experiment a failure, since his status as a worker 'sanctified' the workers in any dispute they had with the management, while the workers themselves regarded him negatively as an 'official Christian'. Jackson found himself caught between unrealistic expectations on both sides.

The Lambeth Conference of 1958 commissioned a report, *The Order of Deacon*, to explore whether the experience of the Episcopal Church in the United States of America (ECUSA), which had a thriving distinctive diaconate, could and should be applied to the Anglican Communion as a whole. As a result, the Conference passed Resolution 88, 'The Office of Deacon', which recommended that 'Each Province of the Anglican Communion shall consider whether the office of deacon shall be restored to its primitive place as a distinctive order in the Church, instead of being regarded as a probationary period for the priesthood'.[2] As Plater has noted, the wording of this resolution seems to imply that the Conference was considering distinctive deacons *instead of* transitional deacons, suggesting that the bishops favoured direct ordination to the priesthood. The Church of England eventually moved to act on the Lambeth Conference's suggestion, and on 19 January 1961, almost a century since the issue had first been discussed there, the Lower House of the Convocation of Canterbury agreed 'that in the opinion of this House the time is ripe for a fresh consideration of the desirability of a wider extension of the diaconate to men who will not normally be proceeding to the Order of Priesthood'. Convocation called for the establishment of a joint committee between the Convocations of York and Canterbury to consider the question,[3] but I have not been able to find any evidence that it produced a report. The Scottish Episcopal Church, by comparison, acted rather more proactively and produced a report in 1965. However, the Scottish experience proved that the best of intentions were not in themselves enough to create a viable distinctive diaconate; of the tiny number of men who took advantage of the possibility of becoming a distinctive deacon after 1965, most were eventually ordained priest.[4]

---

1.  Ibid. pp. 164-5.
2.  Plater (2004), p. 66.
3.  Riley, H. and Graham, R.J. (eds), *Acts of the Convocations of Canterbury and York, 1921-1970* (SPCK: London, 1970), p. 43.
4.  *DMC*, p. 48.

When non-stipendiary ministers finally became a part of the life of the Church of England, following the Welsby Report in 1968, they would all go on to be priests. The idea of voluntary clergy had by this time been debated on and off for 130 years, making the twenty-first century Church of England's debate concerning the consecration of women to the episcopate seem rushed by comparison. In Vaughan's view, the reason for the long delay was 'the uncertain location of authority' within the church and 'the cumbersome structures of Convocation'. However, Vaughan also pointed to the fact that the decentralised nature of the Church of England allowed bishops to experiment on an individual basis with lifelong deacons in a way that would have been inconceivable in the Roman Catholic Church, for example.[1] However, by the time the Church of England at large accepted the principle of non-professional clergy, attitudes had changed so much that non-professional priests who could preside at the parish Holy Communion were far preferable to non-professional deacons.

## After Vatican II

After 1968, the idea of lifelong or distinctive deacons was a somewhat *avant-garde* notion in the Church of England, given that there was no practical or legal reason why voluntary clergy could not be priests. However, developments in the Roman Catholic Church provided the impetus for further consideration of the issue. When asked about the revival of the diaconate in 1957, Pope Pius XII declared that 'the time was not yet ripe' for such a move, but he instructed theologians to examine the issue more closely.[2] Before the opening session of the Second Vatican Council in 1962, no less than ninety proposals were received by the Vatican, many of them signed by bishops, for the restoration of the diaconate. The Council voted to revive the order as a lifelong ministry in September 1964, opening it to married men over the age of thirty-five.[3] Pope Paul VI implemented the decision of the Council by the decree *Sacrum Diaconatus Ordinem* in 1967.[4]

The ecumenical atmosphere of the 1960s, combined with the cumulative influence of the Oxford Movement, resulted in a widespread consensus within the mainstream of the Church

---

1. Vaughan (1987), pp. 307-8.
2. O'Rourke, J.J., Riley, J. and Ditewig, W.T., 'Deacon' in *The New Catholic Encyclopedia*, 2nd edn (Catholic University of America: Washington DC, 2003), vol. 4, pp. 550-54.
3. O'Rourke, Riley and Ditewig (2003), pp. 550-54.
4. Paul VI, *Sacrum Diaconatus Ordinem*, *Acta Apostolicae Sedis* 59 (1967), pp. 697-704.

of England that the Second Vatican Council was an important moment in the life of the universal church, even if only Roman Catholic bishops were actively participating. Whilst few Anglicans would have ascribed formal dogmatic authority to the Council, the prevailing belief that the Holy Spirit was moving Pope John XXIII, Pope Paul VI and the Fathers of the Council to modernise the church made Vatican II a significant event for many Anglicans. One obvious consequence of this was the effect that the liturgical reforms of Vatican II had on Anglican worship, which extended far beyond self-consciously Anglo-Catholic parishes. Many features of worship taken for granted in cathedrals and parish churches today are all legacies of Vatican II,[1] not to mention the heavy influence of the original ICEL English translation of the Roman mass on the *Alternative Service Book* and, later, *Common Worship*.

If Vatican II commanded a certain degree of respect from most Anglicans, it was also representative of an era that gave permission for radical reappraisals of Christian life and ministry. Liberals saw the Roman Catholic Church's new enthusiasm for permanent deacons as a symptom of that church's failure to embrace the modern world as fully as it could have done, by removing the requirement of clerical celibacy altogether. On this reading, the opening of the diaconate to married men was a fudge, a way of increasing the number of ministers in the church while not compromising on the outdated requirement for priestly celibacy. The sense that the Roman Catholic permanent diaconate really existed primarily for political rather than theological reasons may have been one reason why Anglican theologians were reluctant to engage with the issue of the diaconate in the 1960s, even though the theology of the diaconate in Roman Catholicism was experiencing a miniature renaissance.

In 1974, a report prepared for General Synod by the Advisory Committee for the Church's Ministry (ACCM) entitled *Deacons and the Church* argued that the diaconate should be abolished altogether, largely on the grounds that 'we have . . . others who, between them, can do anything in worship that a deacon can'.[2] The report argued in favour of direct ordination to the priesthood. The report's conclusions were rejected by General Synod in 1977, which opted to keep the diaconate and took note of a different report that set out three options for the future of the diaconate: its continuation as a

---

1. West-facing celebrations of the eucharist, priestly concelebration, cassock-albs and large hosts for sharing with the congregation are just a few examples.
2. Quoted in *DMC*, p. 1.

short intermediate stage on the way to priesthood, its discontinuation in the Church of England or its expansion to include lay workers, deaconesses and others.[1] This latter option was not really the same as subsequent proposals to introduce a 'permanent' diaconate, since it was primarily a proposal to give sacramental recognition to existing ministries by diaconal ordination, a 're-labelling' of ministries.

Stephen Platten saw the 1970s as a low point in the church's 'functionalisation' of ministry.[2] Because the roles of deaconesses and Readers were expanded from 1972 onwards, it was thought that there was nothing left that deacons alone could do; therefore deacons were pointless. For John N. Collins, the Church of England's drift towards the abolition of the diaconate was an inevitable consequence of the flawed definition of *diakonia* exclusively in terms of service.[3] As a 'closely allied tradition' to Roman Catholicism, which had nevertheless come under significant influence from the German Evangelical Lutheran deacon movement through Elizabeth Ferard, Anglicanism was burdened with the same misconceptions as those traditions. As service to the church was opened up to lay people, the idea that ordination was necessary in order to commission someone to service came to seem increasingly inappropriate within a utilitarian and functionalist understanding of ministry.

## *From deaconesses to women deacons*

In contrast to deacons, deaconesses continued to develop as a force within the Church of England during the first half of the twentieth century. The first service for the ordering of deaconesses had been published in 1898, and in 1920 deaconesses moved a step closer to recognition as the equals of male deacons when the Lambeth Conference resolved that 'the Diaconate of women should be restored formally and canonically'.[4] The Conference declared deaconesses to be ordained servants of the church, and they were thereafter permitted, with the approval of their bishop and incumbent, to read morning and evening prayer and the litany, effectively giving them the same authority and functions as Readers.

However, the 1930 Lambeth Conference proved resistant to any further development of the liturgical role of deaconesses, and the service for the ordering of deaconesses proposed for inclusion in

1. Ibid.
2. Ibid. pp. 94-5.
3. Collins (1990), p. 44.
4. Blackmore (2007), p. xlix.

the Prayer Book in 1941 made no reference to holy orders.[1] Maud Christian Synge, writing in 1927, was entirely convinced that holy orders were conferred on deaconesses,[2] although at the same time she recognised that the church had not granted any authority to deaconesses that lay people did not have. Synge confidently expected the status of deaconesses to develop with time, and the title of her booklet on deaconesses (*The Diaconate: A Call to Women*) suggests that she would have liked to see deaconesses recognised as the equals of male deacons. Synge was justified in her expectations, in the sense that the question of women's admission to the diaconate was eventually to dominate twentieth-century Anglican thought about deacons.

Renewed discussion of the diaconate in the 1970s and '80s emerged not so much from a recognition of the intrinsic value of deacons, but from a consciousness that the Church of England needed to consider its position on the issue of women in ministry. The issue was made pressing by the fact that other provinces of the Anglican Communion were ordaining women to the diaconate and, indeed, to the priesthood. One question that arose concerned the status of these ordained women if they visited England: were they allowed to officiate as priests and deacons in England? In 1978, General Synod debated, but failed to reach any agreement on, the issue of whether women ordained as priests in other parts of the Anglican Communion could be granted permission by diocesan bishops to officiate as priests in England.[3] The debate rekindled the question of whether deaconesses were simply women deacons or something else, which had been debated at the Lambeth Conferences of 1968 and 1978. The 1968 report *Women in Ministry* proposed the recognition of deaconesses as deacons in the true sense as one possibility among several, and several churches in the Anglican Communion moved forward on the basis of this decision to ordain women as deacons. The first woman deacon in Canada was ordained in 1969, following through the logic that if deaconesses could now serve as deacons, women could therefore be ordained intentionally *as* deacons. However, the Church of England did not follow through this logic and only allowed deaconesses to act *like* deacons. One reason for this was that conservatives considered the ordination of women to the diaconate a 'slippery slope' towards the ordination of women to the priesthood.

---

1. Ibid.
2. Synge, M.C., *The Diaconate: A Call to Women* (SPCK: London, 1927), p. 15.
3. Francis, L.J. and Robbins, M., *The Long Diaconate 1987-1994: Women Deacons and the delayed Journey to Priesthood* (Gracewing: Leominster, 1999), p. 15.

However, the issue of women deacons was coming ever closer, and in 1980 the Church in Wales ordained its first female deacons.[1] In 1981, the Deaconess Community of St Andrew, led by Sister Teresa White, organised an ecumenical consultation on the diaconate at the Royal Foundation of St Katherine in Limehouse. In October 1981, the House of Bishops in General Synod published the report *The Deaconess Order and the Diaconate* (the so-called 'Portsmouth Report'), which paved the way for General Synod's approval of the ordination of women deacons in July 1985. Amongst other recommendations, *The Deaconess Order and the Diaconate* urged 'that the Church of England make provision for, and encourage, men and women to serve in an ordained distinctive diaconate'.[2] General Synod accepted the Bishop of Portsmouth's report and a standing committee was set up to prepare legislation that would allow the admission of men and women to a distinctive diaconate and representation of deacons at General Synod. However, the report was also criticised; Christine Hall noted that its use of the term 'diaconal ministry' 'was so all-embracing as to be, theologically, seriously misleading'.[3] In other words, the term 'diaconal ministry' did not necessarily entail a distinctive diaconate.

A standing committee of General Synod produced a further report entitled *The Ordination of Women to the Diaconate*, which was received by General Synod in 1982.[4] Rather like Paul VI's assertion that permanent deacons could be either married or celibate, the Portsmouth Report's suggestion that distinctive deacons could be both men and women was a political gesture, intended to deflect liberal criticism that the revived diaconate was a form of 'second-class priesthood' for women. In reality, there was little prospect of many men joining a distinctive diaconate in the 1980s, just as there was little prospect of many celibate men choosing to become permanent deacons in the Roman Catholic Church. The exceptional case was the Diocese of Portsmouth, where in 1983 Bishop Ronald Gordon set up a training programme designed to prepare men for the distinctive diaconate. The candidates were selected by the diocese's

1. Robbins, M., 'A Matter of Age or Experience? Parishioners' Attitudes toward Women Vicars in the Church in Wales' in Pope, R. (ed.), *Honouring the Past and Shaping the Future: Essays in Honour of Gareth Lloyd Jones* (Gracewing: Leominster, 2003), pp. 253-64, at p. 253.
2. *DMC*, pp. 16-17.
3. Hall, C., 'Introduction' in Hall, C. (ed.), *The Deacon's Ministry* (Gracewing: Leominster, 1991), pp. 1-8, at p. 6.
4. *DMC*, pp. 16-17.

own internal selection programme and, after studying a core curriculum of theology for two years, they spent a year in diaconal formation. The training programme set out to develop pastoral skills that would allow deacons to reach out into the community, but by 1987 it was clear that the role of these deacons was primarily church-based. In the view of Alison White and Di Williams, 'The style of ministry of most of the Portsmouth deacons is personal rather than enabling. Working with a high view of "being deacon", most of the deacons see their ministry in terms of what they do rather than in terms of facilitating the ministry of the laity'.[1]

White and Williams analysed the work of four specific deacons in the Church of England: Brother Victor SSF in the Diocese of London, and Don Verney, Bob Diaper and Roy Overthrow in Portsmouth. Brother Victor was a Franciscan lay brother until he attended an ecumenical conference on deacons, which convinced him that the renewal of the diaconate required public examples and motivated him to train as a deacon, although he had been engaged in 'diaconal service' long before this point.[2] Verney, an electrical engineer, ministered primarily to 'young Christians' in the context of his parish church, while Diaper, a manager at a tax office, was even more closely involved in his local church. A former Reader, he preached every Sunday. Overthrow, who was a verger at Portsmouth Cathedral, thought that ordination as a deacon was appropriate because he found himself engaged in an increasingly diaconal ministry to people in need who came into the cathedral seeking advice and pastoral ministry.[3] The small band of male distinctive deacons in the 1990s encountered misunderstanding from the laity. As Christine Hall noted, 'That a man should remain a deacon permanently is a concept which is often greeted with incredulity. . . . A doctor, who is a non-stipendiary deacon and does not intend to be ordained to the priesthood, tells how he is repeatedly asked by incredulous people whether he is still a deacon "because he failed his examinations"'.[4] The number of male deacons was so small that disabusing people of these misconceptions proved all but impossible.

John Tiller, Chief Secretary of ACCM 1978-85, reflected on the nature of deacons in 1983, on the eve of the creation of a large 'permanent' diaconate in the Church of England:

1. White, A. and Williams, D., *Deacons at your Service* (Grove Books: Cambridge, 1987), p. 21.
2. Ibid. p. 20.
3. Ibid. pp. 21-2.
4. Hall (1991), p. 5.

Deacons are ordained as a focus of diaconal ministry, which is the call of God to serve the Church in Christ's name. Perhaps the most essential vision, therefore, is to see the deacon as a community servant. Diaconal ministry should not be so tied conceptually to the parochial context as is true generally of the presbyterate. . . . The deacon as community servant needs to be operating firmly within the context of the witness of the whole church, and one Christian community in particular.[1]

For Tiller, the test of whether a person should be ordained to the diaconate was whether their ministry was merely 'local' to a parish, or was taking on broader proportions within a benefice, deanery or diocese, and he recommended that some Readers should consider ordination as deacons:

Some Readers might see their ministry as something much wider than leadership in one particular local Church. If this calling has substance, they ought to be selected and trained for the Order of Deacons, and serve as something akin to public preachers. . . . The line adopted in this strategy is that where a lay ministry serves the whole diocese (e.g. stewardship advisor) it should be considered for inclusion in the diaconate: all local lay ministries should be recognised locally and require no further authorization.[2]

Tiller's use of the distinction between local and diocesan ministry to define the difference between the 'accredited' ministry of the Reader and the 'ordained' ministry of the deacon had its weaknesses. In the first place, what exactly counted as 'local' ministry? Was ministry in a deanery, or in a large benefice consisting of many parishes, still 'local'? Furthermore, Tiller did not make clear whether he was making a merely *moral* case for Readers to consider the diaconate, or whether he was arguing that the church should steer Readers in the direction of diaconal ordination as a matter of course if their ministry exceeded the bounds of the parish. What if Readers did not want this? According to Tiller's logic, roles such as diocesan stewardship advisor should be undertaken by deacons, but such an approach raises the question of why a deacon should be preferred for such a role, even over a gifted lay person. Tiller seems to have

1. Tiller, J., *A Strategy for the Church's Ministry* (CIO Publishing: London, 1983), pp. 112-13.
2. Ibid. pp. 130-31.

been determined to produce a clear guideline on the boundaries between diaconal and lay ministry because he felt the need to define the diaconate functionally, an approach later rejected by Stephen Platten. Perhaps most troublingly of all, Tiller did not seem able to provide any theological justification for his division of lay and diaconal ministry.

Between 1983 and 1984, General Synod amended the draft measure prepared by the standing committee. These amendments provided for a new canon to amend matters of doctrine and worship to allow the ordination of women, so as to ensure that Parliament was not required to debate such issues, which was thought inappropriate. A clause was also added, stipulating that 'nothing in this measure shall make it lawful for a woman to be ordained to the office of a priest'.[1] The motion was passed in the Diocesan Synods of every diocese of the Church of England, with the exceptions of Exeter and Gibraltar in Europe, and was finally passed by General Synod in July 1985. Parliament's Ecclesiastical Committee delayed the implementation of the measure, however, and the first distinctive deacons were not ordained until February 1987.

As a consequence of the measure for the ordination of women deacons, Canon Law was amended to allow licensed deaconesses (who already held the bishop's licence to officiate) to apply to their bishop for ordination to the diaconate, waiving the usual requirement for an examination of their learning. The canons required that the collect beginning 'Almighty God, giver of all good things . . .', containing the reference to the diaconate as an 'inferior office', should be omitted if a woman was being ordained according to the *Book of Common Prayer*, and provided for the alteration of masculine to feminine pronouns in the liturgy.[2] The canons were further amended to allow a deacon who had been ordained for more than six years to be

> capable of receiving the appointment of canon residentiary of a cathedral church notwithstanding anything in the statutes or customs of that cathedral church to the contrary, but nothing in any such statutes or customs shall be construed as authorising or requiring a person in deacon's orders so appointed to preside at or celebrate the Holy Communion or pronounce the Absolution.[3]

1. *DMC*, p. 123.
2. Canon C4A (*Canons*, p. 83).
3. Canon C21 §1A (*Canons*, p. 107).

The canons also closed the Order of Deaconesses to new members who began training after 1986.[1] By June 1987, there were 750 female and 13 male distinctive deacons in England.[2] The largest number of male distinctive deacons was to be found in Portsmouth, where there were 7.[3] In a survey of dioceses on the distinctive diaconate in 1987, responses ranged from a lack of enthusiasm and an indication that there was no intention to ordain more distinctive deacons to considerable enthusiasm from the Diocese of Portsmouth, which reported that 'It is intended that deacons look outward to the wider community, but that there also be a liturgical focus too. They may be licensed to preach'.[4]

In the view of Leslie Francis and Mandy Robbins, by adopting the Portsmouth Report, 'The church had created a permanent diaconate with very little thought as to how it would integrate it into the church'.[5] The theological thought behind the revival of the diaconate was retrospective at best, and superficial at worst. The diaconate was primarily a vehicle for meeting the demand for women to be admitted to ministry without outraging conservative opinion, and women's diaconal ministry was defined negatively: women deacons were clerks in holy orders who were deacons because they *could not* be priests.[6] Much of the official literature on the diaconate produced up to 1994 has the feel of having been hastily assembled, and many writers were much more interested in the future development of the ministry of women than they were in the diaconate for its own sake.

Some did continue to argue for the intrinsic value of the diaconate at this time, however. Alison White and Di Williams, in a pamphlet entitled *Deacons at your Service* (1987), attempted a qualitative analysis of the actual experience and practice of deacons in England. This was in contrast to the approach of subsequent official reports. White and Williams noted with distaste that the diaconate was being used by different people for different purposes: 'It is a temporary stopping-place for an annual intake of men on the way to priesthood. It is a

1. Canon D2 §2A (*Canons*, p. 118).
2. *DMC*, p. 123.
3. Ibid. p. 135.
4. Ibid. p. 62.
5. Francis and Robins (1999), p. 15.
6. For a sociological analysis of the anomalous position of women deacons in the Church of England after 1987, see Aldridge, A., 'Discourse on Women in the Clerical Profession: The Diaconate and Language-Games in the Church of England', *Sociology* 26 (1992), pp. 45-57; Aldridge, A., 'In the Absence of the Minister: Structures of Subordination in the Role of Deaconess in the Church of England', *Sociology* 21 (1987), pp. 377-92.

siding for women who want to test their vocation to the priesthood. It is a convenient ticket for varieties of "full-time ministry"'. Little attention was being paid, however, to 'those men and women who are actually called to be deacons'. The issue of deacons needed to be 'disentangled' from the different issue of the ordination of women to which it had become attached.[1] The authors sounded a note of caution, however: 'There is a real danger of the appeal of the diaconate being seen as a rather romantic one, potent for those who catch on but of little use to the world which is untouched by the Church in action'. Theological images used for the diaconate 'lose their strength if they circumvent the daily frustration and drudgery involved in diaconal ministry'.[2]

Nevertheless, White and Williams suggested two images useful for forming a theological understanding of the diaconate: the deacon as servant and the deacon as bridge.[3] Use of a term like 'drudgery' in relation to the diaconate was soon to become unfashionable, but White and Williams's conception of the deacon as bridge foreshadowed some of the later theology in *For Such a Time as This*. The deacon is a 'bridge' because by representing the church to the world and the world to the church, the deacon provides a way for the clergy to travel towards the laity and the laity to travel towards the clergy.[4] White and Williams linked the revival of the diaconate to Vatican II's renewed emphasis on the dignity of the laity in *Lumen Gentium*:

> The renewal of the diaconate is not an attempt to muscle in on the proper ministry of the laity and take it over. The deacon's role is not so much to do the serving as to work alongside God's people and encourage and facilitate their implementing 'the mandate from Jesus Christ' to be servants.[5]

White and Williams noted that the major conflicts over the diaconate in the ECUSA and the Anglican Church in Canada centred on the deacon's involvement in the liturgy, where the laity felt that deacons threatened to undermine the 'hard-won participation' of the laity. In Canada, this had even led to a moratorium on the further development of the diaconate. However, the authors drew attention to the possibility that deacons might be deployed in the

1. White and Williams (1987), p. 3.
2. Ibid. p. 6.
3. Ibid. pp. 5-7.
4. Ibid. p. 7.
5. Ibid. p. 8.

'Urban Priority Areas' identified as the church's central focus in the report *Faith in the City* (1985): 'The deacon might be instrumental in restoring responsibility and power to the Church in the city for its mission'. However, as in the Victorian period, such deployment would require financial investment from the church since, unlike youth workers, the salaries of deacons could not be paid by local authorities. Deacons represented an opportunity for the church to minister to people in a way other than 'from a position of benevolent superiority'.[1]

Another important theological contribution to discussion of the diaconate to emerge during this time was an article by Robert Hannaford, then a tutor at St Stephen's House in Oxford, which appeared in a collection of essays on the diaconate edited by Christine Hall. Hannaford saw deacons as representatives of, and spokespersons for, the poor, yet he maintained that it was not what deacons did that made them 'diaconal' but rather their ordination, which made them a 'focal point' of the church's ministry to the marginalised. He also upheld the need for a distinctive diaconate:

> The sacred ministry as a whole reflects the diaconal nature of Christ's mission. However, because of their clear identification with the cult and their obvious place of honour and authority, the priesthood and the episcopate tend to stress the permanence of the Church's visible structures. . . . [This] needs to be balanced by the sign of discontinuity provided by the diaconate. The apostolic college is essentially incomplete without the presence of deacons whose particular role it is to signify that the Kingdom is not of this world. It is open to serious question whether such a role is adequately fulfilled by deacons whose main ambition is to become priests or by deacons who are also priests and in some cases bishops as well.[2]

Hannaford concluded that 'the contemporary diaconate is ill-suited to its task as a sacramental focus of the diaconal ministry of Christ in Church and Kingdom', and noted that 'real recognition must be given to its distinctive and unambiguous place in the apostolic college'.[3]

The most significant official report on the diaconate produced between 1987 and 1994 was *Deacons in the Ministry of the Church* (1988) by Stephen Platten and Mary Tanner, which remains a major resource

1.  Ibid. pp. 10-11.
2.  Hannaford (1991), p. 38.
3.  Ibid. p. 43.

on Anglican thinking on the diaconate. However, the question of whether women would be allowed to proceed to ordination to the priesthood was clearly the elephant in the room in the text of the 1988 report, which attempted to balance a re-envisioning of the role of women in the church with a call for the revival of a distinctive diaconate for both men and women. The report was in two parts, a historical and ecumenical review of the diaconate authored by Tanner and a theological reflection by Platten. Platten's most significant theological move was to reject the functionalism that had hitherto prevailed in the Church of England's understanding of ministry, for instance in Tiller's writings. Drawing on Karl Rahner's theological thought on the diaconate, Platten argued that ordination to the diaconate was of value in its own right, since 'ordination calls out individuals to represent both Christ to the Church and, through that, the Church's ministry in Christ to the world'.[1] Whilst Platten stopped short of arguing that all existing lay ministers should be ordained to an order of distinctive deacons, he strongly defended the appropriateness of ordained deacons.

Platten emphasised the role of the deacon as a servant and an embodiment of servanthood in the church, giving a secondary position to preaching and teaching in the deacon's ministry.[2] He suggested that the two 'poles' of the deacon's ministry were likely to be pastoral care – perhaps in a hospital or prison rather than a parish – and liturgical worship, where the deacon 'becomes a sacramental representation of the Church's ministry of service'.[3] Platten rejected the idea that the diaconate should merely be treated as a way to make sense of the diversity of lay ministries in the church by subsuming them within a single order, because to be a deacon is to be invested with holy orders and therefore means that a specific calling must be discerned by the individual who aspires to the diaconate.[4] He suggested that the criteria for selecting a deacon should not necessarily be the same as those for selecting a priest, and that separate training courses should be provided.[5] In reality this never happened, partly because there was insufficient funding, but also because to train women deacons differently from men destined for the priesthood seemed discriminatory, especially since many believed that women would eventually be ordained priests

1. *DMC*, p. 90.
2. Ibid. pp. 92-3.
3. Ibid. p. 96.
4. Ibid. pp. 104-5.
5. Ibid. pp. 106-7.

anyway. One recommendation made by Platten that was later taken up, however, was the expansion of the bishop's explanation of the role of the deacon in the *ASB*, which was considerably augmented in *Common Worship*.

Criticism of *Deacons in the Ministry of the Church* came from Christina Baxter, who protested against the clericalisation of diaconal ministry. For Baxter, the representational 'focus' and ontological model of the diaconate adopted by Platten 'tends to be centripetal rather than centrifugal, drawing all service ministries to itself, and depriving others of such tasks'.[1] However, the momentum of a 'permanent' diaconate could not now be arrested, and in 1990, an ACCM working party produced a further document investigating the practical implications of having a large number of deacons in the Church of England, *Deacons Now*. The report made clear that at the time, there was no expectation that male candidates for ordination would train specifically for the distinctive diaconate; rather, it claimed that 'a few men choose to continue in the diaconate as a matter of conviction after the first year'.[2] There were only thirty-two male distinctive deacons in October 1990.[3] Only women, therefore, consciously chose to continue as deacons prior to ordination, and even here, there was no expectation that dioceses would have different criteria for the selection of priests and deacons. The authors of the report conceded that 'Women have been ordained deacon in the Church of England without there being a clear agreement in the mind of the Church about the theology of the diaconate', and identified six 'aspects of diaconal ministry' that the newly ordained women deacons might participate in: preaching, teaching, leading liturgy, participating appropriately in the administration of the sacraments, pastoral work and leadership.[4] Hall was critical of *Deacons Now*, pointing out that it dealt almost exclusively with practical problems created by the ordination of women, and did little or nothing to advance theological understanding of the diaconate itself.[5]

---

1. Baxter, C., 'Doing Truth: A Consideration of *Deacons in the Ministry of the Church*', *Anvil* 5 (1988), pp. 233-42, at p. 238.
2. *Deacons Now: The Report of a Church of England Working Party Concerned with Women in Ordained Ministry* (Advisory Council for the Church's Ministry: London, 1990), p. 2.
3. Treasure, C., *Walking on Glass: Women Deacons Speak Out* (SPCK: London, 1991), p. 20.
4. Ibid. pp. 7-8.
5. Hall (1991), p. 6.

The church's unpreparedness for the ordination of women deacons was vividly demonstrated by the fact that although 10 places were reserved for women deacons in a special constituency in General Synod, 25 deacons were elected to General Synod in November 1990.[1] What bishops may have envisaged as a minority ministry rapidly became a major section of the clergy, and by November 1990 there were 999 women deacons in the Church of England, of whom 511 were stipendiary and 256 were non-stipendiary parish deacons. Only 56 were non-stipendiary deacons in secular employment, so most of these 256 were women who had been working as paid lay workers in churches for years before their diaconal ordination.[2] 5 deacons were serving as cathedral clergy, 41 as team ministers, 28 as 'deacons-in-charge', 318 as assistant curates, 353 as parish deacons and 1 as a deanery deacon.[3]

The authors of *Deacons Now* found no evidence that the ordination of women as deacons was having a negative impact on Licensed Lay Ministry, which chimed with the experience of ECUSA, where a thriving diaconate exists alongside licensed lay readers.[4] The report found instead that the number of women offering themselves for non-ordained ministry in the church had increased, and suggested that this might have been a consequence of laywomen being inspired to serve by seeing other women in more prominent and public ministry roles. *Deacons Now* noted that four deacons were already serving as rural deans,[5] and argued in favour of the appointment of deacons to positions of senior responsibility on the grounds that all of the church's authority ought to be grounded in *diakonia*.[6]

The report's most radical recommendations concerned the authority it suggested should be extended to women deacons. They should be titled 'assistant curates' while serving their initial year in ministry, then subsequently 'parish deacons'. Furthermore, women deacons serving in team ministries should be entitled to use the title 'team vicar', and the report urged the Church of England to amend legislation 'to make it legally possible for the licence to describe adequately the work of a deacon in a post of responsibility'.[7] This seems to have been a coded call for Parliament to amend the 1662 Act of Uniformity to allow deacons to hold an incumbency.

---

1. Treasure (1991), p. 9.
2. Ibid. p. 13.
3. Ibid. p. 15.
4. Ibid. pp. 27-8.
5. Ibid. p. 19.
6. Ibid. pp. 45-6.
7. Ibid. pp. 61-2.

The report's other radical suggestion concerned the deacon's role in the eucharist; it noted that a report produced by the Diocese of Southwell envisaged that in parishes led by a deacon,

> Although the priest . . . would be liturgical president, the bishop as Ordinary would have delegated ordinary jurisdiction not to any priest, but to the deacon in charge of the parish. She would be the 'minister conducting worship' as far as the Canons were concerned, and to her would fall the discretion permitted both to incumbents and to ministers conducting worship.[1]

'Suggestions for Extended Communion' submitted by the Diocese of Southwell were attached as an appendix to the report.[2] The distribution of consecrated elements outside of the celebration of the eucharist was to be permitted only by the bishop, for periods of a year or less. Licences were likely to be granted to:

1. Churches in a team ministry wanting to celebrate a central eucharist
2. Parish churches whose minister-in-charge was a deacon, participating by extension in the eucharist of a neighbouring church
3. Churches where a second congregation met later on the same day as a eucharist celebrated earlier.

There was to be no distribution in one kind at these services of 'Extended Communion', which were not to be called 'Holy Communion', so as not to confuse congregations. They were not to take place unless preceded by a service of the word, and had to always be linked to a specific eucharist taking place on the same day, preferably explicitly in the notice advertising the service. In this respect, the Church of England laid down stricter guidelines than the Roman Catholic Church, which in the absence of a priest permits deacons to lead eucharistic services at any time, using consecrated wafers. Services of Holy Communion led by deacons are an ancient feature of the Eastern Orthodox tradition, in the form of the 'Liturgy of the Pre-sanctified Gifts' which regularly replaces weekday celebrations of the Divine Liturgy during the Great Lent.

For the Church of England, the severe restrictions placed on deacons with respect to communion by extension reflect the Prayer Book's emphasis on the importance of communion in both kinds,

1. Ibid. p. 63.
2. Ibid. pp. 89-91.

as well as the significance of the eucharist as a communal rather than private celebration in Anglican theology. There has never been a significant debate in the Church of England about diaconal presidency of the eucharist, in contrast to some other parts of the Anglican Communion. Where diaconal presidency is discussed, it is usually in the same breath as lay presidency, rather than as an *alternative* to lay presidency. Nicholas Taylor has argued that the Church of Kenya's authorisation of diaconal presidency in 1985 was founded on an understanding of the diaconate as a probationary year for the priesthood. By permitting a deacon to preside at the eucharist, 'the bishop confers, by his own mandate, an authority he would normally confer at ordination to the presbyterate'.[1] Taylor's analysis presupposes, however, that the capacity to consecrate the eucharistic elements is primarily a matter of *authority* rather than sacramental reality.

By 1991, the number of women deacons in the Church of England may have been as many as 1200.[2] Still, the elephant in the room remained the question of whether women would be ordained as priests, which official reports such as *Deacons Now* were unable to address, but individual theologians and women deacons were considering with increasing urgency. Catherine Treasure complained that most laypeople at this time still did not understand the difference between a deacon and a deaconess, thus undermining women's status as ordained ministers. Of the thirty-eight women deacons she interviewed for her 1991 study, Treasure found that none opposed the ordination of women to the priesthood in principle, and she observed that 'those women who oppose the priesting of women also oppose their ordination to the diaconate'.[3]

Treasure found deacons working as everything from department store chaplains to teachers, social workers and church administrators. Many of these women had spent so long waiting to be deacons that they already had fully developed lay ministries by the time they were ordained.[4] Already in the early 1990s it was quite usual for parish deacons to perform weddings, even though, according to Canon Law, weddings performed by deacons are considered canonically irregular because the wedding service includes a blessing.[5] Treasure

1. Taylor, N.H., *Lay Presidency at the Eucharist? An Anglican Approach* (Mowbray: London, 2009), pp. 177-8.
2. Treasure (1991), p. 1.
3. Ibid. p. 2.
4. Ibid. p. 6.
5. Ibid. pp. 7-8.

highlighted the level of insecurity experienced by deacons, who felt that their 'jobs were in the balance' each time there was a new incumbent.[1] This was because most deacons were licensed as curates, and therefore the nature of their ministry (and even their ability to have a ministry at all) depended on the incumbent's good grace.

Treasure found that a ministry of listening was a common factor in the diverse roles performed by women deacons, which included training church choirs, facilitating discussion groups, running Sunday Schools, making home visits, caring for the sick, keeping bookstalls stocked, counselling department store sales assistants, chairing diocesan and parochial committees, and selecting and training ordinands. Some deacons even presided at the eucharist, only stepping aside for a male priest to say the words of institution, a practice that went further than the recommendations of *Deacons Now*.[2] Ironically, many women deacons passionately wanted to become priests, but found themselves frustrated by the fact that the incumbents they worked with frequently did not know what a deacon did, or understand the church's tradition regarding the diaconate.[3] Thus, women whose ultimate aspiration was the priesthood became enthusiastic advocates of a renewed theology of the diaconate.

The issue of whether women deacons should explore their diaconal ministry or regard themselves as priests-in-waiting divided opinion; Stephen Platten lamented in *Deacons in the Ministry of the Church* that deacons tried to do as much of what a priest did as their order permitted, rather than exploring the riches of their own diaconal tradition.[4] However, the tenor of *Deacons Now* was clearly in favour of women deacons taking on as many traditional priestly roles as Canon Law permitted. Only 20 per cent of the 894 women deacons surveyed by the Movement for the Ordination of Women in 1989-90 reported a specific vocation to the distinctive diaconate rather than a vocation to the priesthood. To Treasure, this suggested that the distinctive diaconate would not die out if women were ordained priests, since a sizeable minority felt a specific call to this ministry.[5] What Treasure did not anticipate was that once women were admitted to the priesthood, some women deacons would experience pressure to be ordained priest in order to make themselves more 'useful' to the church.

1. Ibid. p. 10.
2. Ibid. p. 34.
3. Ibid. p. 70.
4. *DMC*, pp. 94, 116.
5. Treasure (1991), pp. 70-71.

Treasure noted that in spite of the development of a large body of women deacons, the distinctive diaconate remained unpopular amongst men, who made up around 2.5 per cent of all distinctive deacons in 1991. She speculated that this unpopularity could be related to the perception that the work being undertaken by deacons, such as ministries of listening and pastoral care, was 'unmanly' or feminine. Treasure argued that 'The redefinition and recognition of priesthood and diaconate as distinct but equal ministries depend on the Church and all its people seriously examining their approaches to sexuality and, with that, their concepts of masculine and feminine'.[1] This 'gendered' aspect of the distinctive diaconate remains an issue, yet it has not been significantly explored and was addressed in neither of the reports on the diaconate produced in the first decade of the twenty-first century. Just as the question of whether women would be ordained as priests was an elephant in the room in the 1990s, today's 'elephant' is perhaps the fact that women significantly outnumber men in the distinctive diaconate.

## Deacons in the liturgy

The *Alternative Service Book* (*ASB*) of 1980 contained the first revision of the service for the ordination of deacons since 1662, which was approved for use in 1978. The structure of the service was similar to that of 1662, except that it was anticipated that it would include a celebration of Holy Communion. The service began with the liturgy of the word, followed by the creed and then the presentation of the deacons to the bishop by the archdeacon. The bishop then described the role of the deacon:

> A deacon is called to serve the Church of God, and to work with its members in caring for the poor, the needy, the sick, and all who are in trouble. He is to strengthen the faithful, search out the careless and the indifferent, and to preach the word of God in the place to which he is licensed. A deacon assists the priest under whom he serves, in leading the worship of the people, especially in the administration of the Holy Communion. He may baptize when required to do so. It is his general duty to do such pastoral work as is entrusted to him.[2]

---

1. Ibid. pp. 73-4.
2. 'The Ordination of Deacons' in *The Alternative Service Book 1980* (Cambridge University Press: Cambridge, 1980), pp. 339-50.

This was little more than a paraphrase or rendering in modern language of the 1550 Ordinal. In the intercessions that followed, the 'servant' role of the deacon was emphasised: 'Bless your servants now to be made deacons, that they may serve your Church and reveal your glory in the world'. Likewise, the prayer of ordination itself identified the deacons with Christ the servant:

We praise and glorify you, most merciful Father, because in your great love of mankind you sent your only Son Jesus Christ to take the form of a servant; he came to serve and not to be served; and taught us that he who would be great among us must be the servant of all; he humbled himself for our sake, and in obedience accepted death, even death on a cross; therefore you highly exalted him and gave him the name which is above every name. . . . Almighty Father, give to these your servants grace and power to fulfil their ministry. Make them faithful to serve, ready to teach, constant in advancing your gospel; and grant that, always having full assurance of faith, abounding in hope, and being rooted and grounded in love, they may continue strong and steadfast in your Son Jesus Christ our Lord.[1]

The emphasis on servanthood continued in the post-communion prayer: 'Father, you have taught the ministers of your Church to be the willing servants of others. Give to these your deacons skill and gentleness in the practice of their ministry, and perseverance always in prayer'. Under the influence of the ordination rite of the Church of South India, the precatory form 'Send down the Holy Spirit upon your servant N for the office and work of a deacon in your church' was substituted for the imperative 'Take thou authority . . .'. The inclusion of a reference to the Holy Spirit suggests 'that it is God, rather than the Church, who ordains (or one could say: God ordains through the instrumentality of the Church)'. Furthermore, the *ASB* refers to the 'ordaining' rather than 'making' of deacons.[2]

The major difference between the *ASB* liturgy of 1978 and the original Ordinal was the omission of any reference to the diaconate as an 'inferior office' (although, as I have noted, this omission had already been made in the proposed 1928 Prayer Book). However, the development of the theology of the diaconate in the aftermath of Collins's *Diakonia* made the *ASB* ordinal's almost exclusive emphasis on servanthood seem outdated very quickly. Indeed, the greater ambiguity of the 1550 Ordinal about the deacon's role

1.  Ibid.
2.  Avis (2005), p. 101.

was perhaps preferable to the *ASB*. R.G. Leggett has noted that in ordination liturgies across the Anglican Communion, 'Language describing the diaconate as an "inferior" order is increasingly being replaced by language that speaks of the deacon as one who animates the *diakonia*, the "servanthood" of the whole body, and who serves as an agent of the church's ministry to the world'.[1]

When it came to the deacon's participation in the celebration of Holy Communion, Elaine Bardwell insisted that a deacon should always be at the bishop's right hand when he presided at Holy Communion in cathedrals and parish churches. This was the 'normative celebration', and the place of the deacon should not be 'usurped' by the incumbent acting as deacon.[2] Likewise, lay people such as Readers should not take on the role of deacon in the liturgy, since by doing so they 'misunderstand the nature of ordination and the true place of the diaconate within the ecclesial community, [and] they also belittle their own important ministry and that of other laypeople . . . indicating that the ministry of a lay person has value only to the extent of its apparent clericalization'.[3] Andrew Burnham noted that whereas the canons in South Africa, Canada, the USA and Wales describe the reading of the Gospel as a privilege of deacons, in the Church of England the most common minister of the Gospel is a lay person.[4] In 1987, a 'discussion document' prepared for General Synod entitled *The Liturgical Ministry of Deacons* described the deacon as the assembly's 'guide and mentor', and as 'the servant of the assembly'.[5]

Through the addition of a deacon, 'the President is freed from a confusing multiplicity of roles and functions'. The deacon will be available to the congregation as they arrive, will learn their needs and will know their concerns well enough to incorporate them in the intercessions; he or she will prepare the people for worship, supervise the preparation of the sacred vessels and give out notices. The deacon will bring in the book of the Gospels and will be responsible for 'enabling touches' in the course of the service, such as announcing pages and hymns, inviting the people to confess their

---

1. Leggett, R.G., 'Anglicans and Liturgical Revision' in Hefling, C. and Shattuck, C. (eds), *The Oxford Guide to the Book of Common Prayer: A Worldwide Survey* (Oxford University Press: Oxford, 2008), pp. 445-50, at p. 448.
2. Bardwell (1991), p. 59.
3. Ibid. p. 65.
4. Burnham (1991), p. 81.
5. Ibid. p. 84.

sins and helping them to welcome the children. Burnham noted that liturgical directions for the role of the deacon are more fully developed in the Roman Catholic Church, and in the Prayer Books of Anglican churches in the USA, Canada and South Africa than they are in England, and these might provide sources for further development of the deacon's liturgical involvement.[1]

Anglican thought on the diaconate in the period 1987-94 was hampered by the fact that John N. Collins's argument concerning *diakonia* was not then widely known. In 1991, Jill Pinnock did not hesitate to describe the diaconate as 'a ministry of service' with a liturgical aspect,[2] and she and other commentators were left with the well-nigh impossible task of reconciling the traditional understanding of the diaconate as a ministry of humble service with women deacons' aspirations to church leadership. With the benefit of hindsight, documents such as *Deacons in the Ministry of the Church* and *Deacons Now* may appear an enormous waste of energy; after all, women deacons proved a largely transient phenomenon that had necessitated a great deal of soul-searching on the part of the church. However, there were those who profoundly believed that the theological insights on the diaconate of the late 1980s and '90s were of permanent value, and could be applied to a broader project to revive a distinctive diaconate for both men and women in the twenty-first century.

---

1.  Ibid. p. 84.
2.  Pinnock (1991), pp. 9-10.

# 5

# *Deacons in the Church of England Today*

By the 1990s, congregations had begun to feel the impact of the crisis in vocations to the priesthood that occurred in the Church of England, the Roman Catholic Church and other churches in the 1960s and '70s. An earlier generation of priests was starting to retire, and it became apparent that there were not enough clergy to replace them. In response to this crisis in clergy numbers, the Roman Catholic Church in England and Wales, and indeed in Europe as a whole, has come to be increasingly reliant on permanent deacons, usually married men who are trained for four years and serve as part-time, non-stipendiary clergy. In the Church of England, by contrast, attention turned to the idea of admitting those women who were already deacons to the priesthood. This is not to suggest that the only reason women were ordained priests was to make up numbers, but the falling number of male clergy and the willingness of women to serve as priests were factors that motivated change. Deacons, however, did not form part of the Church of England's solution to the vocations problem, for much the same reasons that deacons were not encouraged in England in the second half of the twentieth century: the need, so it was thought, was for priests.

In the second half of the 1990s, interest in the diaconate expanded globally and ecumenically, culminating in the Hanover Report of 1996, which represented an ecumenical declaration on the diaconate by the Anglican Communion and the Lutheran World Federation.[1]

---

1. *The Diaconate as Ecumenical Opportunity* (Anglican Communion Publications: London, 1996). On the growing ecumenical consensus on the need for a revival of the diaconate see Brodd, S-E., 'An Escalating

Anglican churches that had already approved the ordination of women to the priesthood began to return to the idea of the diaconate, since their experience of women deacons had naturally raised theological questions about what deacons should be. In Canada, for example, where the first women deacons were ordained in 1969, women were first ordained as priests in 1985. As early as 1989, a proposal was brought forward to revive the distinctive diaconate in Canada.[1] However, the debate was overtaken by the issue of consecrating women to the episcopate, which took place in Canada in 1994. This course of events, which has been mirrored to some extent in the Church of England, reveals a problem underlying any attempt to revive the distinctive diaconate. Over the past forty years, churches in the Anglican Communion have moved to expand the personnel involved in ministry in a hierarchical direction. Individuals in secular employment, women and gay people have been allowed to become first deacons, then priests and, finally, bishops. The momentum of this hierarchical expansion has made any attempt to expand a ministry lower down the 'ranks' of the church difficult, because the energy of the church's synodical government is directed to advancing (and sometimes opposing) the enlargement of offices further up the hierarchy. In the Church of England, the campaign for the expansion of the distinctive diaconate has certainly been a poor relation to the campaign for the consecration of women to the episcopate. As H.J.M. Turner has observed, 'the need to revive a "permanent diaconate" has not been keenly felt, largely because it is not at present an urgent practical matter'.[2] One might add that it is also not politically fashionable.

The churches in the Anglican Communion where the distinctive diaconate has flourished are generally those in which it was established at an early date, usually in the mid-nineteenth century. The Episcopal Church in the United States of America and the Anglican churches in Jamaica and Brazil are cases in point. In the case of the ECUSA, ordination as deacons was thought to be appropriate for Native Americans and individuals on the frontier who would otherwise have been unauthorised 'lay preachers', and it provided a means for Episcopalians

---

Phenomenon: The Diaconate from an Ecumenical Perspective' in Borgegard, G. and Hall, C. (eds), *The Ministry of the Deacon* (Nordic Ecumenical Council: Uppsala, 1999), pp. 11-50.

1. *A Plan to Restore the Diaconate in the Anglican Church of Canada* (Anglican Church of Canada: Ottawa, 1989).
2. Turner (2005), p. 9.

to legitimise the ministry of the less educated. In colonies like Jamaica, it was considered unacceptable for indigenous people to serve in positions of authority like the priesthood, and yet it was becoming increasingly obvious that an all-white clergy was practically impossible. Ordination of black Christians as deacons served as a convenient compromise. Thus, ironically, racism and colonial attitudes sometimes contributed to the flourishing of the diaconate in overseas churches. However, the fact that literacy and advanced education were not widespread in these countries also meant that the diaconate had a clear place in society that ·it did not have in England. So, in spite of a flourishing of the diaconate within and beyond the Anglican Communion, the Church of England's stance on deacons remained ambivalent at the start of the twenty-first century. A report recommending the development of the distinctive diaconate, *For Such a Time as This*, was debated by General Synod in 2001 but referred for more work (it has yet to be debated again). A subsequent report, *The Mission and Ministry of the Whole Church* (2007), recognised that distinctive deacons have a place as part of the church's overall ministry strategy, but the number of distinctive deacons in the Church of England remains tiny, and encouragement of vocations to the diaconate varies greatly across dioceses. On the other hand, efforts are being made to render the year that curates spend in deacon's orders a more meaningful exploration of diaconal ministry.

An ecumenical theological symposium on the diaconate at Stuttgart in November 2003, whose proceedings were published in 2006, brought together representatives of the Roman Catholic Church, the Church of Sweden, the ECUSA and the Church of England. At the time, there were 2,273 distinctive deacons in the ECUSA and 1,300 deacons in the Church of Sweden.[1] By contrast, there were only about 75 distinctive deacons in England, mostly confined to the dioceses of Chichester, London and Portsmouth,[2] as noted by Paul Avis, who summarised *For Such a Time as This* for the benefit of the symposium's participants. Distinctive deacons underwent a decline in numbers between 1998 and 2003; in 1998, 4 years after it became

1. Epting, S.W. and Epting, C.C., 'Deacons and the Episcopal Church in the United States of America' in Hilberath, B.J. and Mascini, R. (eds), *Diakonia and Diaconate as an Ecumenical Challenge* (Lit Verlag: Berlin, 2006), pp. 39-46; Smedburg, N., 'Church of Sweden Contribution' in idem, pp. 19-34.
2. Avis, P., 'Deacons and the Church of England' in idem, pp. 35-8.

possible for women to be ordained priest, there were a total of 155 distinctive deacons (41 men and 114 women).[1] The disappearance of almost half of these deacons within 5 years can only be adequately accounted for by their having been ordained priest.

The most recent research on numbers of distinctive deacons in the Church of England that I am aware of was carried out by R.P. Clement between July 2007 and January 2008. Clement found that three people had been accepted for training as stipendiary deacons between 2002 and 2006, and twenty-seven people had been accepted for training as non-stipendiary deacons or ordained local ministers. From replies returned by dioceses, Clement found that there were eighty-seven distinctive deacons. Sixteen dioceses had no distinctive deacons at all, while only the dioceses of Chichester, London, Portsmouth, Ripon, Salisbury and Wakefield had more than two deacons. Clement found that the Diocese of Chichester offered the most detailed information on the distinctive diaconate, although Wakefield had an information leaflet for enquirers. Clement tracked down the jobs of seven stipendiary deacons and found a diocesan director of ordinands, a diocesan urban officer, a DAC secretary, a part-time ministry development officer, a parish deacon-in-charge and diocesan vocations advisor, a full-time deacon-in-charge and rural dean, and, finally, a full time deacon in a team ministry.[2] These figures suggest that the composition and popularity of the distinctive diaconate changed little between 2003 and 2008.

On the other hand, efforts are underway at the time of writing to give deacons within the Church of England a higher profile. On 21 and 22 February 2014, a conference entitled 'Discovering Deacons' took place at Wydale Hall in the Diocese of York, and a new website, *Deacon Stories*, was set up early in 2014 to allow distinctive deacons to share their experiences.[3] The 'Discovering Deacons' conference, aimed at distinctive deacons (Anglican and Methodist) and those discerning a diaconal vocation, was addressed by Dr Andrew Orton of Durham University, who undertook a two-year research project on deacons in the Methodist Church of Great Britain. A day of reflection, with Paul Avis as the keynote speaker, was organised for deacons and their incumbents (distinctive and transitional)

---

1. Plater (2004), p. 72.
2. Clement, R.P., 'Is a Permanent Diaconate a realistic proposition, practically and pastorally, for the Church of England at the present time?', MA Dissertation, Anglia Ruskin University, 2008, pp. 7-8.
3. *Deacon Stories*, accessed on 2 February 2014: http://deaconstories. wordpress.com.

in the Diocese of Exeter on 7 June 2014. These developments are indicative of growing confidence amongst the Church of England's small number of distinctive deacons, and a desire for their ministry to be more public. The active support for the distinctive diaconate of prominent theologians, such as Avis, is undoubtedly increasing the pressure on the Church of England to do more to promote this ministry.

## 'For Such a Time as This'

The history of the contemporary distinctive diaconate, in the form in which it exists in the Church of England today, began in 1998 at a meeting of St Neots Deanery Synod. A motion originating there that the Church of England should reconsider the direction of the distinctive diaconate in the aftermath of the admission of women to priest's orders then made its way to Ely Diocesan Synod, and from there to the House of Bishops of General Synod.[1] Richard Noble, then Lay Chair of St Neots Deanery Synod, who originally proposed the motion, was reacting to a concern shared by the then Bishop of Ely, Stephen Sykes, that the ordination of women deacons as priests risked depriving the church of an important ministry.[2] An initial report was prepared during the course of 1998,[3] and Sykes opened the debate on distinctive deacons in General Synod on 18 November, noting the development in understanding of the original meaning of the word *diakonos* in the work of John N. Collins, published in 1990 after the Church of England's last official report on deacons in 1988. Sykes emphasised the 'plural and diverse' traditions concerning the diaconate, and appealed to Richard Hooker's argument that 'tract of time' justified the re-definition of diaconal ministry.[4]

In light of Collins's theological insights, Sykes appealed for 'a broader concept of a *diakonos* as an ambassador, or agent, a person on an errand, a go-between, a mediator, not just as a humble person doing menial tasks'. He asked whether the diaconate could be 'a ministry largely beyond the boundaries of the worshipping congregation in the messy and complex life of the working world', implying that distinctive deacons would not necessarily be licensed as curates working within well-defined parochial boundaries.

---

1. *FSTT*, p. vii.
2. Richard Noble, pers. comm. 15 August 2013.
3. *The Diaconate*, GS MISC 535 (Church House Publishing: London, 1998).
4. I am grateful to Richard Noble for providing me with a copy of Stephen Sykes's original speech.

Finally, Sykes asked whether there could be 'a way of developing the diaconate, whether in stipendiary or self-supporting form, which could be an enhancement of the mission of the church, and at the same time an enrichment of lay vocations'.

Sykes anticipated future controversy by warning that 'the issue of whether or not there is a distinctive work for life-long deacons...ought not to become a moment for raising general anxieties about the devaluing of lay vocation or the so-called clericalization of lay people'. He endorsed Noble's vision of deacons as 'the go-between or agent of the church, ministering in a pro-active, practical way as educator/envisioner/facilitator with an instrumental role in building missionary congregations', and set out a blueprint for the nature of the ministry of future deacons:

> Many new-style deacons would pursue a normal career with the object of applying their theological training and insight to their main occupation. In this way they will build the experience that will enable them to teach, lead, encourage and support the members of their home church and enable them in turn to go out into the world and live their faith as confident, visible Christians. Thus in the gathered churches these new style deacons would have the real capability to equip the members to be missionary congregations.

Barry Rogerson, Bishop of Bristol, insisted that 'a renewed diaconate would fit into developing patterns of collaborative ministry',[1] thereby anticipating the emphasis on collaboration that would be incorporated into the service for the ordination of deacons in *Common Worship*. General Synod approved the original motion, which was to commission a committee of the House of Bishops to compile a report on the distinctive diaconate. At around the same time, Rowan Williams, who was then Bishop of Monmouth and Archbishop of Wales, issued *A Note on the Diaconate* which he circulated to the bishops of Wales, calling for the ordination of people to a non-stipendiary diaconal ministry.[2]

This was led by Rogerson, and it prepared the text of *For Such a Time as This*. *For Such a Time as This* describes the diaconate as 'essentially a ministry involving word and sacrament and compassionate pastoral care. . . . The text of the Ordinal suggests a movement of reaching out from the liturgical heart of parish life to those who are estranged by poverty or sickness, rallying the resources of the

---

1. *MMWC*, p. 4.
2. Turner (2005), p. 78.

parish to meet their need'.[1] The report draws on the Ordinal and the canons to define the diaconate as 'a non-presidential representative ministry of word, sacrament and pastoral care', noting that

> It is theologically important that all clergy are ordained deacon. In the catholic understanding of holy order, presbyters and bishops do not leave their diaconal ordination behind them. . . . The diaconate remains a fundamental stratum, so to speak, whatever more is added to one's ministry. This truth is often invoked to emphasize the servant nature of presbyteral and episcopal ministry. . . . But the diaconal foundation of all ordained ministry becomes all the more important when it is seen in the light of the recent rediscovery of the biblical idea of *diakonia*.[2]

The historical analysis within *For Such a Time as This* is wanting; the report relied heavily on Mary Tanner's work for *Deacons in the Ministry of the Church* (1988), the defects of which have been outlined in the chapters above. The report noted that the nineteenth-century model of the diaconate as a professional apprenticeship strengthened the 'transitional' model,[3] and whilst this is true to an extent, it misses out the entire history of the influential movement for lifelong deacons between 1839 and 1884.

Like previous reports on the diaconate, *For Such a Time as This* strove to balance innovation with tradition, insisting that there existed 'sufficient theological resources in the current ordinal to support the thrust of the present report'. The diaconate was 'a fundamental expression of apostolic ministry', and the 'go-between character' of deacons allowed interface between the world and the church but also between the laity, clergy and bishops:

> The calling of deacons is to focus, to encourage and to help coordinate the *diakonia* (the divine commission of the whole church within the mission of God in the world and to do this in three ways: through the liturgy, through pastoral outreach and through catechetical work. . . . Deacons can help the church to connect.[4]

Echoing Sykes, who had originally emphasised the importance of the development of the diaconate in an ecumenical context across churches, *For Such a Time as This* suggested that deacons'

---

1. *FSTT*, p. 7.
2. Ibid. p. 9.
3. Ibid. p. 7.
4. Ibid. pp. 51-2.

ministry 'may particularly lend itself to ecumenical collaboration'.[1] On a pastoral level, the report suggested that deacons might take a particular responsibility for care of the poor, the sick and the lonely, for 'breaking new ground' in the church's ministry, being 'an authorised prophetic voice' and setting up networks. Deacons might also model and encourage outreach, for example by leading and coordinating pastoral visiting or having a special concern for young families. They might also be involved in ministry in schools and youth groups or as the 'focal ministry person' in a parish of a benefice where the incumbent is not based.[2]

As far as the deacon's involvement in the liturgy was concerned, the report suggested that the deacon could

> [minister] at the celebration of the Eucharist in ways that are appropriate to the life of the community and without excluding the ministry of lay people: reading the Gospel, leading the prayers of penitence, the intercessions and the acclamations of the people, inviting the exchange of the peace, serving at the altar, administering Holy Communion, and sending out the people with the liturgical dismissal.[3]

The deacon could also lead the daily offices, baptise with the parish priest's permission and order the church for liturgical worship, especially the altar and font, giving guidance to the sacristan or verger. The deacon might also administer house and hospital communions and officiate at services of the word with Holy Communion ('extended communion'), and he or she might assist or officiate (except in the first year after ordination) at marriages, funeral services and burials, as well as ministering to the sick and dying with prayers.[4]

The deacon's catechetical ministry might include coordinating and monitoring faith development courses, preparing adult candidates for baptism, preaching, conducting confirmation preparation and preparing couples for marriage. Deacons might also train lay people for catechesis, support lay involvement in children's activities, offer specialist counselling or train volunteers to befriend families in need. The deacon should also represent the church's priorities on behalf of the bishop in areas of community action. He or she might even appropriately assume training and teaching roles within diocese,

1. Ibid. p. 53.
2. Ibid. pp. 54-5.
3. Ibid. p. 55.
4. Ibid. p. 56.

archdeaconry and deanery contexts: 'It would seem appropriate for a person carrying out this form of the ministry of the word, with the bishop's commission, and who was not called to oversight and to presidency at the Eucharist, to remain a deacon'.[1] Deacons might thus serve as diocesan directors of education or ministry, or even as rural deans, a practice that has already been seen in the Diocese of Chichester.[2]

## Subsequent debate

In the debate that followed the publication of *For Such a Time as This* in 2001, the accusation that a revived diaconate risked clericalising the laity came to the fore. The Central Readers' Council, concerned that distinctive deacons would detract from longstanding patterns of lay ministry, opposed the adoption of the report as a blueprint for the future encouragement of distinctive deacons. This was on the grounds that the best way to energise lay ministry in the church was for lay people to continue to minister as laity, rather than to encourage individuals engaged in lay ministry to enter holy orders. The motion to endorse the report foundered in the House of Laity, therefore, and in the end General Synod 'took note of' the report's recommendations, meaning that it had no official status, but might nevertheless be drawn upon by individual dioceses. *For Such a Time as This* was 'referred back for further work, seeking to relate ordained and lay forms of ministry to each other', and the following motion was passed:

> That this Synod, disappointed that the report . . . has not taken the opportunity to examine thoroughly the offices of Reader, Pastoral Assistant and Church Army Officer, request that the report is referred to the Ministry Division for further consideration.[3]

In the event, the Bishops' Committee for Ministry declined to take the issue any further in 2002, and the task of responding to General Synod's request was passed to the Faith and Order Advisory Group.[4]

However, *For Such a Time as This* did not go unnoticed in individual dioceses. The Diocese of Salisbury's 2003 report on the distinctive diaconate, prepared by Rosalind Brown, drew heavily upon the

---

1.  Ibid. pp. 56-7.
2.  Ibid.
3.  *MMWC*, p. xi.
4.  Ibid. p. 4.

earlier report. One diocese that had invested more than any other in its deacons was the Diocese of Chichester. After General Synod's decision to return *For Such a Time as This* to the Ministry Division for more work, the Bishop's Council in Chichester commissioned its own report on how the ministry of its deacons might relate to lay ministries within the diocese. The committee reported in 2003. The Chichester Report noted that priests could still act as deacons, 'but there is something about the flexibility of a distinctive and permanent diaconate, accountable directly to the bishop but working collaboratively with the presbyter in a local situation, which has a different feel'.[1] The report abandoned the idea of 'defining' diaconal ministry and instead recommended a more intuitive discernment of whether a candidate for ministry was a 'deacon-shaped' rather than a 'priest-shaped' person,[2] providing seven discernment criteria for diaconal candidates.

The Chichester Report noted that the traditional ministerial flexibility of deacons meant that they could be particularly important in the 'emerging church', which might be based on a 'cell' structure rather than the traditional parish.[3] According to the report, 'The service of a deacon, conceived as envoy and spokesperson entrusted with important tidings, as an ambassador and mediator with authority and as a person who performs tasks on behalf of another, is the Church's service sacramentalised'.[4] Deacons might operate at the deanery and diocesan levels as well as parish level, and therefore criteria similar to those applied to the selection of rural deans, archdeacons and bishops should be applied to these senior deacons.[5] Chichester envisaged the appointment of stipendiary deacons, instead of curates in some cases, and recognised that parishes would need to be educated about the difference between a curate and a deacon. Indeed, the report goes so far as to suggest that non-stipendiary deacons 'should not be considered the norm'.[6]

Some women priests, who had been forcibly confined to the diaconate by law between 1987 and 1994, were unenthusiastic about the idea of a revived distinctive diaconate. Even after the Church

---

1. *Deacons in the Church: Report of a Diocesan Working Party* (Diocese of Chichester, 2003), p. 6.
2. Ibid. p. 8.
3. Ibid. p. 20.
4. Ibid. p. 10.
5. Ibid. p. 24.
6. Ibid. p. 25.

of England began to ordain women, it seems that some bishops preferred them to remain in deacon's orders. One female candidate for ministry, who approached her diocese in 1999, reported that 'there was . . . a strong presumption that you would be sponsored (if at all) for the permanent diaconate',[1] and another felt 'betrayed' by a woman who was training alongside her for the diaconate and refused to attend communion services celebrated by a woman.[2] The Diocese of Chichester is known for its Anglo-Catholic tradition, and the majority of its distinctive deacons are women, although it is unclear to what extent this is due to the theological concerns of those individuals, or of the diocese as a whole, about women priests. The authors of *For Such a Time as This* noted that the Bishop Otter Centre for Theology and Ministry within University College, Chichester was the only Anglican institution in Britain offering formation for distinctive deacons, although it was not accredited to do so by the House of Bishops. The only other way to receive formation specific to the diaconate was to attend an ecumenical course designed to train Methodist deacons at Queen's College, Birmingham.[3] Although the course at the Bishop Otter Centre was originally set up as a collaborative project between the southern dioceses, the other dioceses later withdrew to leave Chichester as the only diocese involved.[4]

On the other hand, there have been positive reactions from the laity to the idea of a revived distinctive diaconate. The lay theologian Margaret Selby has argued that the revival of the diaconate is a welcome reflection of the 'mutuality' of lay and clerical ministry in the church:

> Traditionally, the deacon is the one who links the people to the priest at the altar, who symbolizes the bringing of the world by the congregation to lay it before God and his transforming love. Many of the traditional tasks of the deacon are now shared by the laity, but it is the servant task of the whole Church, symbolized by the deacon, to carry in the Gospel and to read it – to be the bearer of the Good News to the people of God, to intercede for the world as its servant, to call the people to peace with one another, to send them out into the world as

---

1. Green, A., *A Priesthood of Both Sexes: Paying Attention to Difference* (SPCK: London, 2011), pp. 25-6.
2. Ibid. p. 32.
3. *FSTT*, p. 10.
4. *Chichester Report* (2003), p. 27.

its servants. This allows the laity to see themselves mirrored not only in the priestly ministry, but also in that of the deacon. Christ is both Priest and Servant in his Church, and this must be reflected both in the priestly intercession of the whole people of God and also in their diaconal service in the world.[1]

While it may not have gained universal acceptance, *For Such a Time as This* undoubtedly changed the terms of the debate about distinctive deacons in the Church of England. Before 1998, the diaconate was rarely given sustained theological consideration for its own sake, but rather considered as a stop-gap to the ordination of women as priests. After that milestone was passed in 1994, it was possible for the church to return to what was essentially the same question as Thomas Arnold first asked in 1839: what might lifelong deacons be able to bring to the church?

The weightiest contributions to the debate about deacons immediately after the publication of *For Such a Time as This* came from two theologians, Paul Avis and Rosalind Brown. Avis argued that a purely 'quantitative' analysis of what a deacon does can never get to the heart of what a deacon is. A deacon is not significantly different from a Reader in what he or she can do, but he or she is 'qualitatively' different insofar as he or she is marked by a sacramental character. By emphasising the sacramental character of deacons, Avis echoed an earlier argument by Robert Hannaford that 'the primary significance of these orders is . . . found in what they represent and not in the functions that their members perform'.[2] Ordained ministry, of whatever kind, is necessarily related to all three missiological tasks of the church: word, sacrament and pastoral care. Ordained ministry is lifelong and indelible, and ordination 'involves a formal intention, on the part of the Church, in making that ministry that it should be a ministry of the Christian Church as such, not simply a local ministry'.[3]

Avis further suggests that, at least in theory, an ordained minister is a minister of the church in general and not just a person authorised by the Church of England (as a Reader is), and this remark points to the diaconate's considerable ecumenical possibilities. The deacon's indirect relationship with the eucharist (as opposed to the priest's direct relationship as president) means that the deacon is not a divisive figure in the way that a priest might be. The interchangeability of

---

1. Selby, M., 'A Word from one of the Laos', in Guiver, G. (ed.), *Priests in a People's Church* (SPCK: London, 2001), pp. 51-9, at pp. 52-3.
2. Hannaford (1991), p. 25.
3. Avis (2005), p. 106.

diaconal ministry between the Methodist church and the Church of England, and even between the Roman Catholic Church and the Church of England, presents fewer obvious problems than the interchangeability of priestly ministry. Avis noted that when the diaconate is understood almost exclusively in terms of servanthood, direct ordination makes more sense than the sequential or cumulative ordination practised from the earliest times. However, once *diakonia* is understood primarily as an 'ecclesial sign', the basis for all other ordained ministries, the case for cumulative ordination becomes compelling: '*Diakonia* is the sine qua non of ordained ministry because in the ordination of deacons the divine commission that is the essence of the apostolicity of the Church is signified sacramentally'.[1]

The role of the deacon is 'not simply liturgical or simply pastoral, but involves holding the two together on behalf of the Church', as an 'apostolic envoy'. However, Avis does not believe that the revival of the diaconate necessitates the resurrection of a distinctive diaconate, although this might be one aspect of revival. What matters is that ordinands recover the significance of the diaconate by spending at least two years (preferably three) in deacon's orders alone.[2] The idea of resurrecting *diakonia* in the church, without necessarily restoring the distinctive diaconate as a ministry with its own sacramental identity, is an idea that has also been picked up by Steven Croft in his book *Ministry in Three Dimensions* (1999), in which he argues that bishops, presbyters and deacons represent three aspects of the ministry of all the baptised.[3] However, in Avis's view, the revival of the diaconate would have a knock-on effect on priests and bishops: 'The renewal of the diaconate could blaze a trail for the transformation of presbyteral and episcopal ministry also into a fully missiological mode, while lighting a beacon for all the royal priesthood'.[4]

Avis has acknowledged the Church of England's paradoxical position with regard to deacons: 'On the one hand it knows that it cannot be right to see deacons merely as probationary priests, but on the other hand, the Church of England on the whole is not geared up to take advantage of the ministry of distinctive deacons'. Furthermore, Avis points to a more fundamental problem with defining the function of the diaconate: the difficulty of interpreting the sources for it:

1. Ibid. p. 107.
2. Ibid. p. 108.
3. Croft, S., *Ministry in Three Dimensions: Ordination and Leadership in the Local Church* (Darton, Longman and Todd: London, 1999).
4. Avis (2005), p. 110.

In interpreting the diaconate, reason, tradition and Scripture have a contribution to make. It would seem sensible to try to respond to the needs of the Church and the needs of the world within which it ministers. But these are impossibly diverse. It would also be responsible to be guided as far as possible by the Church's tradition. But this too is extremely varied: the diaconate has meant many things in the past two thousand years. Above all, therefore, it is necessary to be guided by the New Testament. But this too is far from straightforward.[1]

Avis argues that the church's response to this ambiguity of meaning should not be to 'improvise' a diaconate that meets whatever needs are felt at the time – rather like the suggestion put before General Synod in the 1970s that lay ministers should simply be 're-designated' as deacons. The church does not adopt this approach to priests and bishops. Instead, the church must pay close attention to the application of the terms *diakonia* and *diakonoi* in the New Testament. For Avis, St Paul's use of *diakonia* to refer to his 'God-given, Christ-centred, gospel-focused ministry' sets the benchmark for our use of the terms 'deacon' or 'diaconal'. In this way, 'we find ourselves speaking of the deacon as a herald of the gospel and a steward of the mysteries of Christ, as an envoy or ambassador on behalf of Christ and his Church'.[2]

In his most recent writings on the diaconate in the Church of England, Avis has described the diaconate as 'the most problematic but, at the same time, the most promising of all the ministries of the Church'.[3] However, Avis expresses concern that the Church of England might be 'imposing its anxiety about outreach and evangelisation on to deacons',[4] as if the existence of a small band of deacons exonerates the rest of the church from prioritising these concerns. According to Avis,

> Deacons lead the way for the Church in reaching out to the unchurched, in all their physical, social and spiritual needs, and in seeking to draw them, in the name of Christ, back into the blessed fellowship of Christ's Church and ultimately, through the stepping stones of Christian initiation, to share fully in the celebration of the Eucharist.[5]

1. Avis, P., 'Wrestling with the Diaconate', *Ecclesiology* 5 (2009), pp. 3-6, at p. 4.
2. Ibid. pp. 6-8.
3. Avis, P., 'The Diaconate: a flagship ministry', *Theology and Ministry* 2 (2013), pp. 1-14, at p. 1.
4. Ibid. p. 5.
5. Ibid. p. 11.

Avis deliberately distances himself from 'theologising' about the diaconate based on interpretations of church history, and returns to the New Testament sources for diaconal ministry, arguing that this is the only way to overcome the problematic nature of the diaconate.

Rosalind Brown's book *Being a Deacon Today* (2004), which was stimulated by her work on a report on the distinctive diaconate for the Diocese of Salisbury, is currently the only book in print on the subject of the diaconate from a British Anglican perspective that is not an official report. Brown picked up on Avis's insistence that the revival of the diaconate is not exclusively a matter of encouraging more distinctive deacons, and her book is intended to provide spiritual resources to transitional as well as distinctive deacons in an effort to fulfil the aspiration that ordinands should take the diaconate more seriously. *Being a Deacon Today* eschews the historical approach adopted by *Deacons in the Ministry of the Church* and *For Such a Time as This* and approaches the spirituality of *diakonia* more broadly. Brown notes that a distinctive Anglican spirituality of *diakonia* does exist, but owing to the insignificance of the diaconate it is often subsumed within the spirituality of priesthood.[1]

Brown acknowledged that deacons and Readers might find themselves reduplicating each other's ministry, 'but this can be seen as an expression of the perichoretic dance of the Trinity, in which we are caught up and at times find ourselves with our various callings dancing the same steps together for a while, before continuing the dance in different ways'. Deacons are 'enablers of the ministry of the bishop and the Church', like 'old retainer' servants who 'take the initiative and keep [the church] running smoothly'.[2] Brown gives the example of Roy Overthrow, a deacon who served as 'bishop's deacon' to the Bishop of Salisbury.[3] According to Brown,

> The deacon need not be a priest but should have theological training and an immersion in the Church that enables him or her to understand its needs and its ways. The deacon should be content to be behind the scenes, facilitating the public ministry of the bishop. Care and attention to detail are paramount, along with unflappability and an ability in administration.

In a review of Brown's book, Sister Teresa White noted that 'most writings from the permanent-deacon movement decry or ignore the far more numerous transitional deacons', and thus she welcomed

1. Brown (2004), p. xii.
2. Ibid. p. 8.
3. Ibid. n. p. 128.

Brown's focus on this group. However, she wondered whether emphasis on the liturgical role of transitional deacons obscured their social role: '[A]re our deacons overly involved in leitourgia and the pastoral at the expense of social serving?'[1] Teresa White is the editor of *Distinctive Diaconate News*, a newsletter she founded in 1981 that summarises developments in the distinctive diaconate internationally and across denominations.[2] Her comments on Brown's book reflect one of Paul Avis's concerns, that the debate on the meaning of deacons should not stagnate around an uncritical acceptance of Collins's redefinition of *diakonia*, as it previously stagnated around a definition of the deacon as servant; it is always perilous for the church to found its ecclesiology on the insights of one scholar. The debate about deacons must continue, and the balancing act the church must perform is having a theology of the diaconate coherent enough to inspire vocations, but at the same time open enough to accommodate new scholarly insights.

The issue of deacons was raised again at General Synod in November 2006 in the context of a debate on Readers. The Bishop of Carlisle, Graham Dow, rejected the idea that Readers should be ordained deacons:

> But why should they not just be ordained? Were they diaconal? A steady stream moved on to become deacons and priests, and it was natural to wonder whether a gifted Reader might be called to ordination. But the Bishop did not want to clericalise all church services. What message would it give the laity if public worship was led only by priests and deacons? Readers were 'a natural sign to lay people of what their ministry can be'.[3]

Since 2001, the terms of discussion about non-priestly ministry in the Church of England have largely been set by Readers. There are certainly many more Readers than there are deacons, and they are better represented in the church's synodical government. Whilst there are dozens of Readers in General Synod's House of Laity, at the time of writing there is only one deacon in the House of Clergy. The Diaconal Association of the Church of England (DACE), founded on 29 November 1988,[4] is a professional association for 'diaconal

---

1. White, T., 'Review: Being a Deacon Today', *The Church Times*, 2 November 2006.
2. On Teresa White see Plater (2004), p. 73.
3. 'Readers feel neglected and ill-used', *The Church Times*, 2 November 2006.
4. Plater (2004), p. 73.

ministers' including, but not limited to, distinctive deacons; it also includes Church Army officers, for example. However, DACE lacks the status of the Central Readers' Council, which is a charity within the Ministry Division. The cause of distinctive deacons depends for its advancement on the sympathy of individual bishops: Stephen Sykes of Ely, Barry Rogerson of Bristol, David Stancliffe of Salisbury, John Hind of Chichester and Stephen Platten of Wakefield particularly stand out as supporters of the diaconate over the last thirty years. The voices of distinctive deacons themselves are rarely heard in the media or in scholarship on the subject.

## 'The Mission and Ministry of the Whole Church'

In 2007, the Church of England's Faith and Order Advisory Group produced the report *The Mission and Ministry of the Whole Church*, which was intended as a reappraisal of the roles of all involved in ministry, whether bishops, priests, deacons or lay ministers, and as a follow-up to *For Such a Time as This*. However, *The Mission and Ministry of the Whole Church* was avowedly not a report about the distinctive diaconate *per se*, but rather a report 'about the diaconal calling of the whole church'.[1] The authors of the report made a conscious effort to incorporate Collins's insights about the meaning of the word *diakonos*. In the preface to the report, John Hind, then Bishop of Chichester, was reluctant to substitute the translation 'minister' for the traditional translation 'servant', but he did conclude that 'on the basis of New Testament usage, "diaconal" language about the Church and the ministry is primarily "missional"',[2] with the implication being that an understanding of the diaconate based solely on humble service is impoverished.

Hind conceded that 'The Church of England has not been alone in not knowing quite what to make of the diaconate', and acknowledged the confusion and hostility that the encouragement of vocations to the distinctive diaconate could elicit from lay ministers such as Readers.[3] The main text of the report itself alluded to practical questions regarding the position and function of deacons, for instance 'whether it would be right for Canon B12 to be amended to allow deacons, Readers and other lay ministers to be allowed to preside at Holy Communion', and 'whether it is right to see the diaconate as primarily a stepping stone to the priesthood, or whether

---

1. *MMWC*, p. vii.
2. Ibid. pp. vii-viii.
3. Ibid. p. ix.

it should be given greater emphasis as a distinctive form of ministry in its own right'. Furthermore, the report promised to consider 'how the ministry of deacons should relate to that of Readers and other recognized lay ministers'.[1]

The authors of the report drew attention to the ambiguity of the Greek word *diakonia*, which can be translated either very narrowly as 'diaconate' or very widely as 'ministry'. Since the idea that all baptised Christians should be involved in ministry is now widely accepted, this raises important questions about the meaningfulness of the word *diakonia*: 'If *diakonia* (ministry) is understood as referring to the whole Church, what then is the distinctive role of a deacon? Attempts to define the diaconate can all too easily appear to be attempts to remove legitimate ministries from the whole people of God'.[2] The report's authors argued that accepting Collins's expanded definition of the diaconate did not require the church to abandon the idea that the diaconate was concerned with humble service, but rather to emphasise that humble service is required of all Christians, in imitation of Christ.[3]

*The Mission and Ministry of the Whole Church* acknowledged the predominance of women over men amongst existing distinctive deacons, and noted two major reasons for people choosing to be ordained as lifelong deacons:

> First, there were those who felt called to a distinctive diaconal ministry which they saw as a particularly well suited to establishing links between the Church and the wider world. Secondly, there were a number of women who felt called to ordained ministry but on theological grounds did not believe that it was right for them to be priests.[4]

Although the authors of the report did not comment on these motivations for seeking ordination to the diaconate, the implication of the report's recommendations is that the diaconate should not be seen primarily as a suitable ministry for women whose theological views do not allow them to proceed to ordination to the priesthood. The diaconate has long been an option favoured by women in the Anglo-Catholic tradition who feel called by God but remain uncertain of the legitimacy of their ordination to the priesthood. More recently, however, the conservative evangelical group Reform has also

1. Ibid. p. 3.
2. Ibid. p. 17.
3. Ibid. p. 26.
4. Ibid. p. 76.

promoted the ordination of women to the diaconate. In 2010, Mike Smith, Vicar of Hartford, published an article on Reform's website arguing that ordination to the diaconate might be appropriate for women, since there was no requirement in the 1550 Ordinal that deacons should preach to the congregation (which, in Smith's view, is inappropriate for a woman). Smith does not make clear exactly what he would envisage a female deacon doing, and the thrust of his argument seems to be that the diaconate is a convenient vehicle for dealing with women who feel called by God to ministry, because it can be defined in ways suitable to his conservative evangelical theology.[1] This kind of 'instrumental' use of the diaconate seems to be excluded by the thrust of the 2007 report.

A major recommendation of *The Mission and Ministry of the Whole Church* was the call for greater weight to be given to the 'transitional' diaconate, which is 'an opportunity for the ordained minister to discover and live out in practice what it means to be conformed to the Deacon Jesus Christ, to partake of his apostolic calling and to be entrusted with the stewardship of the mystery of the gospel'. The report noted that one reason why people were calling for the restoration of the distinctive diaconate was the neglect of the 'transitional' diaconate, yet 'If the diaconate is indeed fundamental, nothing is more important and time spent discovering what it means in practice is time well spent. If the diaconate is a full and equal calling, any impatience to move on to something supposedly more advanced [i.e. the priesthood] is misplaced'.[2] By the same token, however, a greater emphasis on the importance of a priest's year as a deacon might remove the need for encouraging vocations to the distinctive diaconate.

The report advised that individuals called to the distinctive diaconate itself should have 'a calling and aptitude for a life-long ministry that is inextricably related to the word, the sacraments and pastoral care, but is suited more to an assisting than to a presiding role in relation to both the sacraments and the leadership of the community'. Furthermore,

The distinctive diaconate is particularly appropriate where an individual feels strongly drawn to the missionary, go-between ministry, seeking out the lost sheep and bringing both the message of the gospel and the practical care that goes with it to

1.  Smith, M., 'A Case for Permanent Female Deacons', *Reform*, accessed on 19 November 2013: http://reform.org.uk/resources/media-downloads/src/article/27/title/report-a-case-for-permanent-female-deacons.
2.  *MMWC*, pp. 131-2.

the unchurched and, therefore, may be reluctant to proceed to priesthood with its additional responsibilities and constraints. The distinctive diaconate appears to be suited to those with an evangelistic gift, provided this is clearly related to the three basic dimensions of ministry, tied into the liturgy and directed towards the full sacramental initiation of new converts.[1]

In response to these recommendations of the report, Paul Avis and Stephen Ferns produced a set of guidelines for Diocesan Directors of Ordinands to consider when evaluating vocations to the distinctive diaconate. Avis and Ferns recommended that a candidate should have 'a strong sense of vocation to the ministry of the deacon, not a failed or thwarted sense of vocation somewhere else'. Furthermore, he or she should show 'engagement with a servant ministry, [as] a responsible behind the scenes person, able to be hidden, to get on with things out of the limelight, to oil the wheels'. The potential deacon should also be 'comfortable occupying space on the boundaries, a liminal person who is at ease alongside people on the edges of the church and of society yet who is also secure and centred for themselves'. Finally, the would-be deacon should have 'an attitude that reflects a vocation to be a servant without being a doormat', and 'leadership gifts that reflect a willingness to be a leader who assists rather than always takes the lead, and does not unsettle or unseat others who have either long term or short term responsibilities'.[2]

*The Mission and Ministry of the Whole Church* argued that diaconal ordination was particularly suited to individuals called to Pioneer Ministry. To argue that deacons are of limited value because they cannot preside at the eucharist assumes that the primary purpose of a minister is to serve the gathered congregation, whereas

> there is now a growing realization that the top priority is to grow more Christians by reaching out to the unchurched and to those hovering on the fringes. Deacons, considered as agents of God's mission through the Church, are eminently well placed to do this within the parochial structures.[3]

1. Ibid. p. 133.
2. Avis, P. and Ferns, S., 'Discerning the Diaconate', *Diaconal Association of the Church of England*, accessed on 19 November 2013: http://www.dace.org/literature/docs/Discerning-the-Diaconate.pdf. It should be noted that these guidelines do not have official status, and candidates for the diaconate continue to be assessed against the general criteria for selection for ordained ministry.
3. Ibid. p. 164.

At his or her ordination, the deacon receives 'authority from Christ', but is not 'set apart for humble service any more than any other Christian, lay or ordained'. The deacon is 'a person on a mission, a messenger or ambassador', and 'a sign of what the whole Church essentially is and is called to become more and more'. The ministry of the deacon '"promotes, releases and clarifies" what is true of the Church as such. The ordination of a deacon may be regarded, therefore, as an ecclesial sign'.[1] The report's authors associate deacons with the prophetic nature of the church, 'her calling to convey the word of God to those who are meant to hear it', while priests are associated with the priestly, and bishops with the pastoral nature of the church.[2] These attributes are in turn features of Christ's threefold messianic identity.

*The Mission and Ministry of the Whole Church* reached three conclusions that are important to the future of the diaconate in the Church of England. In the first place, it suggested that 'some Readers should be encouraged to seek ordination to the diaconate and so receive the authority to administer baptism and to solemnize marriages (and to officiate at funerals *ex officio*)'.[3] The report's rationale was that many Readers were already engaged in traditionally 'clerical' ministries anyway, so a transition to the diaconate might make sense for them. Secondly, the report suggested that a greater emphasis should be placed on the diaconal calling of candidates for the priesthood. Individuals should be encouraged to spend more than one year as deacons only, and selection for ordination training should 'be focused more than it generally does on the calling of a deacon and ordination to that order, rather than tending to take the diaconal period for granted and focusing almost entirely on the priesthood'.[4]

Finally, the report concluded that 'the distinctive diaconate should be actively encouraged', adding that 'ministry as a distinctive (that is to say, on-going, though not necessarily permanent) deacon is one that the Church of England recognizes and honours'. The distinctive diaconate needs to be 'more widely recognized as a valid calling', through the nature of vocations advice and selection of ordinands, 'where the training pathway for distinctive deacons could be more clearly and prominently signposted than it has been in the past'.[5]

---

1. Ibid. p. 134.
2. Ibid. p. 135.
3. Ibid. p. 148.
4. Ibid. pp. 161-3.
5. Ibid. p. 163.

Implicit in this statement is a criticism of vocations advisers, who sometimes steer individuals away from the distinctive diaconate out of a lack of knowledge of, or respect for, the diaconal vocation.

Some reactions to *The Mission and Ministry of the Whole Church* were less than enthusiastic. The *Church Times* leader of 29 August 2007 complained that the report failed to convey 'any idea strong enough to compete with the prevailing view that a deacon is someone training to be a presbyter. Much of the new report would make just as much sense if the words "lay minister" were substituted for "deacon"'. The same confusion could result over diaconal ministry as currently besets Reader ministry, and 'As long as confusion continues over what constitutes a diaconal ministry, it would be as well to appoint people to particular tasks, and to leave ordination out of it. Until there is a greater enthusiasm for a distinctive *diakonia*, there is little point in reviving the term, even if only to relabel existing branches of ministry'.[1]

The 2007 report was a carefully balanced document that succeeded in commanding a broad consensus where *For Such a Time as This* had failed, by gaining the approval of General Synod. However, a report from the Faith and Order Advisory Group did not have the same force as a report from the Ministry Division would have done, and the report's recommendations for the encouragement of the distinctive diaconate are arguably so deeply embedded in a diffuse document that it hardly comes across as a charter for the full-scale revival of distinctive deacons. The report is primarily an elucidation of the current status quo and of the theology underlying the emphasis on collaborative ministry in the Ordinal of *Common Worship*. Its most radical recommendation is perhaps the idea that some Readers should be encouraged to become deacons, yet even this is presented as a somewhat tentative suggestion. The report's emphasis on deacons as an 'ecclesial sign' simultaneously elevates deacons in importance and risks evacuating the office of deacon of any specific meaning.

A consultation on the diaconate organised by the Scottish Episcopal Church in Edinburgh in March 2012 was attended by a deacon representing the Church of England, Frances Hiller, who is the chaplain to the Suffragan Bishop of Gibraltar. Hiller argued that there is a need for both clergy and laity to understand better the differences between Readers and deacons. The future development of the distinctive diaconate depends a great deal on the policies

---

1. 'Leader: Deacons, not doormats', *The Church Times*, 29 August 2007.

of individual dioceses and the attitude of local bishops. Hiller argued that in general, 'there is little appetite in the dioceses for a renewed diaconate, and permanent deacons are often seen as "an inconvenient irritant"'.[1] Hiller's observations point to the fact that the recommendations contained within *The Mission and Ministry of the Whole Church* can be implemented only at the discretion of individual bishops, who often do not see the development of distinctive deacons as a priority, or even a matter worthy of consideration. By contrast with the Church of England, the Scottish Episcopal Church placed the renewal of the diaconate close to the top of its agenda for General Synod in June 2013. The SEC's Diaconate Working Group should produce a report on how the diaconate is to be taken forward in Scotland by 2016.[2]

## *Deacons in the liturgy*

Paul Avis has argued that it was the realisation that the *ASB*'s liturgy for the ordination of deacons was inadequate that persuaded bishops to overhaul the entire Ordinal for *Common Worship* (2004).[3] The liturgy in *Common Worship* made some attempt to correct the *ASB*'s excessive emphasis on the servant ministry of deacons. In the preface to the service, the bishop declares that 'Deacons are ordained so that the people of God may be better equipped to make Christ known. Theirs is a life of visible self-giving. Christ is the pattern of their calling and their commission; as he washed the feet of his disciples, so they must wash the feet of others'. Here the servant nature of the diaconate is implied rather than explicitly stated, and the deacon's role in equipping the laity is emphasised instead. *Common Worship*'s description of the role of the deacon is considerably richer than the one found in the *ASB*:

> Deacons are called to work with the Bishop and the priests with whom they serve as heralds of Christ's kingdom. They are to proclaim the gospel in word and deed, as agents of God's purposes of love. They are to serve the community

1. Comerford, P., 'Edinburgh Seminar on Deacons and the Diaconate', *Patrick Comerford*, accessed on 11 December 2013: http://www. patrickcomerford.com/2012/04/edinburgh-seminar-on-deacons-diaconate.html.
2. 'General Synod 2013 – Saturday 8th June', *The Scottish Episcopal Church*, accessed on 19 April 2014: http://www.scotland.anglican.org/general-synod-2013-saturday-8th-june.
3. Avis (2005), p. 96.

in which they are set, bringing to the Church the needs and hopes of all the people. They are to work with their fellow members in searching out the poor and weak, the sick and lonely and those who are oppressed and powerless, reaching into the forgotten corners of the world, that the love of God may be made visible.

Deacons share in the pastoral ministry of the Church and in leading God's people in worship. They preach the word and bring the needs of the world before the Church in intercession. They accompany those searching for faith and bring them to baptism. They assist in administering the sacraments; they distribute communion and minister to the sick and housebound.

Deacons are to seek nourishment from the Scriptures; they are to study them with God's people, that the whole Church may be equipped to live out the gospel in the world. They are to be faithful in prayer, expectant and watchful for the signs of God's presence, as he reveals his kingdom among us.[1]

The keynote of this description of diaconal ministry, which is founded ultimately on the words of the 1550 Ordinal, is the collaborative nature of the deacon's work, both with the priest and the laity. The 2004 Ordinal does not single out any task as exclusively that of the deacon, thereby conferring on the deacon a holistic and representative rather than functional ministry. As Avis summarises it, 'Deacons have an assisting, not a presiding, ministry. . . . They assist the priest and the bishop. They have a sacramental ministry, but not a presidential one'.[2] Nevertheless, the ordination prayer continues to emphasise a servant ministry for deacons: 'And now we give you thanks that you have called these your servants, whom we ordain in your name, to share as deacons in the ministry of the gospel of Christ, who came not to be served but to serve, and to give his life as a ransom for many'. The Ordinal of *Common Worship* represents a cautious adoption of a broader conception of the diaconate, derived from Collins's work, but without abandoning entirely the earlier emphasis on the diaconate as a ministry of service.

---

1. This and subsequent quotations from the Ordinal of Common Worship are taken from the online version of the text, 'Common Worship: Ordination Services', *The Church of England,* accessed on 30 July 2013: http://www.churchofengland.org/prayer-worship/worship/texts/ordinal.aspx.
2. Avis (2005), p. 103.

## The canonical position of deacons

It is a historical accident that the ministry of deacons is more fully regulated by canon in the ECUSA and the Anglican churches of Brazil, Puerto Rico, Mexico, the Philippines, the West Indies and South India than it is in the Church of England. Because distinctive deacons have long existed in these former colonial churches, the role of deacons was carefully defined, and deacons were usually placed under the authority of incumbent priests.[1] In England, by contrast, there is very little Canon Law governing the ministry of deacons. This has the consequence that the limits of what deacons can and cannot do in the Church of England are not always clearly defined. In almost every case, the canons of the Church of England include deacons in their provisions through the use of the inclusive term 'clerk in holy orders'.

It has not been possible for deacons to hold benefices since 1661, but the question of whether a deacon can be 'in charge' of a parish or benefice is more controversial. A deacon can certainly be the minister of a proprietary chapel, and may therefore be 'in charge' of such a chapel. It is also possible for the charge of a parish to fall to a curate (who may not be in priest's orders) as a result of the withdrawal of an incumbent. However, Lynne Leeder argued in 1991 that this does not constitute legal grounds for the existence of 'deacons in charge'.[2] Yet in practical terms, many deacons were already taking on such roles by 1991. It is unclear whether a deacon could be a team vicar within a team ministry.

As noted in Chapter 4 above, deacons may be admitted as residentiary canons of cathedral churches, but the same canon implicitly forbids deacons from pronouncing absolution. The highest ecclesiastical office that a deacon may hold is that of a canon or rural dean; archdeacons and deans of cathedral churches must be priests. Apart from the fact that deacons are forbidden to preside at Holy Communion and (more controversially) to pronounce absolution, there are restrictions on the solemnisation of marriages by deacons. According to guidelines issued jointly by the Archbishops of Canterbury and York and appended to the canons, the ordinary minister of marriage should be a priest or bishop. However, 'A deacon may officiate at a marriage only if the consent of the incumbent and/or minister is first given'. Even if the officiating minister is a deacon, 'The authorized services should be

1. Doe, N., *Canon Law in the Anglican Communion: A Worldwide Perspective* (Clarendon Press: Oxford, 1998), pp. 145-6.
2. Leeder (1991), p. 127.

used without variation', including the blessing of the congregation. If a priest or bishop is present, he or she should perform the blessing. Furthermore, 'In the first year following ordination as deacon . . . a deacon should rarely, if ever, solemnize a marriage and should only do so for exceptional reasons', since training for the solemnisation of marriages usually takes place in the year after ordination.[1]

On the other hand, the guidelines allow that a deacon may be permitted to perform the blessing of the rings, even if a priest is present. This suggests that deacons may canonically bless individual objects, whilst a blessing of the congregation by a deacon (although possible) is irregular. This chimes with the official teaching of the Roman Catholic Church, according to which deacons may administer the sacramentals of the church (such as blessings) to individuals, but not to congregations. In 1991, a collection of forms of service approved by the House of Bishops, *Ministry at the Time of Death*, permitted 'a deacon authorized for this ministry' to anoint the sick or dying with oil consecrated by a bishop or priest, even though the Canons make clear that a priest is the minister of anointing.[2] However, in Andrew Burnham's view, the provision in *Ministry at the Time of Death* amounts to an official interpretation of this canon in favour of deacons.[3] Deacons have not been permitted to perform exorcisms (another class of sacramental) in the Roman Catholic Church since the revision of Canon Law in 1917. In the Church of England, there is no such restriction on exorcism and deliverance ministry by deacons, but Canon 72 of the Canons of 1604 (which stipulates that a specific licence must be obtained from the bishop for such an extraordinary rite) may be presumed to apply.

Even for a church that is renowned for its indecisiveness, for the Church of England to have vacillated on the question of deacons for 175 years is a remarkable, if dubious, achievement. Only a tiny number of the laity who regularly attend church are aware of the existence of distinctive deacons, and those that are may be largely confined to churches that experience the ministry of a deacon directly. It seems probable that even a large number of the clergy are unaware of the existence of lifelong deacons, unless they happen to have read *The Mission and Ministry of the Whole Church*. Whatever view one takes on the question, it is clear that a meaningful debate on the future of lifelong deacons will never take place while discussion of the issue remains confined to official church reports and the work of academics.

1. *Canons*, p. 201.
2. *Canons*, p. 58.
3. Burnham (1991), pp. 72-3.

# Conclusion

Deacons, in one form or another, are set to remain in the Church of England. It seems unlikely that the idea that deacons should be abolished altogether, which last surfaced in General Synod in the 1970s, will return in the near future; the same can be said of the idea of direct ordination to the diaconate or priesthood. The affirmation of belief in the threefold order of bishops, priests and deacons that is part of the Declaration of Assent, together with the status of the *Book of Common Prayer* and the Ordinal as doctrinal and liturgical norms, mean that a blanket abolition of the diaconate in favour of direct ordination to the priesthood would strike at the roots of Anglican tradition. The contemporary debate on the diaconate in the Church of England is not about whether the diaconate should exist or not, but about the *form* in which it should exist. Is it necessary or desirable that vocations should be encouraged to a distinctive diaconate, or should the existing distinctive deacons be allowed to fade away, as deaconesses have been since the late 1980s, since the ordination of distinctive deacons was a failed experiment? To conclude this book, I shall draw on the evidence presented within it to argue the cases both for the discontinuation of the distinctive diaconate and for its enlargement.

## The case against distinctive deacons

The case against distinctive deacons is really the case *for* transitional deacons. To expect individuals to remain in deacon's orders for their entire lives is unrealistic in the contemporary Church of England. In the same way that many vocations to the priesthood come from amongst former Readers, so it is not possible for an individual to be certain that a vocation to the diaconate will not evolve into a vocation to the priesthood. Furthermore, the church has a duty to serve the world as it is, rather than the world as the church would like it to be.

The institution of lifelong deacons may date back centuries, but that does not mean that it is suited to the modern world. Richard Hooker argued that the diaconate must adapt to suit the times, and one way in which the diaconate has adapted in the twentieth century has been by becoming almost exclusively transitional in character.

To suggest that there is no need for a distinctive diaconate does not presuppose that the transitional diaconate, in the form in which it exists today, is perfect. Indeed, as Paul Avis has suggested, it may be appropriate for a much greater emphasis to be given to the 'diaconal' nature of curacies, with curates spending two or three years in deacon's orders alone, rather than the one year that is now normative. The historical evidence for long-term deacons presented in this book makes the mechanical one-year interval now expected of clergy seem inappropriate. It seems odd that curates in the supposedly decadent eighteenth century spent far longer in deacon's orders than deacons in the 'mission-shaped' twenty-first century. While the interval of one year is specified in the Ordinal, the idea of curates spending *exactly* a year in deacon's orders is a recent innovation adopted in the twentieth century, partly as a result of the concentration of both diaconal and priestly ordinations at Petertide. To expect an ordinand to have explored their diaconal ministry after a calendar year is just as absurd as expecting someone to discern their vocation to ministry in a set time, and if individuals feel that they need to remain in deacon's orders for longer than one year, they should surely be given that opportunity.

In addition to transitional and distinctive deacons, the other group of deacons in the church are clergy who are also ordained priest (and in some cases bishop) whose ongoing diaconal character has been emphasised in recent church documents. The institution of distinctive deacons detracts from attempts to foster the diaconal ministry of priests who are also deacons, creating the impression that diaconal ministry is somehow the exclusive domain of the distinctive deacon. The argument that there must be distinctive deacons to 'represent' the diaconate, or to provide a 'focus' for diaconal ministry, denigrates the diaconal ministry and diaconal character of other ordained ministers.

It is already the practice of priests to act as 'liturgical deacons' in circumstances of concelebration of the eucharist, especially when a bishop is present. One possibility for the future, little discussed, is that some priests might choose to take this identification with their diaconal character beyond the liturgy and into their everyday ministry. This is something that occasionally happens in the

Methodist Church, when presbyters choose to be deacons. Some priests in the Church of England, whose primary role is already diaconal, might choose to exercise their diaconal functions more or less permanently. If ordination really is cumulative, and diaconal ministry is the foundation for all ministry, there is no reason in theory why a priest might not choose to define him or herself primarily as a deacon, and revert to priestly ministry if the need for it should arise. Retired bishops cease to exercise their episcopal ministry and often take on priestly roles, such as chaplain and assistant curate; therefore there is no reason why some priests should not cease to exercise their priestly ministry and become full-time deacons. Such an arrangement would proclaim the equality of priestly and diaconal ministry far more effectively than the ordination of distinctive deacons.

Whilst a greater emphasis on the significance of the transitional diaconate is only right, encouraging individuals to discern vocations to the distinctive diaconate is inappropriate. The very existence of a distinctive diaconate undermines the status of transitional deacons – who make up the vast majority of members of the order of deacons at any one time – as 'real' deacons. The institution of lifelong deacons is a relic of a church divided by class and gender that is best forgotten, and although deacons existed in the Church of England before the 1990s, they existed only for negative reasons. Men remained in deacon's orders because they were considered insufficiently well-educated to proceed to priest's orders, or because they were of a lower social status than other clergy. Women remained in deacon's orders in the 1980s because the church was not prepared to ordain them as priests.

Whatever its significance in the early church, the diaconate in the Church of England has only ever been a form of 'second-class' ministry in a status-obsessed church. The diaconate's relegation to a form of probation for priesthood is to be welcomed in a church that ought to strive to be more egalitarian. The revival of the distinctive diaconate has never taken hold in the Church of England, in spite of many attempts at revival, and the church should attend to that failure. Distinctive deacons represent a failed experiment in ministry, and their tiny numbers and minimal growth rate testify to that fact. The existence of distinctive deacons only serves to handicap the diaconal ministry of others, whether bishops, priests or lay people, by attempting to make an aspect of the church that belongs equally to all its members the particular domain of one category of ministers.

The point that the renewal of the diaconate undermines the ministry of the laity has been raised time and time again since the 1980s, both in England and other parts of the Anglican Communion. The revival of the diaconate comes primarily from the clergy themselves, and stems from a combination of mimicry of the Roman Catholic Church and a sense that the diaconate is 'fashionable' and 'ecumenical'. However, the Church of England has evolved non-priestly ministries of its own, and it is impossible to impose a new level of clericalisation on the church without detracting from lay ministries, particularly that of Readers, but also the ministry of lay workers and youth workers. Time and time again, experience has demonstrated that a clear definition of the ministerial role of Reader is impossible, and in parishes throughout the country, Readers frequently take on roles that go far beyond their original preaching and teaching ministry. Readers and other lay people are often the glue that keeps local churches together, especially in rural areas where ministers are few and far between. The renewal of the diaconate would be a retrograde step, an inappropriate clericalisation and an affront to the work carried out by Readers.

## The case for distinctive deacons

The case for a revival of the diaconate put forth in documents such as *For Such a Time as This* and *The Mission and Ministry of the Whole Church* is not especially persuasive to individuals unfamiliar with the theology of the diaconate. Furthermore, church insiders often find it hard to appreciate the sheer depth of the laity's indifference to official church documents, many of whom do not know or care what the General Synod is, quite apart from being familiar with the reports prepared for it. Admittedly, reports such as *For Such a Time as This* and *The Mission and the Ministry of the Whole Church* were not written with a mass readership in mind, and it could be argued that their value lies in encapsulating 'the mind of the church' on the issue. However, it is surely legitimate to ask whether a report that is incomprehensible to the average layperson can possibly express the mind of the church.

An honest advocate of deacons in the Church of England must acknowledge that any ministry that could be done by deacons is currently undertaken by priests and lay people, often extremely effectively. Arguing for the distinctive diaconate in the Church of England is difficult, because most people in the church have never experienced it; it is almost like trying to explain the usefulness of money to a society that has only ever experienced a barter economy. The Church of England has adapted itself to a deaconless existence. Of course it seems that deacons are not needed – because the church has evolved so as not to need them. Deacons can therefore appear like an ecclesiological luxury, something worthy and commendable but hardly necessary to the church's survival. Unless people have direct experience of something in their own parish, it can easily seem exotic and alien.

Honesty is important in advancing a successful case for the revival of the distinctive diaconate, because the Church of England is inured to effusive bluster about the amazing possibilities offered by a renewed distinctive diaconate and the possible ministries of putative deacons. Unfashionable though it may seem, proponents of the diaconate must acknowledge that the most compelling case for the existence of a diaconate to which men and women are specifically called will always be historical. The Church of England proclaims a threefold order of ministry, and the fact that deacons have no permanent, independent existence in the church will therefore always raise questions about the Church of England's faithfulness to its own formularies and the tradition of the universal church. As Robert Hannaford noted, deacons are an intrinsic part of the 'apostolic college'. In a church that claims to be Catholic and reformed, logic surely dictates that vestigial remnants of earlier practices should either be discarded in their entirety, or revived in a form appropriate for the present time. The diaconate is one such vestigial remnant. Since the Church of England has never discarded the diaconate, and commitment to the threefold order of bishops, priests and deacons is a relatively uncontroversial and basic part of the church's patrimony, it remains incumbent on the church to revive the diaconate in more than a truncated form.

Related to the fact that the case for the diaconate is historical is the fact that the diaconate may matter more to some Anglicans than others. Mike Smith of Reform's suggestion that the distinctive diaconate should be revived for women is the exception, and evangelical churches are generally far less aware of the diaconate than those in the sacramental or Catholic tradition. The distinction between a deacon and Reader is all but invisible in churches that are liturgically minimalist and do not lay much stress on the theology of orders. It is no accident that the two English dioceses in which distinctive deacons are most numerous, Chichester and London, are renowned for their Anglo-Catholic tradition. Supporting the ordination of distinctive deacons means affirming the intrinsic value of ordination itself, which may prove offensive to some Readers and to certain shades of theological opinion within Anglicanism.

When Paul Avis notes that the ordination of deacons makes them ministers of the universal church, and not just authorised ministers of the Church of England, he highlights an important feature of the distinctive diaconate in the Church of England today, which is its ecumenical and international outlook. Distinctive deacons do not see themselves primarily as a marginalised category of ministry within the Church of England, but as a growing category of ministry within the church as a whole. They feel they have as much, if not more, in common with Roman Catholic and Methodist deacons as they do with priests in their own church. The outward-looking and ecumenical character of Anglican distinctive deacons in England is one demonstration of their authenticity and faithfulness to diaconal ministry.

A further issue on which an honest discussion needs to take place concerns how deacons relate to existing structures of authority. It was commonly assumed in the past that deacons are under the authority of the parish priest, and to some extent this is implied in the Ordinal. This was clearly not the case in the early church, however, in which deacons were equal in status to presbyters and enjoyed a special relationship with the bishop. J.M. Barnett's rhetoric of the diaconate as a 'full and equal order', which was widely adopted in the 1980s, drew on this historical analysis of early deacons, but, as Martyn Percy has pointed out, Barnett failed to take account of the possibility that the church's structures of ministry undergo a process of gradual evolution.[1] Barnett's egalitarian rhetoric may seem very appealing, but in the case of deacons, it is clear from the historical record that in the Church of England they have always been ministers under the authority of priests. The late twentieth-century's anxiety about status-specific language led the phrase 'this inferior office' to be removed from the *ASB* Ordinal, but the word 'inferior' does not necessarily imply 'despised'. 'Inferior' may mean 'under authority' or 'under obedience', and while the monastic idea of 'holy obedience' may not be a fashionable one in the contemporary church, it is one of the ancient foundations of the church's effective functioning. If, as Collins suggests, deacons are to be individuals on a mission with an urgent message for the world, they must also be people under authority. It is impractical and unrealistic to insist that all deacons will be the equals of priests, under the authority of bishops; some will inevitably

---

1.  Percy (2006), pp. 19-20.

find themselves under the authority of parish priests. In the twenty-first century's mixed economy of ministry, in which non-stipendiary priests and Ordained Local Ministers (usually priests) are subordinate to incumbents and priests-in-charge, it would seem perverse for deacons to consider themselves outside of incumbents' authority.

Distinctive and transitional deacons need to acknowledge that they are, indeed, 'inferior' ministers. This should be a liberating realisation, as it will lead to deacons fulfilling their own destiny rather than trying to be like other ministers. On the other hand, it is important that deacons do not become victims of the whims of an incumbent. As clerks in holy orders and ordained ministers, deacons exercise their sacred functions as of right, which is a crucial difference between deacons and Readers. The Chichester Report's suggestion that stipendiary deacons should be the norm is wildly unrealistic, not just because most dioceses lack the resources to employ deacons but because all dioceses would prioritise paying for priests over deacons. The church should not have the characteristics of a 'supply and demand' economy, but all too often the allocation of stipendiary clergy in deanery pastoral plans is determined by congregational demands for a priest to celebrate Holy Communion as often as possible. This preoccupation with the weekly eucharist is a very recent innovation and not part of historic Anglican tradition, and therefore the church should not be brow-beaten into allocating all resources to the employment of ordained priests. However, there is also a theological case for all deacons to be non-stipendiary by definition. If the deacon is to be a bridge or link between the church and the world, representing the needs of the laity to the church, then there is a strong argument for most deacons to be in secular employment.

A feature of church life in the twenty-first century is the increasingly 'episcopal' ministry undertaken by incumbents, in the sense that most incumbents now have oversight of a number of parishes and are obliged to delegate the everyday running of local churches to lay leaders, such as Readers and churchwardens. At the same time, priests are often expected to be the focus of everything. Without distinctive deacons, priests are forced to take on an unmanageable range of tasks and ministries, and laypeople are forced to take on roles of spiritual leadership that they execute admirably, but may never have signed up for. Other priests in the benefice often act primarily as stand-in presidents at Holy Communion, rather than shouldering part of the incumbent's administrative burden. Fashionable talk of the 'priesthood of all believers' and the ministry of all the baptised obscures the fact that foisting roles on laypeople can give outsiders the impression that the church undervalues those roles. Ordination may be 'clericalisation', but it is also a form of official recognition historically practised by churches with Catholic order.

The twentieth century saw an ever increasing emphasis on the parish service of Holy Communion on a Sunday as the centre and focus of church life, and this contributed to the sense that deacons were redundant. However, this focus implies that 'the church' is co-extensive with 'the congregation', an outdated ecclesiological assumption that is increasingly being questioned. As the worshipping community dwindles as a percentage of the parish community in many places, the church risks losing its credibility and its role in the life of the community if it defines itself primarily as a 'chaplaincy to churchgoers'. Consequently, many churches in the second decade of the twenty-first century are shifting their time and resources away from Sunday worship and towards other activities during the week. Churches may provide café spaces and run food banks, host rural post offices or co-ordinate parish nursing. Archbishop Justin Welby has even called upon local churches to set up credit unions to provide an alternative to pay-day lenders. The future of the church lies in serving the entire community and not just in serving the spiritual needs of congregations, those who happen to turn up to church.

In this environment, deacons are more keenly needed than they have ever been. It is by no means *necessary* that the church's outreach into the world should be put in the hands of ordained ministers, but if the church were to do this, it would send a message that such outreach is not merely a bolt-on to Sunday worship, but something *for which the church exists*. Furthermore, it would make clear that the church's service to the world is sacramental, and break down the division between work and worship. There is a place in the contemporary church for clergy whose primary role is to administer church-based projects in the community rather than leading worship and conducting occasional offices in the traditional way. The church may expect priests to do all of this – the chaplaincy to churchgoers and the outreach to the unchurched – but if it does so, it expects too much of them and stretches the boundaries of priestly ministry so far that the role of the priest becomes indefinably broad. Alternatively, the church may pass all of the responsibility to Readers, Authorised Lay Ministers and lay workers, leaving a 'rump' of clergy to serve the church's sacramental functions. Yet both of these possible futures seem ecclesiologically and spiritually impoverished in the light of the church's ancient practice of ordaining fully authorised agents of the church in the world: deacons.

# *Appendix A*

## Cambridge alumni ordained deacon
## 1560-1642, Abbes-Ayscough

(from John Venn, *Alumni Cantabrigienses*,
digitised as the ACAD Database[1])

| Name | Ordained deacon | Ordained priest | Interval between ordinations (days) |
|---|---|---|---|
| Abbes, Christopher | 30 July 1580 | - | - |
| Abbott, Robert | 11 June 1609 | 24 September 1609 | 105 |
| Abell, John | 17 December 1615 | 19 September 1624 | 3561 |
| Abington, John | 8 March 1593 | - | - |
| Abraham, Thomas | 16 September 1584 | 16 September 1584 | 0.5 |
| Acrodd | [22 May] 1584 | 22 May 1586 | 730 |
| Acroyde, Anthony | 7 June 1623 | 8 June 1623 | 1 |
| Acrod, Roger | 29 April 1576 | 12 August 1576 | 105 |
| Acworth, William | 30 November 1564 | - | - |
| Adams, Alexander | 5 October 1577 | 6 October 1577 | 1 |
| Adams, George | 19 March 1609 | - | - |
| Adam, Michael | 24 August 1598 | 25 August 1598 | 1 |
| Adams, Thomas | 23 September 1604 | 23 September 1604 | 0.5 |
| Adams, Thomas | 20 September 1628 | - | - |

---

1. All dates are Old Style, with the year taken to begin on 1 January throughout. Where the day of the month on which an ordination took place is unknown, I have inserted the first day of the month. Where both the day and month are unknown, I have assumed that exactly a year elapsed between diaconal and priestly ordination. '0.5' indicates that the candidate was ordained deacon and priest on the same day.

| Name | Ordained deacon | Ordained priest | Interval between ordinations (days) |
|---|---|---|---|
| Adams, Thomas | 25 September 1636 | 24 September 1637 | 729 |
| Adamson, Richard | 29 September 1570 | 29 September 1570 | 0.5 |
| Adamson, William | 31 March 1588 | 31 March 1588 | 0.5 |
| Addison, Philip | 19 June 1614 | 25 September 1614 | 98 |
| Adlam, John | 8 December 1642 | - | - |
| Adlard, Michael | Sept. 25, 1642 | - | - |
| Adrian, Bartholomew | 31 May 1618 | 1 June 1618 | 1 |
| Agas, Anthony | 24 September 1609 | - | - |
| Aggas, Edward | 29 September 1604 | 21 September 1607 | 1087 |
| Agmondesham, Philip | 20 September 1586 | 20 September 1586 | 0.5 |
| Ailesbury, William | December 1632 | - | - |
| Ainsworth, George | 3 December 1578 | [3 December] 1579 | 365 |
| Ainsworth, Robert | 31 May 1618 | 20 September 1618 | 113 |
| Ainsworth, Thomas | 24 September 1626 | 24 September 1626 | 0.5 |
| Alchon, Edward | 24 February 1585 | - | - |
| Alcock, John | 17 December 1620 | 31 May 1629 | - |
| Alcock, Robert | 23 August 1583 | - | - |
| Alcock, Thomas | 19 September 1619 | 20 September 1619 | 1 |
| Alderman, Francis | 22 December 1639 | - | - |
| Aldred, Benjamin | 15 October 1618 | 16 October 1618 | 1 |
| Aldrich, James | 23 December 1632 | 24 May 1635 | 546 |
| Aldridge, Thomas | 21 December 1568 | 22 April 1570 | 487 |
| Aldridge, Thomas | 22 December 1605 | 22 December 1605 | 0.5 |
| Aldus, William | 20 September 1628 | - | - |
| Aldus, William | 22 September 1633 | - | - |
| Alford, Robert | 29 July 1624 | 30 July 1624 | 1 |
| Allaley, James | 19 August 1585 | - | - |
| Allanson, Thomas | 17 February 1611 | - | - |

| Name | Ordained deacon | Ordained priest | Interval between ordinations (days) |
|---|---|---|---|
| Allen, Alexander | 21 September 1628 | 22 September 1628 | 1 |
| Allen, Francis | 2 December 1599 | 2 December 1599 | 0.5 |
| Alleyn, Giles | 20 December 1612 | 20 December 1612 | 0.5 |
| Allen, John | 20 September 1618 | 21 September 1618 | 1 |
| Allen, John | 19 September 1619 | 20 September 1619 | 1 |
| Allen, John | 20 September 1620 | - | - |
| Allen, John | 16 June 1633 | - | - |
| Allen, Jonathan | 22 May 1630 | 23 May 1630 | 1 |
| Allen, Judas | 22 February 1624 | 23 February 1624 | 1 |
| Allen, Peter | 26 May 1616 | 26 May 1616 | 0.5 |
| Allen, Robert | 9 June 1639 | - | - |
| Allen, Thomas | 24 February 1605 | - | - |
| Allen, Thomas | 11 June 1620 | 12 June 1620 | 1 |
| Allen, William | 26 November 1594 | 26 November 1594 | 0.5 |
| Allen, William | 2 November 1589 | 2 November 1589 | 0.5 |
| Allen, William | 28 February 1613 | 30 May 1613 | 92 |
| Allens, John | 20 December 1607 | - | - |
| Allenson, John | 22 May 1581 | - | - |
| Allenson, William | 19 September 1619 | - | - |
| Allerton, John | 11 May 1620 | - | - |
| Allott, John | 15 May 1625 | 16 May 1625 | 1 |
| Aliot, Thomas | 8 June 1628 | - | - |
| Almond, George | 20 September 1640 | 25 April 1643 | 916 |
| Alpinas, Christian | 19 December 1563 | - | - |
| Alsopp, George | 31 May 1618 | 1 June 1618 | 1 |
| Alston, Henry | 25 March 1601 | - | - |
| Alvey, Edward | 26 May 1616 | 15 June 1617 | 384 |
| Ambrose, Daniel | 15 May 1625 | 16 May 1625 | 1 |
| Ambrose, Edward | 25 February 1616 | 25 February 1616 | 0.5 |

| Name | Ordained deacon | Ordained priest | Interval between ordinations (days) |
|---|---|---|---|
| Americke, William | 9 March 1628 | 10 March 1628 | 1 |
| Amies, Peter | 6 April 1600 | - | - |
| Amyh, Henry | 18 June 1584 | - | - |
| Anderson, Alexander | [29 March] 1577 | 29 March 1578 | 365 |
| Anderson, John | 24 December 1609 | - | - |
| Andrew, Bartholomew | 6 January 1574 | 21 December 1576 | 1079 |
| Andrews, Bartimeus | 9 September 1604 | 23 September 1604 | 14 |
| Andrews, Edward | 20 March 1614 | 21 March 1614 | 1 |
| Andrewes, Roger | 14 November 1602 | 14 November 1602 | 0.5 |
| Andrews, William | 19 September 1602 | 19 September 1602 | 0.5 |
| Anger, Ambrose | 15 August 1624 | 16 August 1624 | 1 |
| Angier, Edward | 9 March 1628 | 10 March 1628 | 1 |
| Ansell, Reginald | 6 April 1623 | - | - |
| Anstey, Stephen | 18 December 1641 | 8 December 1642 | 355 |
| Anthony, Charles | 16 September 1636 | 16 September 1636 | 0.5 |
| Anthony, John | [1] March 1562 | - | - |
| Anton, Robert | 23 December 1610 | 31 May 1618 | 2714 |
| Appleyard, Thomas | 24 November 1608 | 25 November 1608 | 0.5 |
| Archer, John | 21 December 1569 | 21 December 1569 | 0.5 |
| Archer, Thomas | 24 September 1585 | 24 September 1585 | 0.5 |
| Archer, Thomas | [17] March 1639 | 17 October 1641 | 944 |
| Archer, Thomas | 18 December 1641 | 22 February 1646 | 1526 |
| Archer, Timothy | 18 December 1641 | - | - |
| Arme, John | 12 November 1629 | 13 November 1629 | 1 |
| Arme, William | 16 September 1597 | 17 September 1597 | 1 |
| Armitage, Anthony | 15 July 1593 | 15 July 1593 | 0.5 |
| Armitage, John | 15 June 1606 | 31 May 1607 | 350 |

| Name | Ordained deacon | Ordained priest | Interval between ordinations (days) |
|------|-----------------|-----------------|-------------------------------------|
| Armitage, William | 21 December 1581 | 21 December 1582 | 365 |
| Armitsted, William | 22 December 1605 | 22 December 1605 | 0.5 |
| Armstrong, John | 15 May 1577 | 25 March 1578 | 314 |
| Arnall, Henry | 27 February 1632 | 23 September 1632 | 208 |
| Arrowsmith, John | 22 February 1624 | 22 February 1624 | 0.5 |
| Arthur, Thomas | 1 June 1634 | 21 September 1634 | 113 |
| Arwin, John | March 1610 | - | - |
| Arwin, Thomas | 21 September 1570 | - | - |
| Ashe, Richard | 1 March 1618 | 20 December 1618 | 295 |
| Ash, Simeon | 5 October 1619 | 6 October 1619 | 1 |
| Ashbold, William | 23 March 1567 | 27 September 1567 | 188 |
| Ashborne, Alexander | 18 February 1638 | 10 March 1639 | 385 |
| Ashburne, Francis | 2 June 1570 | - | - |
| Ashbourne, John | 24 April 1630 | - | - |
| Ashley, John | 23 May 1624 | 20 May 1627 | 1092 |
| Ashton, Abdias | 8 March 1591 | 8 March 1591 | 0.5 |
| Ashton, Anthony | 8 March 1591 | 8 March 1591 | 0.5 |
| Ashton, Edmund | 22 December 1611 | 22 December 1611 | 0.5 |
| Ashton, John | 7 July 1560 | 24 August 1560 | 48 |
| Ashton, Peter | 18 September 1613 | 19 September 1613 | 1 |
| Ashton, Walter | 4 March 1610 | - | - |
| Aspden, Miles | 7 December 1609 | - | - |
| Aspden, Thomas | 19 September 1624 | - | - |
| Aspinall, James | 30 November 1565 | 9 March 1566 | 100 |
| Astell, John | 21 September 1634 | 20 September 1635 | 364 |
| Atkinson, Edward | 30 September 1612 | 20 December 1612 | 82 |
| Atkinson, Edward | 2 December 1616 | 21 February 1619 | 811 |
| Atkinson, John | [1] September 1620 | [1] June 1626 | 2099 |

| Name | Ordained deacon | Ordained priest | Interval between ordinations (days) |
| --- | --- | --- | --- |
| Atkinson, Peter | 11 June 1609 | - | - |
| Atkinson, Thomas | 11 June 1609 | 11 June 1609 | 0.5 |
| Atkinson, Thomas | 19 May 1583 | 7 June 1584 | 384 |
| Atkinson, Thomas | 8 June 1628 | - | - |
| Atterbie, Thomas | 19 March 1578 | 27 October 1580 | 952 |
| Attersall, William | 6 October 1588 | 6 October 1588 | 0.5 |
| Attersall, William | 24 December 1615 | 26 May 1616 | 153 |
| Auburne, Matthew | 19 September 1630 | 23 September 1632 | 734 |
| Auder, William | 12 March 1609 | 12 March 1609 | 0.5 |
| Audley, John | [1] September 1627 | [1] September 1627 | 0.5 |
| Audley, John | 27 September 1629 | 28 September 1629 | 1 |
| Audley, Lewis | 28 December 1641 | - | - |
| Audley, Robert | 24 September 1620 | 25 September 1620 | 1 |
| Audsley, Roger | 19 September 1624 | 13 March 1625 | 175 |
| Aumont, Robert | 22 June 1596 | 22 June 1596 | 0.5 |
| Austin, Francis | 27 May 1599 | 27 May 1599 | 0.5 |
| Austin, Francis | 17 July 1609 | 24 September 1609 | 69 |
| Austin, Robert | 23 May 1624 | 23 May 1624 | 0.5 |
| Averey, Richard | 3 January 1626 | 4 January 1626 | 1 |
| Aylmer, John | 15 May 1617 | 16 May 1617 | 1 |
| Aylmer, John | 4 June 1626 | 4 June 1626 | 0.5 |
| Ailmer, Theophilus | 12 October 1583 | - | - |
| Ailmer, Theophilus | 15 May 1617 | 16 May 1617 | 1 |
| Aylward, Thomas | 10 November 1560 | 20 December 1560 | 40 |
| Ayrie, James | 26 May 1616 | 15 September 1616 | 82 |
| Ayscough, Henry | [1] April 1595 | - | - |
| Ayscough, Henry | 18 December 1641 | - | - |
| Ayscough, Thomas | 11 June 1620 | - | - |

# Appendix B

## Cambridge alumni ordained deacon 1660-1758, Abbott-Ayscough

(from John Venn, *Alumni Cantabrigienses*,
digitised as the ACAD Database[1])

| Name | Ordained deacon | Ordained priest | Interval between ordinations (days) |
|---|---|---|---|
| Abbott, Edward | [1] June 1699 | - | - |
| Abbott, Edward | 1 March 1725 | - | - |
| Abbott, Henry | 18 September 1703 | - | - |
| Abbott, John | 22 September 1711 | 15 June 1712 | 264 |
| Abbott, John | 15 June 1712 | 23 December 1716 | 1618 |
| Abbott, Nicholas | 7 June 1696 | 30 May 1697 | 356 |
| Abbot, William | 13 June 1756 | 26 December 1757 | 408 |
| Abdy, Stotherd | 22 December 1750 | 24 December 1752 | 721* |
| Abell, John | 26 May 1678 | 29 May 1681 | 3 |
| Abell, William | 2 June 1710 | 11 June 1713 | 374 |
| Abson, Samuel | 13 June 1742 | 19 February 1744 | 616 |

1. All dates before 14 September 1752 are Old Style, and those after are New Style, with the year taken to begin on 1 January throughout. I have adjusted for the eleven days eliminated from the calendar between 2 and 14 September 1752 by the adoption of the Gregorian Calendar (marked *). Where the day of the month on which an ordination took place is unknown, I have inserted the first day of the month. Where both the day and month are unknown, I have assumed that exactly a year elapsed between diaconal and priestly ordination. '0.5' indicates that a candidate was ordained deacon and priest on the same day.

| Name | Ordained deacon | Ordained priest | Interval between ordinations (days) |
| --- | --- | --- | --- |
| Adams, George | 13 March 1720 | 23 September 1722 | 924 |
| Adams, George | 20 September 1741 | 29 May 1743 | 924 |
| Adams, Robert | 24 September 1664 | - | - |
| Adams, Samuel | 18 December 1669 | - | - |
| Adams, William | 24 September 1738 | [1] June 1740 | 616 |
| Adamson, James | 17 June 1753 | 22 December 1754 | 553 |
| Adamson, John | [7 February] 1666 | 7 February 1670 | 1460 |
| Adamson, Samuel | 16 March 1685 | - | - |
| Adamson, William | 12 July 1662 | 12 July 1662 | 0.5 |
| Adamson, William | 22 February 1730 | 14 March 1731 | 385 |
| Adcock, John | 22 September 1745 | 14 June 1747 | 630 |
| Addenbrooke, Benjamin | 22 September 1745 | 14 June 1747 | 630 |
| Addenbrooke, Nicholas | 2 March 1735 | 1 June 1735 | 91 |
| Addenbrooke, Samuel | 8 June 1707 | 19 December 1708 | 559 |
| Addenbrook, John | 12 June 1715 | 16 June 1717 | 734 |
| Addington, Charles | 23 May 1725 | 25 September 1726 | 490 |
| Addison, Leonard | 9 June 1723 | [1] March 1724 | 265 |
| Addison, Robert | 22 June 1718 | [1] September 1722 | 1166 |
| Adkin, William | 25 September 1737 | 2 March 1740 | 888 |
| Adrian, Richard | 21 September 1661 | 18 October 1662 | 392 |
| Affleck, Gilbert | 21 March 1736 | [1] July 1736 | 102 |
| Agar, Moses | 22 February 1741 | 29 May 1743 | 826 |
| Agar, William | 18 February 1733 | 21 December 1735 | 1036 |
| Aggas, Anthony | 24 September 1670 | - | - |
| Aggas, William | [1] June 1696 | [1] December 1697 | 549 |
| Ainsley, Ralph | 31 May 1702 | - | - |
| Ainsworth, Samuel | 5 July 1713 | 14 July 1717 | 1834 |

| Name | Ordained deacon | Ordained priest | Interval between ordinations (days) |
|---|---|---|---|
| Albright, William | 23 May 1714 | 17 March 1715 | 298 |
| Alcock, Christopher | 21 September 1755 | 19 September 1756 | 726 |
| Alcock, John | 15 October 1662 | - | - |
| Alcock, John | [1] December 1670 | [1] September 1672 | 608 |
| Alcock, Robert | 5 June 1737 | 21 December 1740 | 1294 |
| Alcock, Thomas | 24 December 1710 | 21 February 1714 | 1154 |
| Alders, James | December 1671 | - | - |
| Alders, James | 4 July 1710 | 24 September 1710 | 81 |
| Aldersey, Samuel | 6 March 1737 | 24 December 1738 | 658 |
| Alderson, Richard | 5 March 1710 | - | - |
| Alderson, Samuel | 20 December 1668 | - | - |
| Aldhouse, Stephen | 22 December 1700 | - | - |
| Aldrich, William | August 1756 | - | - |
| Aldwinckle, Thomas | 20 September 1674 | - | - |
| Alfounder, Robert | 23 September 1710 | - | - |
| Alexander, John | 24 December 1721 | [1] June 1723 | 493 |
| Alexander, John | 6 March 1748 | 23 September 1750 | 931 |
| Alexander, Joseph | 18 December 1675 | 4 August 1677 | 594 |
| Alexander, Joseph | [1] February 1719 | [1] June 1720 | 486 |
| Alexander, Maurice | [1] March 1709 | 24 September 1709 | 208 |
| Alexander, Thomas | June 1674 | - | - |
| Algor, Richard | January 1673 | - | - |
| Alanson, James | 23 December 1722 | 29 June 1723 | 188 |
| Allen, Charles | 5 June 1737 | 21 December 1740 | 929 |
| Allen, Cuthbert | 21 September 1673 | 28 September 1673 | 8 |
| Allen, Cuthbert | 19 September 1742 | 19 December 1742 | 90 |
| Allen, Edward | 15 July 1661 | 18 July 1661 | 3 |

| Name | Ordained deacon | Ordained priest | Interval between ordinations (days) |
|---|---|---|---|
| Allen, James | 16 June 1717 | 8 June 1718 | 357 |
| Allen, John | [1] December 1663 | 20 September 1667 | 1420 |
| Allen, John | 19 September 1674 | - | - |
| Allen, John | 25 September 1720 | - | - |
| Allen, John | 19 September 1725 | 19 December 1725 | 90 |
| Alleyne, Jonathan | [1] September 1722 | [1] December 1723 | 455 |
| Alleyne, Richard | 22 December 1728 | 22 December 1734 | 2190 |
| Allen, Thomas | 21 September 1673 | 28 September 1673 | 8 |
| Allen, Thomas | 30 May 1697 | 22 December 1700 | 1301 |
| Allen, Thomas | [1] February 1716 | [1] September 1717 | 578 |
| Alleyne, Thomas | 24 December 1727 | 17 March 1728 | 84 |
| Allen, Thomas Scargill | 21 September 1679 | - | - |
| Allen, William | 22 September 1700 | | - |
| Allen, William | 21 December 1718 | 4 June 1721 | 895 |
| Allen, William | September 1724 | 24 September 1727 | 1095 |
| Allen, William | 11 November 1750 | 23 December 1753 | 761* |
| Allenson, Allen | 18 March 1709 | 31 May 1713 | 1534 |
| Allenson, Gilbert | 23 September 1733 | 2 December 1734 | 404 |
| Allenson, Marmaduke | 1 June 1684 | - | - |
| Allgood, Bartholomew | 23 September 1676 | [23] September 1677 | 365 |
| Allgood, James | 21 September 1701 | 12 April 1702 | 203 |
| Allison, William | 23 February 1745 | 20 December 1747 | 1030 |
| Allistone, Matthew | [1] December 1663 | [1] June 1664 | 152 |
| Allix, John Peter | 16 May 1705 | 19 May 1706 | 367 |
| Allott, James | 21 September 1746 | - | - |
| Allott, Robert | 19 June 1709 | 18 December 1709 | 192 |
| Allott, Robert | 25 April 1716 | 27 May 1716 | 33 |

| Name | Ordained deacon | Ordained priest | Interval between ordinations (days) |
|---|---|---|---|
| Allsopp, John | May 1668 | May 1670 | 730 |
| Alsop, John | 20 December 1691 | 20 December 1696 | 1825 |
| Alsop, Thomas | 7 August 1662 | [1] November 1662 | 86 |
| Alston, Samuel | [1] March 1739 | [1] February 1741 | 699 |
| Alston, William | [1] July 1712 | [1] December 1717 | 1979 |
| Alt, Just | 24 April 1758 | 21 May 1758 | 28 |
| Altham, James | 31 May 1724 | 5 June 1726 | 735 |
| Alvis, Andrew | 23 December 1733 | 24 December 1738 | 1824 |
| Ames, Charles | [1] July 1727 | [1] September 1728 | 428 |
| Amyas, Francis | 10 June 1682 | 25 May 1684 | 714 |
| Amyas, John | 22 September 1678 | 27 February 1681 | 523 |
| Amyas, John | May 1706 | - | - |
| Amy, John | 25 May 1694 | - | - |
| Amy, John | 21 December 1718 | 20 December 1719 | 364 |
| Amos, William | [1] July 1754 | 14 March 1756 | 622 |
| Anderson, Henry | [1] September 1662 | 13 June 1663 | 286 |
| Anderson, Robert | 23 December 1660 | 23 December 1660 | 0.5 |
| Anderson, William | 29 May 1743 | - | - |
| Andrew, John | 21 May 1665 | - | - |
| Andrews, James | [1] February 1727 | [1] June 1728 | 486 |
| Andrewes, John | 27 February 1670 | 27 February 1670 | 0.5 |
| Andrews, John | 24 September 1699 | 22 September 1700 | 363 |
| Andrews, Robert | [1] March 1726 | - | - |
| Andrewes, Thomas | 15 June 1712 | 20 December 1713 | 553 |
| Andrews, William | 22 September 1706 | - | - |
| Andrews, William | 27 May 1716 | - | - |
| Angier, George | 21 June 1699 | 21 February 1704 | 1705 |
| Angier, John | 6 February 1727 | - | - |
| Angier, Thomas | 3 June 1683 | 25 May 1684 | 356 |

| Name | Ordained deacon | Ordained priest | Interval between ordinations (days) |
| --- | --- | --- | --- |
| Annesley, Martin | 5 June 1726 | 10 July 1726 | 35 |
| Ansell, John | 18 September 1669 | 22 September 1672 | 1091 |
| Anstey, Christopher | 5 March 1732 | 29 June 1734 | 846 |
| Antrobus, George | 21 September 1661 | 21 September 1661 | 0.5 |
| Antrobus, William | 19 December 1714 | 18 December 1715 | 364 |
| Archer, Benjamin | 24 May 1719 | - | - |
| Archer, Henry | [23 May] 1712 | 23 May 1714 | 730 |
| Archer, Isaac | 20 September 1662 | 20 December 1662 | 60 |
| Archer, Miles | 25 September 1726 | 28 May 1727 | 245 |
| Ardern, Henry | 18 February 1665 | [1] December 1666 | 651 |
| Ardern James | 10 March 1661 | 13 March 1661 | 3 |
| Armitage, John | [4 March] 1690 | 4 March 1694 | 1460 |
| Armistead, Anthony | [1] February 1681 | [1] September 1681 | 213 |
| Armstrong, Benjamin | 10 June 1682 | 23 September 1682 | 105 |
| Armstrong, John | 20 September 1674 | - | - |
| Arnold, John | 24 May 1719 | 12 June 1720 | 384 |
| Arnald, John | 16 March 1726 | - | - |
| Arnald, Michael | 20 December 1719 | 24 December 1721 | 726 |
| Arnald, Richard | 23 September 1722 | 20 September 1724 | 728 |
| Arnold, Robert | 12 June 1720 | 25 September 1720 | 105 |
| Arnold, William | 25 September 1748 | 24 December 1749 | 424 |
| Arnot, George | 20 December 1702 | 19 May 1706 | 1244 |
| Arrowsmith, Joseph | 12 April 1675 | 12 April 1675 | 0.5 |
| Arrowsmith, Thomas | 21 June 1699 | [1] December 1699 | 163 |
| Artis, Thomas | 24 June 1721 | 20 May 1722 | 330 |
| Arthur, Owen | 17 August 1662 | 17 August 1662 | 0.5 |
| Arundell, William | 23 May 1700 | - | - |

| Name | Ordained deacon | Ordained priest | Interval between ordinations (days) |
|---|---|---|---|
| Ascham, Robert | 24 September 1727 | 16 March 1728 | 173 |
| Ash, Nathaniel | 11 April 1661 | 11 April 1661 | 0.5 |
| Ash, Simeon | 1684 | 1685 | 365 |
| Ashburne, John | 25 May 1673 | - | - |
| Ashburner, Thomas | 19 May 1706 | 21 September 1707 | 460 |
| Ashby, George | [1] December 1746 | 24 May 1752 | 1635 |
| Ashby, Richard | 23 February 1746 | 25 May 1746 | 91 |
| Ashby, Samuel | 5 June 1748 | 21 May 1749 | 350 |
| Ashcroft, John | 22 March 1713 | 15 August 1714 | 511 |
| Ashton, Stephen | 17 March 1715 | 22 September 1717 | 919 |
| Ashton, Thomas | 14 March 1742 | - | - |
| Ashwell, Edward | 3 March 1728 | 19 December 1731 | 1383 |
| Ashwell, Nathaniel | [1] September 1679 | [1] June 1680 | 274 |
| Aspin, Edward | 26 May 1700 | - | - |
| Asplin, Samuel | 19 May 1706 | 21 September 1707 | 490 |
| Astman, John | 5 March 1732 | 17 August 1735 | 896 |
| Atcherly, Thomas | 17 June 1753 | - | - |
| Atherton, Thomas | [1] February 1708 | [1] September 1709 | 213 |
| Atthill, Edward | 7 June 1747 | 21 May 1749 | 348 |
| Athill, John | 13 July 1718 | 20 December 1719 | 556 |
| Athorp, Francis | 20 May 1733 | 10 March 1734 | 294 |
| Athorp, Robert | 4 June 1710 | 21 September 1712 | 839 |
| Athowe, Robert | 23 September 1733 | - | - |
| Atkins, Willis | 16 October 1683 | - | - |
| Atkinson, Gilbert | 31 July 1686 | - | - |
| Atkinson, Peter | [1] December 1678 | [1] March 1680 | 456 |
| Atkinson, Philip | 26 March 1683 | - | - |
| Atkinson, Richard | 16 January 1732 | 4 June 1732 | 139 |

| Name | Ordained deacon | Ordained priest | Interval between ordinations (days) |
|---|---|---|---|
| Atkinson, Thomas | [1] June 1751 | [1] December 1753 | 902* |
| Atkinson, Worsopp | 21 December 1712 | 9 June 1723 | 8200 |
| Atton, George | 29 January 1721 | 20 September 1724 | 1329 |
| Atton, Stephen | 10 August 1668 | 6 June 1669 | 310 |
| Atwood, Clement | 26 May 1678 | 5 June 1680 | 679 |
| Aubrey, Thomas | 21 September 1712 | 20 December 1713 | 424 |
| Audley, John | 14 November 1661 | - | - |
| Ault, George | 3 May 1724 | 19 December 1725 | 595 |
| Austin, Daniel | 23 December 1739 | 24 July 1743 | 1308 |
| Austen, Henry | [1 April] 1748 | 1 April 1750 | 730 |
| Austin, Peter | 23 December 1660 | - | - |
| Austin, Richard | 20 December 1696 | 24 September 1699 | 1008 |
| Austin, Richard | 19 September 1731 | 23 September 1733 | 734 |
| Austen, Thomas | 23 September 1744 | 5 October 1746 | 742 |
| Austin, William | 19 September 1703 | 12 April 1704 | 205 |
| Aveling, William | 5 June 1737 | 2 March 1740 | 972 |
| Ayde, Robert | [1] June 1693 | [1] May 1695 | 700 |
| Aylmer, Francis | [1] November 1722 | 20 December 1724 | 780 |
| Aylmer, John | 22 December 1667 | 27 February 1670 | 797 |
| Ailmer, Justinian | 23 December 1694 | 20 December 1696 | 727 |
| Aylmer, Robert | 22 September 1723 | 20 December 1724 | 423 |
| Aynscough, Thomas | 24 May 1752 | 15 October 1752 | 132* |
| Ayres, John | 7 March 1680 | 4 March 1683 | 1092 |
| Ayrton, William | [1] May 1746 | [1] June 1748 | 760 |
| Ayscough, James | [1] September 1709 | [1] March 1710 | 182 |

# Bibliography

## Manuscripts

Cambridge University Library
Add. MS 4484: Papers regarding Nicholas Ferrar and other matters

Suffolk Records Office, Bury St Edmunds
Papers of the Revd George Ashby, E2/22/1

## Unpublished dissertations and theses

Blackmore, H., 'Autonomous Ministry and Ecclesiastical Authority: The Revival of the Female Diaconate in the Church of England, 1850-1900', DPhil Thesis, University of Oxford, 2004

Clement, R.P., 'Is a Permanent Diaconate a realistic proposition, practically and pastorally, for the Church of England at the present time?', MA Dissertation, Anglia Ruskin University, 2008

Nicholas, D., 'Derwent Coleridge (1800-83) and the Deacon Schoolmaster' PhD Thesis, Institute of Education, University of London, 2007

Vaughan, P.H., 'Non-stipendiary Ministry in the Church of England: A History of the Development of an Idea', PhD Thesis, University of Nottingham, 1987

## Primary printed sources

Ainsworth, H., *The Confession of Faith of certayn English People living in Exile* (n. p., 1607)

Almack, H., *A Plea for Deacons* (Rivingtons: London, 1868)

*The Alternative Service Book 1980* (Cambridge University Press: Cambridge, 1980)

*The Arminian Nunnery: or, A Briefe Description and Relation of the late erected Monasticall Place, called the Arminian Nunnery at Little Gidding in Huntington-Shire* (London, 1641)

Baird, W., *A Plea for the Extension of the Ministerial Office* (Rivingtons: London, 1865)

Beaumont, J.A., *More Bishops, More Priests, More Deacons: How to increase the efficiency of the church* (Rivington: London, 1846)

Bingham, W.P.S., *The Extension of the Diaconate: A Paper read before the Spalding Clerical Association* (Joseph Masters: London, 1862)

Blackstone, R. (ed.), *The Ferrar Papers: containing a life of Nicholas Ferrar* (Cambridge University Press: Cambridge, 1938)

Blakeney, R.P., *The Book of Common Prayer in its History and Interpretation* (James Miller: London, 1870)

*The Book of Common Prayer with the additions and deviations proposed in 1928* (Cambridge University Press: Cambridge, 1928)

Bradford, J., *The Writings of John Bradford, M.A.*, ed. A. Townshend (Parker Society: Cambridge, 1853)

Brett, T., *An Enquiry into the Judgment and Practice of the Primitive Church, In Relation to Persons being Baptized by Lay-men* (London, 1713)

Brewster, J., *Practical Reflections on the Ordination Services for Deacons and Priests, in the United Church of England and Ireland* (London, 1817)

*The Canons of the Church of England*, 6th edn (Church House Publishing: London, 2008)

[Chepmell, C.W.], *Chapters on Deacons* (London, 1849)

Cooke, W., *The Power of the Priesthood in Absolution, and a few Remarks on Confession* (John Henry and James Parker: London, 1858)

Deacon, T., *A Book of Common Prayer or Clementine Liturgy* (London, 1734)

*Deacons in the Church: Report of a Diocesan Working Party* (Diocese of Chichester, 2003)

*Deacons Now: The Report of a Church of England Working Party Concerned with Women in Ordained Ministry* (Advisory Council for the Church's Ministry: London, 1990)

*Decrees of the Ecumenical Councils*, ed. N P. Tanner (Sheed and Ward: London, 1990), 2 vols

Dibb, J.E., *The Sub-diaconate* (William MacIntosh: London, 1866)

*The Divine Right of Convocations Examined* (London, 1701)

Downer, A.C., *The Diaconate: An Ancient Remedy for Modern Needs* (Church of England Book Society: London, 1906)

Eachard, J., *The Grounds and Occasions of the Contempt of the Clergy* (1679) in *The Works of John Eachard* (London, 1772), 3 vols

*The English Church Canons of 1604*, ed. C.H. Davis (H. Sweet: London, 1869)

[Ferrar, J.], *Life of Nicholas Ferrar* in *Nicholas Ferrar: Two Lives*, ed. J.E.B. Mayor (Cambridge University Press: Cambridge, 1855)

*The First Prayer-Book of King Edward VI 1549* (Griffith Farran Browne: London, 1891)

*The First and Second Prayer Books of Edward VI* (J.M. Dent and Sons: London, 1910)

Foxe, J., *Actes and Monuments* (London, 1583), 2 vols

Hale, W.H., *Duties of the Deacons and Priests in the Church of England compared* (Rivington: London, 1850)

——, *Suggestions for the Extension of the Ministry and the Revival of the Order of Sub-deacons* (Rivington: London, 1852)

'H.G.', 'Reply to X.X. on Deacons officiating', *The Christian Observer* 24 (1824), pp. 85-7

Hill, S., *A Thorough Examination of the False Principles and Fallacious Arguments, advanc'd against the Christian Church, Priest-hood, and Religion* (London, 1708)

Hooker, R., *Of the Lawes of Ecclesiastical Politie* (London, 1723)

Irvine, J.W., *The Revival of a True Working Diaconate in the Church of England* (Simpkin, Marshall and Co: London, 1882)

Laurence, R., *Lay Baptism Invalid* (London, 1710)

A Layman, *The Restoration of the Diaconate the only way to increase the supply of ministers in the Church of England* (Edward Stanford: London, 1877)

Lias, J.J., *The Extension of the Diaconate* (J.S. Nicholas: Bristol, 1909)

MacConnel, E.W.J., *A Plea for a Proper Diaconate* (SPCK: London, 1919)

Mackenzie, H., *The Fuller Restoration of the Diaconate, a Means of strengthening the Church* (Smith, Elder and Co: London, 1845)

Mant, R. (ed.), *The Book of Common Prayer, and Administration of the Sacraments* (W. Baxter: Oxford, 1820)

Nicolls, J.H., *Essay on the Subject of the Restoration of the Diaconate* (J. Lovell: Montreal, 1863)

Nightingale, B., *The Ejected of 1662 in Cumberland and Westmoreland* (Manchester, 1911), 2 vols

*A Paraphrase and Notes on St. Paul's Ist Epistle to Timothy: in imitation of Mr. Locke's manner* (London, 1733)

A Parish Priest, *The Diaconate and the Poor: the duty of the laity of England briefly considered with reference to the above two objects* (J. Ollivier: London, 1849)

*The Parliamentary Debates from the Year 1803 to the Present Time*, ed. T.C. Hansard (London, 1812), vol. 9

Paul VI, *Sacrum Diaconatus Ordinem* in *Acta Apostolicae Sedis* 59 (1967), pp. 697-704

Pearse, G.W., *Opening of the Diaconate to Persons engaged in Professions and Trades* (Rivingtons: London, 1875)

*A Plan to Restore the Diaconate in the Anglican Church of Canada* (Anglican Church of Canada: Ottawa, 1989)

*The Prayer Book of Queen Elizabeth 1559* (Griffith Farran: London, 1891)

A Presbyter of the Church of England, *Reasons for the Restoration of the Order of Deacons* (Francis and John Rivington: London, 1845)

*Reformatio Legum Ecclesiasticarum* (London, 1641)

*Reports from Commissioners* (London, 1834), vol. 26

Riley, H. and Graham, R.J. (eds), *Acts of the Convocations of Canterbury and York, 1921-1970* (SPCK: London, 1970)

Robinson, H. (ed.), *Zurich Letters* (Parker Society: Cambridge, 1846)

Strype, J., *The Life and Acts of Matthew Parker* (London, 1711)

——, *Annals of the Reformation* (London, 1709-25), 2 vols

Synge, M.C., *The Diaconate: A Call to Women* (SPCK: London, 1927)

Twells, H., *Extension of the Diaconate: A Speech delivered in the Lower House of the Convocation of Canterbury on Friday, July 8, 1887* (Rivington: London, 1887)

Walton, I., *The Life of Mr George Herbert* (London, 1670)

## Secondary sources

Aldridge, A., 'In the Absence of the Minister: Structures of Subordination in the Role of Deaconess in the Church of England', *Sociology* 21 (1987), pp. 377-92

——, 'Discourse on Women in the Clerical Profession: The Diaconate and Language-Games in the Church of England', *Sociology* 26 (1992), pp. 45-57

Avis, P., 'The Revision of the Ordinal in the Church of England, 1550-2005', *Ecclesiology* 1 (2005), pp. 95-110

——, 'Deacons and the Church of England' in Hilberath, B.J. and Mascini, R. (eds), *Diakonia and Diaconate as an Ecumenical Challenge* (Lit Verlag: Berlin, 2006), pp. 35-8

——, 'Wrestling with the Diaconate', *Ecclesiology* 5 (2009), pp. 3-6

——, 'The Diaconate: a flagship ministry', *Theology and Ministry* 2 (2013), pp. 1-14

Bardwell, E., 'The Pastoral Role of the Deacon' in Hall, C. (ed.), *The Deacon's Ministry* (Gracewing: Leominster, 1991), pp. 15-66

Barnett, J M , *The Diaconate: A Full and Equal Order*, 3rd edn (Trinity Press: Harrisburg, PA, 1995)

Baxter, C., 'Doing Truth: A Consideration of *Deacons in the Ministry of the Church*', *Anvil* 5 (1988), pp. 233-42

Bedard, A.C., 'James II and the Catholic Challenge', in Tyacke, C. (ed.), *Seventeenth-century Oxford* (Oxford University Press: Oxford, 1997), pp. 907-54

Blackmore, H., *The Beginning of Women's Ministry: The Revival of the Deaconess in the 19th-century Church of England*, Church of England Record Society 14 (Church of England Record Society: London, 2007)

Bowmer, G.C., *The Sacrament of the Lord's Supper in Early Methodism* (Dacre Press: London, 1951)

Bradshaw, P.F., *The Anglican Ordinal: Its History and Development from the Reformation to the Present Day*, Alcuin Club Collections 53 (SPCK: London, 1971)

——, 'Ordinals', in Sykes, S., Booty, J. and Knight, J. (eds), *The Study of Anglicanism*, 2nd edn (SPCK: London, 1998), pp. 155-65

Brodd, S-E., 'An Escalating Phenomenon: The Diaconate from an Ecumenical Perspective' in Borgegard, G. and Hall, C. (eds), *The Ministry of the Deacon* (Nordic Ecumenical Council: Uppsala, 1999), pp. 11-50

Brogan, H., 'Clarkson, Thomas' in *ODNB*, vol. 11, pp. 937-41

[Brown, R.], *The Distinctive Diaconate: A Report to the Board of Ministry, the Diocese of Salisbury* (Sarum College Press: Salisbury, 2003)

——, *Being a Deacon Today: exploring a distinctive ministry in the Church and in the world* (Canterbury Press: Norwich, 2004)

Bullock, F.W.B., *A History of Training for the Ministry of the Church of England . . . from 1800 to 1874* (Budd & Gillatt: St Leonards-on-Sea, 1955)

Burdon, A., *Authority and Order: John Wesley and his Preachers* (Ashgate: Aldershot, 2005)

Burnham, A., 'The Liturgical Ministry of a Deacon' in Hall, C. (ed.), *The Deacon's Ministry* (Gracewing: Leominster, 1991), pp. 67-87

Charles, A.M., 'George Herbert, Deacon', *Modern Philology* 72 (1975), pp. 272-6

Childs, J., *God's Traitors: Terror and Faith in Elizabethan England* (Bodley Head: London, 2014)

Cleugh, H., 'The Prayer Book in Early Stuart Society' in Platten, S. and Woods, C. (eds), *Comfortable Words: Polity, Piety and the Book of Common Prayer* (SCM Press: London, 2012), pp. 35-48

Collins, J.N., *Diakonia: Reinterpreting the Ancient Sources* (Oxford University Press: Oxford, 1990)

——, *Deacons and the Church: Making Connections between Old and New* (Morehouse Publishing: Harrisburg, PA, 2002)

Collinson, P., 'Cartright, Thomas' in *ODNB*, vol. 10, pp. 409-13

Cranfield, N.W.S., 'Ferrar, Nicholas' in *ODNB*, vol. 19, pp. 417-19

Croft, S., *Ministry in Three Dimensions: Ordination and Leadership in the Local Church* (Darton, Longman and Todd: London, 1999)

Cullen, J., 'The Educational Ministry of Deacons' in Hall, C. (ed.), *The Deacon's Ministry* (Gracewing: Leominster, 1991), pp. 89-101

Cummings, O.F., *Deacons and the Church* (Paulist Press: Mahwah, NJ, 2004)

*The Diaconate*, GS MISC 535 (Church House Publishing: London, 1998)

*The Diaconate as Ecumenical Opportunity* (Anglican Communion Publications: London, 1996)

Dix, G., *The Shape of the Liturgy* (Dacre: London, 1945)

Doe, N., *Canon Law in the Anglican Communion: A Worldwide Perspective* (Clarendon Press: Oxford, 1998)

Dowland, D., *Nineteenth-Century Anglican Theological Training: The Redbrick Challenge* (Oxford University Press: Oxford, 1997)

Driver, J., 'Restored Diaconate, Restored Church? An Australian Anglican Contribution to an Ecumenical Debate', *St Mark's Review* 161 (1995), pp. 6-11

Duffy, E., *Faith of Our Fathers* (Continuum: London, 2004)

Epting, S.W. and Epting, C.C., 'Deacons and the Episcopal Church in the United States of America' in Hilberath, B.J. and Mascini, R. (eds), *Diakonia and Diaconate as an Ecumenical Challenge* (Lit Verlag: Berlin, 2006), pp. 39-46

Ferguson, R.S., *Carlisle* (SPCK: London, 1889)

Fincham, K., *Prelate as Pastor: The Episcopate of James I* (Oxford University Press: Oxford, 1990)

*For Such a Time as This: A Renewed Diaconate in the Church of England*, GS 1407 (Church House Publishing: London, 2001)

Francis, L.J. and Robbins, M., *The Long Diaconate 1987-1994: Women Deacons and the delayed Journey to Priesthood* (Gracewing: Leominster, 1999)

Gibbs, L.W., 'Life of Hooker' in Kirby, T. (ed.), *A Companion to Richard Hooker* (Brill: Leiden, 2008), pp. 1-26

Griffiths, P., 'Inhabitants' in Rawcliffe, C. and Wilson, R. (eds), *Norwich since 1550* (Hambledon: London, 2004), pp. 63-89

Hall, C., 'Introduction' in Hall, C. (ed.), *The Deacon's Ministry* (Gracewing: Leominster, 1991), pp. 1-8

Hannaford, R., 'Towards a Theology of the Diaconate' in Hall, C. (ed.), *The Deacon's Ministry* (Gracewing: Leominster, 1991), pp. 25-44

Hayes, G.M., 'Ordination Ritual and Practice in the Welsh-English Frontier, circa 1540-1640', *Journal of British Studies* 44 (2005), pp. 713-27

Jago, J., *Aspects of the Georgian Church: Visitation Studies of the Diocese of York, 1761-1776* (Associated University Press: Cranbury, NJ, 1997)

Jones, M.G., *The Charity School Movement: A Study of Eighteenth Century Puritanism in Action* (Cambridge University Press: Cambridge, 1938)

Knight, F., *The Nineteenth-Century Church and English Society* (Cambridge University Press: Cambridge, 1995)

Lake, P., 'Lancelot Andrewes, John Buckeridge and *Avant-Garde* Conformity at the Court of James I' in Peck, L.L. (ed.), *The Mental World of the Jacobean Court* (Cambridge University Press: Cambridge, 1991), pp. 113-33

Lescher, B, '*Diakonia* and Diaconate' in Sheldrake, P. (ed.), *The New SCM Dictionary of Christian Spirituality* (SCM Press: London, 2005), pp. 241-3.

Leeder, L., 'The Diaconate in the Church of England: A Legal Perspective' in Hall, C. (ed.), *The Deacon's Ministry* (Gracewing: Leominster, 1991), pp. 123-45

Leggett, R.G., 'Anglicans and Liturgical Revision' in Hefling, C. and Shattuck, C. (eds), *The Oxford Guide to the Book of Common Prayer: A Worldwide Survey* (Oxford University Press: Oxford, 2008), pp. 445-50

Lynn, A., 'Finding Images' in Hall, C. (ed.), *The Deacon's Ministry* (Gracewing: Leominster, 1991), pp. 103-22

MacCulloch, D., *A History of Christianity*, 2nd edn (Penguin: London, 2010)

McCullouch, P., 'Absent Presence: Lancelot Andrewes and 1662', in Platten, S. and Woods, C. (eds), *Comfortable Words: Polity, Piety and the Book of Common Prayer* (SCM Press: London, 2012), pp. 49-68

Maltby, J., *Prayer Book and People in Elizabethan and Early Stuart England* (Cambridge University Press: Cambridge, 1998)

Marshall, W., *Church Life in Hereford and Oxford, 1660-1760: A Study of Two Sees* (Carnegie: Lancaster, 2009)

*The Mission and Ministry of the Whole Church: Biblical, theological and contemporary perspectives*, GS MISC 854 (Church House Publishing: London, 2007)

Morehen, J., 'Amner, John' in *ODNB*, vol. 1, pp. 964-5

Muir, L.R. and White, L.J., *Materials for the Life of Nicholas Ferrar* (Leeds Philosophical and Literary Society: Leeds, 1996)

Nelson, J.K., *A Blessed Company: Parishes, Parsons and Parishioners in Anglican Virginia, 1690-1776* (University of North Carolina Press: Chapel Hill, NC, 2001)

Nicholas, D., '112 years of professional disability: an under-examined aspect of the 1846 Education Minutes', *History of Education* 39 (2010), pp. 319-41

O'Connor, D., *Three Centuries of Mission: The United Society for the Propagation of the Gospel 1701-2000* (Continuum: London, 2000)

Owen, D.M. and Thurley, D. (eds), *The King's School Ely: A Collection of Documents relating to the History of the School and its Scholars* (Cambridge Antiquarian Society: Cambridge, 1982)

Parry, G., *The Arch-Conjurer of England: John Dee* (Yale University Press: New Haven, CT, 2011)

Percy, M., *Clergy: The Origin of Species* (Continuum: London, 2006)

Pinnock, J., 'The History of the Diaconate' in Hall, C. (ed.), *The Deacon's Ministry* (Gracewing: Leominster, 1991), pp. 9-24

Plater, O., *Many Servants: An Introduction to Deacons* (Cowley Publications: Boston, MA, 1991)

——, *Many Servants: An Introduction to Deacons*, 2nd edn (Cowley Publications: Plymouth, 2004)

Pocock, P.G., 'The Diaconate and the Anglican Church Today', *St Mark's Review* 206 (2008), pp. 29-38

Porter, S., 'University and Society', in Tyacke, C. (ed.), *Seventeenth-Century Oxford* (Oxford University Press: Oxford, 1997), pp. 25-104

Puglisi, J.F., *The Process of Admission to Ordained Ministry: A Comparative Study* (Collegeville, MN, 1998), 2 vols

Redmond Curtis, W., *The Lambeth Conferences: The Solution for Pan-Anglican Organization* (Columbia University Press: New York, 1942)

Robbins, M., 'A Matter of Age or Experience? Parishioners' Attitudes toward Women Vicars in the Church in Wales' in Pope, R. (ed.), *Honouring the Past and Shaping the Future: Essays in Honour of Gareth Lloyd Jones* (Gracewing: Leominster, 2003), pp. 253-64

Roberts, D., 'The Social Conscience of Tory Periodicals', *Victorian Periodicals Newsletter* 10 (1977), pp. 154-69

Savidge, A., *The Origins and Foundation of Queen Anne's Bounty* (SPCK: London, 1955)

Schlenther, B.S., 'Whitefield, George' in *ODNB*, vol. 58, pp. 640-49

Simut, C.C., 'Orders of Ministry' in Kirby, T. (ed.), *A Companion to Richard Hooker* (Brill: Leiden, 2008), pp. 403-34

Smedburg, N., 'Church of Sweden Contribution' in Hilberath, B.J. and Mascini, R. (eds), *Diakonia and Diaconate as an Ecumenical Challenge* (Lit Verlag: Berlin, 2006), pp. 19-34

Smyth, C.H., *Cranmer and the Reformation under Edward VI* (Cambridge University Press: Cambridge, 1926)

[Tanner, M. and Platten, S.], *Deacons in the Ministry of the Church: A Report to the House of Bishops of the General Synod of the Church of England*, GS 802 (Church House Publishing: London, 1988)

Taylor, N.H., *Lay Presidency at the Eucharist? An Anglican Approach* (Mowbray: London, 2009)

Tiller, J., *A Strategy for the Church's Ministry* (CIO Publishing: London, 1983)

Treasure, C., *Walking on Glass: Women Deacons Speak Out* (SPCK: London, 1991)

Turner, H.J.M., *Holy Orders and Completeness of the Church* (Melrose Books: Ely, 2005)

Van't Spijker, W. (trans. Vriend, J. and Bierma, L.D.), *The Ecclesiastical Offices in the Thought of Martin Bucer* (Brill: Leiden, 1996)

Wallwork, C.N.R., 'Lay Ministries' in Bradshaw, P.F. (ed.) *The New SCM Dictionary of Liturgy and Worship* (SCM Press: London, 2005), p. 273

Westerfield-Tucker, K.B., 'Ordination: Methodist' in Bradshaw, P.F. (ed.), *The New SCM Dictionary of Liturgy and Worship* (SCM Press: London, 2005), pp. 352-3

White, A. and Williams, D., *Deacons at your Service* (Grove Books: Cambridge, 1987)

Woodward, L., *The Age of Reform*, 2nd edn (Clarendon: Oxford, 1962)

Wright, D.F., 'Martin Bucer in England – and Scotland' in Krieger, C. and Lienhard, M. (eds), *Martin Bucer and Sixteenth Century Europe* (Brill: Leiden, 1993), vol. 2, pp. 523-32

## Newspapers

'Leader: Deacons, not doormats', *The Church Times*, 29 August 2007

'Readers feel neglected and ill-used', *The Church Times*, 2 November 2006

White, T., 'Review: Being a Deacon Today', *The Church Times*, 2 November 2006

## Online sources

'A Cambridge Alumni Database' (ACAD), *Cambridge University Library*, accessed on 27 September 2013: http://venn.lib.cam.ac.uk/Documents/acad/intro.html.

Avis, P. and Ferns, S., 'Discerning the Diaconate', *Diaconal Association of the Church of England*, accessed on 19 November 2013: http://www.dace.org/literature/docs/Discerning-the-Diaconate.pdf

*The Clergy of the Church of England Database* (CCEd), accessed on 2 February 2015: http://theclergydatabase.org.uk

Comerford, P., 'Edinburgh Seminar on Deacons and the Diaconate', *Patrick Comerford*, accessed on 11 December 2013: http://www.patrickcomerford.com/2012/04/edinburgh-seminar-on-deacons-diaconate.html

'Common Worship: Ordination Services', *The Church of England*, accessed on 30 July 2013: http://www.churchofengland.org/prayer-worship/worship/texts/ordinal.aspx

*Deacon Stories*, accessed on 2 February 2014: http://deaconstories.wordpress. com.

'General Synod 2013 – Saturday 8th June', *The Scottish Episcopal Church*, accessed on 19 April 2014: http://www.scotland.anglican.org/general-synod-2013-saturday-8th-june

Smith, M., 'A Case for Permanent Female Deacons', *Reform*, accessed on 19 November 2013: http://reform.org.uk/resources/media-downloads/src/article/27/title/report-a-case-for-permanent-female-deacons

# Index

*You may be interested in*

# The Web of Friendship
*Nicholas Ferrar and Little Gidding*

By Joyce Ransome

Print ISBN: 9780227173480
Epub ISBN: 9780227900901
PDF ISBN: 9780227900895

This is a biography of Nicholas Ferrar (1593–1637) and his family, focusing on his background, his education and the experiences that shaped his ministry, as well as the circumstances that brought the family to the village of Little Gidding in Cambridgeshire. Relying mostly on contemporary accounts and avoiding the hagiographic tone adopted in previous biographies, Ransome shows how the search for community was central to Ferrar's life, and this becomes the unifying theme around which she has constructed her account.

For its fresh perspective on the unique Little Gidding that Ferrar created, this book will appeal to both an academic and general audience of readers interested in early modern history, church history, English literature, theology, family history (historical sociology) and gender studies.

Available now with more excellent titles in Paperback, Hardback, PDF and Epub formats from James Clarke & Co

www.jamesclarke.co